THE
SCOTLAND YARD

SIR BASIL THOMSON

THE LITERARY GUILD

NEW YORK   1936

PRINTED AT THE *Country Life Press*, GARDEN CITY. N Y , U. S. A.

NEW SCOTLAND YARD

Built of granite quarried by the convicts of Dartmoor, this building on the banks of the Thames houses the working quarters of the world's most celebrated police force.

To

MY FORMER COLLEAGUES OF ALL RANKS
whose devotion to duty in critical times helped to
bring the Criminal Investigation Department to its
present state of efficiency.

A WORD TO THE READER

THE proud and sombre procession of English justice is no innovation of a modern day. The herbs that strew the floor of the judge's bench at the Old Bailey, the bright little bouquets that the judges carry in the administration of their duties, are themselves reminders of times and conditions vanishing into the distant past. Turn some day to the great early eighteenth-century folios in which the state trials of the preceding century were set down verbatim, just as the court stenographer wrote them out in the dusky courtrooms of an ancient Old Bailey. Listen as even much-maligned Bloody Jeffries guides his witnesses—and his criminals— through the mazes of the law, with dignity, with kindness, with a sort of magnificent equity. And you will see that to the Englishman the administration of the law is no light matter, to be tossed about in the hands of a fatly paid lawyer like balls above a juggler's head. What that law has ever been is an attempt to get at the truth. Its end has always been justice. It is doubtful if many American criminal lawyers would feel at home in its atmosphere. In its strange conceptions of libel, of divorce, in its old courts of chancery, English law has not been quite so happy, but in the criminal courts where the lives of men are at stake it is perhaps the best conception of right and justice that modern nations have seen.

But the courts and their judges are only one phase of the law. No criminal can be brought before the bar until he has been caught, and to apprehend him there must be another great arm of legal administration, the police power. It is with the final flowering of that police power, New Scotland Yard, that this book primarily deals.

Sir Basil Thomson took charge of the administrative branch of the Yard, the Criminal Investigation Department, in June of 1913. The world, by comparison, was a quiet place then, lightly sleeping, but Scotland Yard had already won a world-wide reputation in its battle with crime. It had its rivals—the more ancient Sûreté of Paris, slow outgrowth of a French Charles's fourteenth-century detectives; and the police departments of Berlin and Vienna— but it was, and rightly, a magic name wherever English was spoken. From difficult origins, from the antipathy of a free people to whom any police were likely to be looked on as an outrage, it had gathered a reputation with relentless thoroughness. There were setbacks and discouragements; there were defeats; even the writers who were later to create a sort of specialized Balzacian Comédie Humaine around the Yard and its inspectors were, toward the end of the last century, taking the sort of pot shots at it which must have reflected the public opinion of the day. Sherlock Holmes had no truck with the Yard; to him Inspector Lestrade was in the beginning little better than an ordinary flatfoot. In later years Lestrade came off better, but he never grew to be a really admirable figure. Of those times, less meagre in achievement than in reputation, Sir Basil writes with sympathy and understanding.

To put a finger on the exact moment when the feeling for the Yard changed from distaste through tolerance to adulation is impossible. Certainly by the turn of the century the ugly and imposing building by the Thames, built of granite quarried by the convicts at Dartmoor, had begun to fire men's imaginations. Police were an old story by then, the world was getting on, and eighteenth-century individualism was little better than a memory; the romantic criminal, from

Robin Hood to Professor Moriarty, was at a heavy discount, and the certainty that if you were murdered in your
bed certain dour men from the Yard, in bowlers and neatly
rolled umbrellas, were almost sure to catch your murderer,
had its points. What was happening was quite simple: people had learned that the austere honesty of the criminal
judges had an exact counterpart in the austere honesty of
the Yard.

But it was more than honesty; it was patience, it was
brains, it was bravery. Case after case had piled up; you
couldn't buy the Yard, you couldn't use what is politely
known as "influence"; it simply wasn't safe to be a major
criminal in England. No Becker cases disturbed its routine
and uncovered veinous tangles of corruption. No ward-
heelers with the right connections higher up killed and went
free to kill again. Then as now there were no Al Capones
and Jack Diamonds pursuing their carefree ways. Small
wonder that America, even more than England, began to
weave a golden haze about the Yard. No human organization could possibly be as flawless as the Yard began then
to appear in literature, but no organization could have
come closer to deserving the reputation.

Through the years of the war, until his retirement in
1921, Sir Basil carried the Yard to new fame. With quiet
imperturbability he faced the problems of wartime, with its
espionage and its waves of violence; he saw—and smashed
—England's brief flare of kidnapping; he saw new methods
of crime arise and devised new ways of combating them.
He left the Yard very much as it is today, with its Big
Four (a term, not strictly accurate, popularized by the late
Edgar Wallace), its Flying Squads, all its complex panoply
for liming the lawbreaker's birdlike feet.

Now he has written the Yard's story. It is a book to read
for its history, for the sheer fascination of the long record
brought together in its completion for the first time. Here is
the Yard from the inside, here are the men who made it and
fought for it and built it to enduring greatness; here are
the secrets of that greatness. The lure of the detective, the

greatest hunter of them all, the hunter of men, is timeless; and *The Story of Scotland Yard* is the story of the greatest of these hunters. In no book of fiction can be found a more enthralling tale.

M. J.

CONTENTS

PART I

THE YARD AT WORK

PART II

THE NEED FOR SCOTLAND YARD

PART III

THE ESTABLISHMENT OF SCOTLAND YARD

ILLUSTRATIONS

PART I
THE YARD AT WORK

CHAPTER I

The Murder of
Police Constable Gutteridge

Perhaps the best way to begin the story of Scotland Yard is to explain how the Yard works today; to exhibit it, as it were, in action. Having then shown it as it is, it will be better possible to appreciate the record that follows of its inception and growth.

Many cases come to mind that might serve as a model, but perhaps no one of them could serve better than that of the murder of Police Constable Gutteridge of the Essex County police on September 27, 1927. It is not so recent as others that might be chosen, but it offers certain points of procedure that make it of more than ordinary interest.

Here is the story of P. C. Gutteridge and his murderers: A mail-van driver named Ward was the first to find the body, lying by the roadside in a pool of blood. He called a Mr. Perrett to help him, and on opening the tunic they found the body still warm. Another constable named Taylor had met Gutteridge at a "conference point" at 3:30 A.M.: this fixed the hour of the murder at about 3:30 A.M., allowing for the distance between the conference point and the scene of the murder. When the Essex police came to move the body a bullet that had been fired through the dead man's cheek fell out of his clothes; another bullet, fired through one of his eyes, was discovered embedded in the ground. The tarred road surface afforded no useful marks, but there were signs in the grass bank, at the roadside, of a motorcar having collided with it, and there was a deep scratch in a stone.

The chief constable of Essex lost no time in asking for help from Scotland Yard, pointing out on the telephone that the crime had been committed not far from the boundary of the Metropolitan area and that it was probable that the murderer had come from London and would return there. On this, Chief Inspector Berrett and Detective-Sergeant Harris were dispatched to the scene of the crime in a car, and early that same afternoon they took charge of the inquiry in coöperation with the detectives from Essex.

It was easy to reconstruct the crime from the objects found on the spot. Gutteridge was on night patrol duty. He was to have met another constable at a fixed point. He did not keep the appointment. An examination of the body in the coach house to which it had been removed showed that two shots had been fired at the head at close range and after the constable had fallen a shot had been fired into each eye. There was no sign of a struggle, but his whistle had been pulled from his pocket, his pencil was held tightly in his hand, and his notebook was lying close to the body. From these facts it was conjectured that he had sounded an alarm with his whistle and had been about to make an entry in his notebook when he was shot.

Chief Inspector Berrett had already received information that on the previous night a car belonging to a Dr. Lovell had been stolen in the village of Billericay, twelve miles distant from the scene of the crime, and this suggested that the man or men who had stolen this car had shot Gutteridge when he challenged them. On the other hand it is very rare for a motorcar thief in England to resort to murder when the penalty for such a theft is comparatively light. In such a case as this, where local feeling against the guilty is very strongly aroused, the police always suffer from too much rather than too little information. Before the inquiry was completed more than one thousand persons had been interviewed and more than two hundred voluntary statements had been taken. Local prejudices were rife. Most of them centred on an eccentric person against whom possession of firearms was alleged, as well as suspicious behaviour. Berrett was satisfied in his own mind that the suspicions were baseless, but he had nevertheless to expend valuable time in sifting the allegations to the bottom. In another case an old criminal was said to have admitted some connection with the murder: actually he had had nothing to do with it, but he was wanted for another crime, and of this he was convicted a little later. As in most mysterious murder cases, there was a confession by an innocent person. The Hampshire police reported that a man had given himself up at Basingstoke, sixty miles away, as being guilty of the murder. The detective had to drive all night through dense fog to bring this man to Romford in Essex, only to find that he was an epileptic who had given himself up a few months before as guilty of another murder. He was released.

The first real advance was made in the evening of the day following the murder, when the police in the Brixton Division found a derelict car abandoned in a passageway. It was taken to the police station and compared with the description of Dr. Lovell's car stolen at Billericay. Constable Hearn, from the Yard, an expert on cars, went over this car very carefully. Dark spots on the running board were identified as dried human blood; on both the near side wheels there was earth of the same quality as the earth by the roadside on the scene of the crime; dried grass was found adhering to the wheels, and there were other signs that the car had hit something. An expert from the Yard examined the car for fingerprints but could find none sufficient for identification, nor was there any more successful result from an examination of the garage door at Billericay. Dr. Lovell identified his car and remembered that his last recorded mileage on the speedometer had been 40.9 miles. The mileage now stood at 84.3; therefore the thieves had driven about 43 miles through by-lanes. The inquiries at Billericay brought definite information about the car theft. A neighbour had heard it being started up at 2:30 A.M. and being driven down a back lane: the next step was to work up the route taken to Brixton with a mileage that would tally with the speedometer. The officers tackled this problem by visiting more than five hundred houses scattered along the route, and in the end fifteen people were found who had heard a car speeding along the country lanes before daylight, no doubt in order to avoid meeting police on the main road. In the end this proved to have been waste labour, because it was found possible to rely upon more conclusive evidence. Dr. Lovell's car did, however, yield one piece of invaluable evidence—a spent cartridge case.

Berrett now applied to the Criminal Record Office at the Yard for a list of criminals known to resort to violence on arrest. The very first name on that list was that of Frederick Guy Browne, and this was startling because Browne had an intimate knowledge of country lanes in Essex, where he had for a time rented a repairing garage. But it was one thing to entertain suspicions of a man and quite another to obtain evidence for bringing him to justice.

The hunt was now spreading all over England. It was easy to advertise Browne in the columns of the *Police Gazette* as wanted, but Browne was not required to report to the police any more than any other free citizen. It was Dame Fortune who came to the aid of Chief Inspector Berrett, or rather, as he chose to put it, it was ten or twenty thousand police officers in every corner of the kingdom. That is the kind of keen co-operation that Scotland Yard can always count on from other police forces.

In the middle of November, nearly six weeks after the murder, a motor truck in Sheffield was forced against a wall to avoid collision with a passing car in the hands of a reckless driver. The truck driver took the number of the car and complained to the nearest constable, with the result that the car was stopped and a summons was taken out against the driver. This summons was sent to the Metropolitan police for service at the London address shown on the licence, but the address proved to be false and the licence belonged to somebody else. The Sheffield police did not allow the matter to drop, and after patient inquiry and the aid of a local informant they discovered that the driver was Frederick Guy Browne, who had sold in Sheffield a car stolen from a house in Tooting, a London suburb, and that he was carrying on a garage business at Battersea in London.

There was still insufficient evidence for detaining Browne on the murder charge, and unless he could be charged with murder a charge of stealing a motorcar seemed quite inadequate, but at the end of December the C.I.D. received a letter from a writer in Sheffield who offered them information about recent hold-ups at railway stations and ended with the remark that if the police got the two men concerned in these hold-ups it was a "thousand to one" that they had the right man for the Gutteridge murder. This letter was referred to the Sheffield police, who replied that the writer was the man who had been sitting beside Browne when he collided with the truck and that he was the man who had given Browne away as the driver of the car. This informant had met Browne as a fellow convict at Dartmoor, but he was now carrying on an honest business in Sheffield; his motive in writing to Scotland Yard was twofold: to rid himself of a dangerous friend and to earn a reward. (Eventually he received a reward of £2,000 offered by the *News of the World*.)

Berrett and Harris now lost no time. They left for Sheffield by car at 8 A.M. and drove straight on until 8:45 P.M. without stopping for a meal. Their car covered 540 miles. It had to pull up for gas at a wayside station; Berrett's bill was receipted with a rubber stamp which showed the form of a man hanging from a gallows and beneath it the word "settled." For Berrett it was a good omen: the receipt is now in the Scotland Yard museum.

An interview with the Sheffield informant convinced Berrett that he would be a witness of the first importance. Berrett invited him to Scotland Yard, and two days later he appeared there and made a long and detailed statement which left no doubt in Berrett's mind that Browne and a man named "Pat," otherwise Kennedy, were the men of whom he was in search.

The officers in the W Division, which included Tooting, London, were keeping an eye on the Battersea garage. They knew Browne's dangerous character; they determined to arrest him on his return from Dartmoor, where he had gone to meet a discharged convict. The arrest was certain to be a risky job for the police. However, they made preparations by concealing armed officers in different parts of the garage. On January 20, 1928, Browne drove into his garage in his Angus-Sanderson car; armed detectives surrounded the car and seized him while they took away his revolver. In the pocket on the right of the driver's seat was a fully loaded Webley revolver from which one of the shots which killed Gutteridge had been fired. Berrett came forward and invited Browne to account for his movements on the night of the murder and cautioned him. Browne hesitated and then said, "Why should I tell you anything? But there, I might as well." His statement, taken down by Sergeant Harris, was a tissue of lies. He said that he was not interested in the murder, but in the course of the statement he mentioned William Henry Kennedy under the name of "Pat."

Pat was found to be associated with Browne at his garage. Browne was charged with stealing the car sold in Sheffield, and the detectives were then free to go after Kennedy. He was traced to Liverpool. Detectives were keeping observation on his lodgings late on January 25 when they saw a man "creeping along the wall" of the house. Sergeant Mattinson was sent to question him. Kennedy stuck a pistol into Mattinson's ribs and said, "Stand back or I'll shoot you." The other police heard the click of the pistol, but the safety catch had not been drawn. Kennedy was arrested, disarmed, and taken to Scotland Yard. Mattinson afterwards received the King's police medal.

After the usual caution Kennedy was asked to account for his movements on the night of the murder. His wife, who was present, advised him to tell the truth, and he made a very long statement, admitting the theft of the doctor's car but declaring that his share in the murder had been that of an unwilling accessory. He said that all the shots had been fired by Browne; that he, Kennedy, had only reloaded the revolver as they drove away. Some of the details in the statement were verified, but Berrett's opinion was that the first shot had been fired, not by Browne, but by Kennedy.

The antecedents of the two men were of some interest. Browne was forty-five; he had seen some service during the war, but he had been an habitual criminal from boyhood. He was immensely strong and could lift a car without the aid of a jack. He did not drink or smoke. Kennedy, on the other hand, was a feeble creature, a man of Irish ancestry born in Scotland. He had served for two and a half years during the war, and it was thought that Browne associated with him only because he was a man of better education than himself. He had been a jack-of-all-trades—motor mechanic, compositor, etc. In Kennedy's statement he said that after taking the car they avoided the main road for fear of being held up by police, but scarcely had they reached the tarred road when a man flashed a lamp as a signal for them to stop. Browne drove on, but on hearing a police whistle from his rear he pulled up. The policeman then asked for the number of their car: Browne told him that he could read it for himself. Yes, said the policeman, but did *they* know it? The constable pulled out a notebook and was in the act of writing when Browne shot him. Kennedy then tried to break away from Browne, but Browne threatened him, saying, "No, you don't: you'll stop here and face it out with me."

Kennedy also was charged at the Southwestern police court with the theft of the Tooting motorcar, and both he and Browne were remanded, but a day or two later the charge of wilful murder was substituted. Kennedy's lawyer represented that the statement made at Scotland Yard had been "pumped out" of Kennedy by threats when in a state of distress and hunger. This was false: Kennedy had been provided with meals and rest, and the magistrate was satisfield that the statement had been voluntary, made under no pressure of any kind. At the Central Criminal Court the police were vindicated, because Kennedy declined to give evidence on the ground that his statement fairly represented his defence. Of course, this statement was not evidence against Browne. His guilt was proved by what Berrett called "a new science," namely, the identification of the pistol that had fired a given cartridge case. The cartridge case and the revolver found in Browne's own car when he was arrested were submitted to the War Office experts on small arms, who were able, from microscopical examination, to say that the empty cartridge case had been fired from the revolver in question and could have been fired from no other. This was due to the fact that these service revolvers are finished by hand and the file marks leave their impression on the cartridge case.

Browne's Webley was of .455 calibre. It was of government issue, and the bullets were all obsolete. In order to understand why the cartridge case preserved so sharp an impression it is necessary to realize the action of gas pressure in the region of tons per square inch. This enormous pressure, which goes far beyond hydraulic pressure, is not a blow but a true squeeze. Each file mark is peculiar to the weapon which has been filed, and under the microscope one can see every mark reproduced on the copper of the cartridge case. There were dents in the breech case of the Gutteridge murder weapon apparently due to a cleaning rod having been forced down through the muzzle. These dents too were faithfully transferred to the cartridge case.

We are accustomed to meet Mr. Bernard Shaw in many unfamiliar spheres, but his omniscience failed him in this instance. He wrote to one of Browne's relations speaking of "manufactured evidence" and suggesting that someone might have made such marks on pistol and cartridge in order to confuse the jury. If only popular authors would abstain from subjects which they do not understand, the course of justice would be smoother.

The case was tried before Mr. Justice Avery in the Central Criminal Court on April 24, 1928. There were three women on the jury. Both Browne and Kennedy were found guilty. The judge said that there was never any foundation for the suggestions made that Kennedy's statement was obtained improperly. The result testified to police efficiency, and the police deserve the highest commendation.

The two men appealed unsuccessfully. They were executed together on May 31, 1928.

The case was a conspicuous example of the efficacy of teamwork between Scotland Yard and many hundred police officers scattered all over the country. So far from there having been any tendency on the part of provincial officers to "bottle up" information, all were equally keen to bring the case to a successful conclusion. Berrett himself said that when he took over the case he ceased to be Berrett but became "ten, twenty, or thirty thousand police officers in every corner of the kingdom." In his opinion it was Kennedy who fired the first shot and Browne who finished off the unfortunate Gutteridge. It is worth noting that the expert evidence on the pistol and the cartridge case hanged Browne; and that Kennedy hanged himself by his own statement which he said represented his defence.

So much for the Yard as it is. Let us now consider its past.

PART II
THE NEED FOR
SCOTLAND YARD

CHAPTER II

Eighteenth-Century Conditions

T HE INGRAINED LOVE of personal liberty inherent in the British people and their distrust in giving additional power to their governments made Great Britain one of the slowest countries in the world to institute police. Jurists were far in advance of public opinion. Jeremy Bentham (1747–1832) considered police necessary as a means to prevent crimes and calamities as well as to correct and cure them. Blackstone in his *Commentaries* (1765) wrote:

By public police and economy I mean the due regulation and domestic order of the kingdom, whereby the individuals of the State, like members of a well-governed family, are bound to conform their general behaviour to the rules of propriety, good neighbourhood and good manners; to be decent, industrious, and inoffensive in their respective stations.

The French kings seem to have been the first in modern times to establish a police system. As early as the fourteenth century Charles V instituted police "to increase the happiness and security of his people." The police system was destined soon to become an engine of oppression that deprived the people of the commonest rights and privileges, prescribed their diet and their dress, and forbade them to move from place to place without leave. Louis XIV enormously increased the powers of the police, with the excellent object of giving security to a city in which crime, disorder, and dirt flourished unchecked, but in doing this he crushed all freedom and independence out of his people. The lieutenant of police, called into existence in 1667, ruled Paris despotically thenceforward, until the great break-up of the Revolution in 1789. He had summary jurisdiction over criminals, vagabonds, and beggars; he was responsible for the security and good order of Paris. Nevertheless, crime flourished. In the heart of the city—the Cour-des-Miracles —was a criminal Alsatia in which desperadoes of all kinds defied authority. Everyone carried a sword—even the servants of the great nobles—and was quick to use it. Crime was rampant even in the highest ranks. The Chevalier de Rohan was detected in a plot to sell strategic places on the Normandy coast to the enemy; the Marquise de Brinvilliers and others of little less importance were convicted of wholesale poisonings and were executed in 1776.

La Reynie, the first lieutenant of police, did much towards suppressing disorder. He cleared out the Cour-des-Miracles and forbade servants to carry arms. He was press censor; books and pamphlets to which he objected were sent to the Bastille to be destroyed; the printers were arrested and their presses broken up. He had nearly a thousand cavalry and infantry under his orders besides the city watch, or archers, as they were called.

While most of the Continental countries in Europe were overpoliced, Great Britain was content to make shift with her citizens for the maintenance of order. The policy in dealing with crime was to terrorize potential criminals by the savagery of the punishments, which, with that object, were carried out in public. It was no uncommon thing for parents to take young children to such exhibitions as an awful warning against temptation to engage in crime. Public executions were the rule even as late as the childhood of the author.

The office of constable in England was incumbent upon every adult citizen, but many evaded the duty by paying substitutes. One of the earliest attempts to establish a systematic police was the enactment of Statute 13, Edward I (1285), for the purpose of maintaining peace in the City of London. This ancient statute was known as the "Watch and Ward." It recognized the principle that the inhabitants of every district must combine for their own protection. It enjoined that "none be so hardy as to be found going or wandering about the streets of the city with sword or buckler after curfew tolled at St. Martin's le Grand."[1] Any such were to be taken by the keepers of the peace and be put in a place of confinement, to be dealt with and punished if the offence were proved. This Act further prescribed that as such persons sought shelter "in taverns more than elsewhere, lying in wait and watching their time to do mischief," no tavern should remain open after the tolling of curfew. No school to teach fencing was allowed within the city.

As evidence of the traditional British distrust of foreigners, this Act imposed penalties on foreigners who came to England "by reason of banishment out of their own country, or who, for great offence, have fled therefrom." Such persons were forbidden to become innkeepers, unless they could find sureties. The Act sets forth that—

some do nothing but run up and down the streets more by night than by day and are well attired in clothing and array and have their food of delicate meats and costly; neither do they use any craft or merchandise, nor have they lands and tenements whereof to live, nor any friend to find them; and through such persons many perils do often happen in the city and many evils, and some of them are found openly offending, as in robberies, breaking of houses by night, murders, and other evil deeds.

Another police Act, if we may call it so, was that of 27 Elizabeth (1585) for the good government of the city of Westminster which had been recently enlarged. "The people thereof being greatly increased, and being for the most part without trade or industry, and many of them wholly given to vice and idleness," power to correct them was given to the dean of Westminster and the high steward, who were authorized to punish "all matters of incontinencies, common scolds and common annoyances, and to com-

---

[1]Curfew (couvre-feu) was at sunset in the summer and from 8 to 9 P.M. in the winter. It was revived during the Great War.

mit to prison all who offended against the peace." Orders
were issued under this Act to control the bakers, the brewers,
the colliers, the woodmongers and bargemen; none were
suffered to forestall or "regrate" the markets so as to increase the price of victuals by buying them up beforehand.
Cooks and tavern keepers were kept apart; no man might
sell ale and also keep a cookshop. The tavern keepers had to
keep a lanthorn lighted at their street doors from 6 P.M.
until 9 A.M. "except when the moon shall shine and give
light."

The Act contained many other regulations for the cleans-
ing of the streets, the selling of wholesome food, the strict
segregation of persons affected with the plague. It is interesting to note that the great Lord Burleigh was the first
high steward of Westminster and that he was the author of
these excellent regulations.

But it is one thing to pass a law and quite another to enforce it. The powers of the high steward soon fell into disuse, but in the 10 George II (1737) the Elizabethan Act
was re-enacted and its powers enlarged. In that Act a night
watch in the city—"a matter of very great importance for
the preservation of the persons and properties of the inhabitants, and very necessary to prevent fires, murders,
burglaries, robberies and other outrages and disorders"—
was prescribed. The Common Council of the City was to
levy rates to pay for the night watch, whose instructions
were issued through the constables of wards and precincts.
Forty years later 14 George III (1777) was passed to
supersede the last-mentioned Act. It is far more detailed in
prescribing the actual number of watchmen; their wages;
their arms, such as rattles, staves, and lanterns; their duties; how they are to proclaim the time of the night or morning "loudly and as audibly" as they can; they are to see
that all doors are safe and well secured; they are to prevent
"to the utmost of their power all murders, burglaries, robberies, and affraies; they are to apprehend all loose, idle or
disorderly persons and deliver them to the Headborough
of the night at the watchhouse."

But this was only another instance of the failure of the best legislation where there is no will in the public mind to carry it out. The watchmen were too few in number, and their pay was insufficient. Mr. Colquhoun, the police magistrate of the time, declared that "no small portion of these very men who are paid for protecting the public are not only instruments of oppression in many instances, by extorting money most unwarrantably, but are frequently accessories in aiding and abetting, or concealing the commission of crimes which it is their duty to detect and suppress." In June, 1780, when a mob surrounded the Houses of Parliament at the beginning of the Gordon riots, only six out of the eighty constables appointed by the Westminster Court Leet could be found.

Throughout the eighteenth century the position of the poor in London was deplorable. Gregory King, the publicist, estimated that at the end of the seventeenth century paupers amounted to nearly one quarter of the population. The disproportion between wages and prices left the men who were fortunate enough to be in employment little margin above a mere subsistence level. The Statute of Artificers which was in force up to 1813 required the justices to make an annual assessment of wages under the supervision of the Privy Council, but the temper of the time was strongly against the central regulation of industry in any form, and with the decline in the power of the Privy Council the justices became progressively laxer in the performance of their duties in regulating wages. King wrote:

The industrial revolution with its disastrously fluctuating prices and its further displacement of labour fell upon the poor rather as the last straw on the back of a camel that had been living largely on its hump for some hundred and fifty years.

THE WATCHMEN

Night watchmen had been instituted in the reign of Charles II and named after him "Charleys," but they seemed to have served more as a sport for the high-spirited than as a deterrent to lawbreakers. Henry Fielding, the novelist, thus describes them in *Amelia*:

> They were chosen out of those poor old decrepit people who are from their want of bodily strength rendered incapable of getting a living by work. These men, armed only with a pole, which some of them are scarce able to lift, are to secure the persons and houses of His Majesty's subjects from the attacks of young, bold, stout, and desperate and well-armed villains. If the poor old fellows should run away from such enemies no one, I think, can wonder, unless he should wonder that they are able even to make their escape.

The "Charleys," as they were called, rarely complied with their orders to perambulate their districts once in every twenty-four hours. They were facetiously described as "persons hired by the parish to sleep in the open air." Another wit preferred the title "Shiver and Shake" to "Watch and Ward." The watchhouses were dirty, insecure hovels where prisoners were confined in underground cellars secured by a grating.

The justices of the peace were entrusted with the sole responsibility for maintaining order with these poor instruments; and they themselves, in London at any rate, were often men of corrupt morals, incapable of inspiring respect and quite indifferent about the efficiency of their subordinates. In the rural districts there was no difficulty about finding gentlemen of property and repute to serve as justices without emoluments, but in London the duties of a magistrate, if taken seriously, were so much more arduous and less pleasant that candidates were seldom men of distinction and frequently persons whose motive was to exploit rather than to serve the public. For though the justices were not paid, they were entitled to receive certain fees, and some of them deservedly earned the opprobrious name of "trading justices."

Amid the prevailing apathy and corruption of the time, the Bow Street magistrates stood out as striking exceptions, and it was to their initiative and example that all the movements which culminated in the establishment of the Metropolitan Police in 1829 were due.

London under the first four Georges was probably more pre-eminent in crime than any other town in earlier or later history. Little by little the slums in what is now known as Mayfair were cleared out to permit the building of mansions for the rich, and their occupants were sent to swarm in the filthy and unlighted streets in Westminster and Lambeth. There was no work for them. Children of the tenderest years were employed in every kind of crime and depravity; many were compelled to maintain their parents by thieving; girls at the early age of twelve swelled the ranks of prostitutes. There were streets in London which it was not safe for well-dressed people to traverse even in the daytime; pickpockets would dash out, rob, and make off again into the rabbit warren of criminals before any alarm could be given. Murder was rampant, because the addition of homicide to a theft of twelve pence or over could not make the punishment any heavier, while it might decisively favour the chance of escape. "One might as well be hanged for a sheep as for a lamb." There was, moreover, in London, organized co-operation among malefactors, though such organized co-operation was entirely lacking among the guardians of law and order. Sir John Fielding tells of a gang "whose number falls little short of a hundred, who are incorporated in one body, have officers and a treasury: and have reduced theft and robbery to a regular system." The headquarters of such gangs were the labyrinths of narrow, filthy alleys in which the London of the time abounded.

As Fielding tells us, it would have been foolhardy for unarmed constables to venture into such alleys, "for it is a melancholy truth that at this very day a rogue no sooner gives the alarm in certain purlieus than twenty or thirty armed villains are ready to come to his assistance." An officer of the Honourable Artillery Company who was occasionally called upon to assist the Bow Street runners, thus describes Chick Lane, Field Lane, and Black Boy Alley:

The buildings in these parts constitute a sort of distinct town. . . . The houses are divided from top to bottom into many apartments, with doors of communication between them all, and also with the adjacent houses; some have two, others three, nay, four doors opening into different alleys. The peace officers and the keepers of these houses were well acquainted with each other, and on much better terms than is compatible with the distinction between honesty and roguery.

Not only the common footpads of the town but their more romantic brethren of the road profited by the asylum they enjoyed in these unsavoury precincts; a highwayman who had robbed a traveller or a coach in Hendon or Blackheath would make straight for Whitefriars with his booty and would be secure from arrest until he betrayed himself by his own vanity and boastfulness or was betrayed by the treachery of a woman in whom he had confided. According to Sir John Fielding, "most highwaymen keep company with low women who generally spend half the year in Bridewells and they have often impeached their paramours."

The disposal of loot was comparatively easy and safe in those days. Pawnbrokers were under no supervision and could safely carry on a trade in stolen goods. They were entitled to take before a magistrate any who attempted to sell or to pledge any article they believed to have been stolen, but as they ran no risk in accepting it, and to denounce a customer was dangerous, they preferred to take the safer road.

It was from these horrible streets and alleys that the mobs and rioters issued in times of public excitement to burn and pillage London. The government had no means of dealing with these riots except the military, who were called out far too late when the temper of the mob had become unmanageable. During the eighteenth and early nineteenth centuries there were five serious disturbances of this kind— the riots caused by the Gin Act in 1736; the riot of the journeymen weavers in 1765; the Gordon riots in 1780; the riots caused by the arrest of Sir Francis Burdett in 1810; and the riots at the Queen's funeral in 1821. In all but two of these cases the wretched inhabitants of the poor quarters of London had no interest in the questions that were made the excuse for the riots; they did not even understand them. It was inevitable, as Fielding said at the time, that those who starved and froze and rotted among themselves should "beg and steal and rob among their betters."

The destitution in London during the whole of this period was appalling. By the end of the seventeenth century her population amounted to just over half a million, or more than one tenth of that of the whole kingdom. By the beginning of the nineteenth century it had nearly doubled. In 1821 it was 1,167,000 and in 1851, 2,300,000. People had been crowding into the city by thousands without any reasonable hope of finding work. What else could they do but steal, and what could they do with their booty but convert it into liquor to drown their misery? There were from six to seven thousand dramshops in London and Westminster alone. Smollett thus describes these establishments:

The retailers of this poisonous compound set up painted boards in public inviting people to be drunk at the small expense of one penny, and assuring them that they might be dead drunk for twopence and have straw for nothing.

And again:

As his guests get intoxicated they are laid together promiscuously, men, women and children, till they recover their senses, when they proceed to get drunk, or having spent all they had, go out to find wherewithal to return to the same dreadful pursuit, and how they acquire more money the Sessions paper too often acquaints us.

It was not until 1729 that an excise duty of five shillings per gallon on gin and other "compounded" spirits was imposed in the hope of raising the price beyond the means of the poorest. This Act was repealed in 1733, but the problem became so acute that three years later the duty on all spirits was raised to twenty shillings per gallon, and none might retail them who had not taken out a £50 licence. It is on record that only two £50 licences were taken out in seven years, and yet in 1742 excise duty was paid on 7,160,000 gallons of spirit. Nevertheless, in 1780, liquor and spirits were still being sold in 500 out of a total of 2,000 houses in the parish of St. Giles.

The eighteenth century was the great period of the smuggler. The gangs were well organized, as were the bootleggers in the United States before the repeal of the Eighteenth Amendment. These gangs claimed a prescriptive right to a certain coast line and openly defied the revenue authorities. They operated under the protection of armed "fighting men," not only terrorizing the local population but actually inducing by bribes members of the local magistracy to aid them.

Although the British criminals of the eighteenth century had anticipated modern methods, the countermeasures employed against them were still almost entirely medieval. The principle was that the people of a township or parish were answerable for every offence committed within their borders and were bound within forty days either to produce the body of the offender or else to make good the damage and pay a fine. This system had long become unworkable. Expansion of trade and population calls for specialization. "What is everybody's business is nobody's business" applies more closely to communities which are too large for public opinion to exercise pressure on indolence or evasion on the part of officials. The only solution of this problem is for the citizens to delegate their obligations to paid, permanent officials under the direct control of the executive, but for various reasons the eighteenth century was slow to accept this principle. In one of the most important departments of social economy—that of police—it paid dearly for its laxity.

Until the year 1792 constables were still theoretically ordinary citizens, serving unpaid for yearly terms of office in rotation. It is more than probable that those who could afford it paid substitutes to take their places—a practice not beneficial to the public, since these deputies were unlikely to be men of much integrity. Like Elbow in *Measure for Measure,* who, when asked by Escalus how it is that he has been a constable for seven and a half years—"Are there not men in your ward sufficient to serve it?"—replied, "Faith, sir, few of any wit in such matters. As they are chosen, they are glad to choose me for them: I do it for some piece of money and go through with all."

CHAPTER III

Sir Thomas de Veil
and the Fieldings

Iт WAS ALMOST BY CHANCE that the germ of the modern
Scotland Yard planted itself in Bow Street, which was the
first and most famous of the police offices. It chanced that
a certain retired colonel, Sir Thomas de Veil, the son of a
Huguenot minister, born in 1684, had been apprenticed to
a mercer in Cheapside. The business failed, and he joined
the army for a livelihood. He rose to be a captain, but on
his return to civil life he was too poor to indulge his rather
extravagant tastes. Accordingly, he set up an office in Scotland Yard, leading out of Whitehall, where he transacted
business such as preparing memorials to the public offices
and drawing petitions at fixed fees. In 1729 we find him appointed to the Commission of the Peace for Middlesex and
Westminster. It was exactly one century before the passing
of Peel's Metropolitan Police Act.

He was now forty-five, well educated, and well travelled
during his military service, and he had won a good reputation in business after leaving the army. He was thus well
fitted for the responsible work he had undertaken. Throughout his career his guiding principle was to better himself; to
stand well with his superiors, and to do all that tact, sa-
gacity, and conscientiousness could accomplish. As his
biographer says of him:

The case was this. The captain was a very nice economist, and
though he was willing to give his friends any assistance that might be

26

drawn from his time and labour, yet he thought they had no right to his pocket, and therefore he was so punctual in setting down his expenses that a dish of coffee did not escape him.

Those who thought him mean respected his scrupulous honesty in paying his debts. His caution and prudence were shown in his declining to be nominated for the Bench until he had carefully studied the powers and duties of a magistrate.

The reputation he had acquired for conscientious work won him recognition as "Court Justice" in 1735. This office also had been created by chance. From the reign of Queen Elizabeth, if not earlier, it had been the practice for the Court and the Ministry to have recourse to some London or Middlesex magistrate for confidential services. The magistrate so employed came to be known as the "Court Justice." One of De Veil's successors, Henry Fielding, was known as "Principal Justice of the Peace in Westminster." Addington and Ford, who also succeeded him, received special emoluments for attendance at the Home Office, and the Bow Street magistrates came to be recognized as higher authorities than their colleagues, especially in matters of police.

De Veil came into prominence as the author of a pamphlet, "Observations on the Practice of a Justice of the Peace, Intended for Such Gentlemen as Design to Act for Middlesex and Westminster." His reputation was further advanced by his feat in breaking up one of the formidable gangs of criminals which infested London. This gang had long been defying the law. Their leader, a cunning attorney named Wreathock, had conducted their legal defence, but he took alarm when it became known that De Veil was on his track, so they lay in wait for him near his new office in Leicester Fields to murder him. In this they failed, and one of their number, Julian Brown, surrendered himself to Sir Thomas as King's evidence. On his information, Wreathock, the leader, was arrested and the rest dispersed. The case attracted the attention of the Ministry. In the following year Colonel de Veil induced the Middlesex magistrates to petition Parliament on the subject of restraining drunkenness, and in consequence the Gin Act of 1736 was passed. It was quite ineffective, and De Veil incurred much odium in consequence.

In January 1737 he read the Riot Act to disperse a crowd collected outside his house in Thrift Street, Soho. The mob demanded the persons of two informers who were in his house at the time. He could not turn them out without sacrificing their lives, or permit them to remain without danger to his own. He sent for assistance and had the leader of the mob, Roger Allen, committed to Newgate. The man was not tried for six months, and he escaped punishment on a false plea of insanity. On his acquittal he made a speech to his supporters which showed no sign of any derangement.

De Veil had some gift as a detective. A man was being examined by him on a charge that he had stolen plate from an eating house. There was no evidence against him beyond the fact that he had passed more than once through the house to the billiard room. A lock had been picked, and on hearing this De Veil began to talk about other matters. Then, suddenly turning to the prisoner, he asked him to lend him his knife and on opening it discovered that the point had been broken off. On this he sent a constable to examine the lock, and the point of the knife was found in it. On this the man confessed and gave the address of a pawnbroker to whom he had sold the stolen plate.

Few years passed without De Veil coming into public notice for some remarkable instance of detection. He it was who discovered the murderer of Mr. Penny, the principal of Clement's Inn and deputy paymaster of the pensions. The murdered man had a servant, James Hall, "a fellow of a surly disposition and of a very cloudy aspect," who had been with him for six or seven years and was heavily in debt. To pay these debts he resolved to kill and rob his master. Accordingly he bought an oaken knobkerrie and hid it under his master's bed. In the evening, as Penny sat at his bedside, undressing himself, Hall drew out the club and stunned him from behind, then carefully undressed him and

cut his throat with a penknife. He made no attempt to
escape, but told the charwoman that his master had gone out
of town.

Penny's friends decided to have Hall taken before a
magistrate, and that magistrate, unfortunately for him,
was Sir Thomas de Veil. Hall was truculent, but he was no
match for the colonel, who questioned him so closely that
he "fell into confusion." Finally, Hall made a full confession. He was executed on September 14 at the end of Cath-
erine Street in the Strand. At that time hanging in chains in
cases of special barbarity formed part of the sentence. The
custom was not abolished until 1834. Hall was hung in
chains at Shepherd's Bush.

On March 10, 1744, De Veil's house was again assaulted by a mob. The footmen of London were meeting
on a Saturday afternoon to protest against the unfair
competition of French footmen. De Veil was instructed to
prevent the meeting, and the proprietor was craven enough
to inform the mob that De Veil had the key to the room
they had hired. Thereupon they went in a body to his house
in Bow Street and demanded the key. Obtaining no satisfaction, they proceeded to break his windows and beat down
his front door with hatchets, he meanwhile standing on the
staircase, armed with pistols and a blunderbuss, for three
hours, before the military made their appearance. The
ground floor of the colonel's house was entirely wrecked,
and only one arrest was made. A month later he received the
honour of knighthood.

His last recorded exploit was keeping London quiet
whilst Charles Edward was advancing to Derby. He was
taken ill while examining a prisoner on October 6, 1748, and
died early the following morning. He had been four times
married and had twenty-five children. His biographer records that "his greatest foible was a most irregular passion
for the fair sex, which, as he freely indulged, he made it
often a subject of his discourse."

Sir Thomas de Veil was succeeded by Sir Henry Fielding
after a space of two years when a magistrate named Poul-

sen held the office. Like De Veil, Fielding's motive in taking office was lack of means, for he was a barrister, a journalist, and a playwright by profession. His appointment to
the Bench is dated October 25, 1748; six weeks later he was
dispensing justice in Bow Street. Living with him was his
blind half-brother, John, who succeeded him at his death
in 1764.

One of Fielding's first actions on his appointment was to
get himself nominated as a magistrate for Middlesex as
well as for Westminster, but he lacked the necessary qualification as a property owner until the Duke of Bedford made
up the deficiency. The fees due to him were supposed to
amount to about £1,000 a year, but much of this income
had to go to his clerk. He received, besides, a small yearly
pension out of the public service money, and this was made
the precedent for the system of stipendiary magistrates
which came into being in 1792.

Fielding was in fact the instrument out of which grew
the institution of the Metropolitan Police in 1829, for very
early in his service he found it necessary to institute a body
of paid police who came to be known as the Bow Street runners. Some idea of how hard he worked can be formed from
his statement that fifty commitments a week were not unusual. Often he was compelled to sit up all night, as when
a gambling house in the Strand was raided and forty-five
accused were taken into custody. More serious than this
was the prevalence of gangs of street robbers. He broke up
one such gang during his first year in office.

These activities quickly brought him into prominence. He
was elected chairman of Quarter Sessions for Westminster,
and a month later he wrote his "Charge to the Grand
Jury," which was published three weeks later "by order of
the Court and the unanimous request of the grand jury." It
was at this time that he submitted to the government a draft
of necessary legislation. His apprehensions were soon justified by the riots of 1749. He had gone away for the week-
end on Saturday, July 1. That night three sailors from the
Grafton visited a house in Westminster, where they were

robbed of thirty guineas by women. They were turned out of the house, but they came back with a large body of comrades, broke all the windows, demolished the furniture, ripped the clothing from the backs of the inmates, piled up their spoils in the streets, and set the heap ablaze. A huge crowd gathered to encourage them, and the parish fire engines were called to stop the blaze from spreading, but they never appeared. No magistrate could be found who cared to interfere with the angry mob. Towards midnight soldiers were called in, and after desperate fighting the streets were cleared. Only a few of the rioters were arrested; two were placed in a cellar under the house of a beadle named Munns. On the following night the mob again assembled, wrecked two houses and burned the goods, wrenched the bars out of the beadle's cellar and rescued the two prisoners. But it happened that when the riot was at its worst a magistrate named Welch met the mob about midnight and with the aid of a military force succeeded in driving the rioters from the streets. Several of the ringleaders were arrested and lodged in prison. On the Monday morning rioters pressed into Bow Street to rescue their comrades.

This was the position when Henry Fielding returned about noon on Monday. In no way intimidated, he sent for a company of the Guards to bring the ringleaders to his house, where they arrived amid shouts of "To the rescue!" Fielding addressed them from an upper window, and failing to induce them to disperse, sent a messenger to the War Office for a reinforcement to protect the Court. Nine of the prisoners were committed to Newgate. That was not the end. All that night the dwellers on the Strand were in consternation. Threatening mobs were gathering at points as far east as the Tower; all the streets in the danger zone were patrolled by soldiers and peace officers; Fielding himself sat up all night, ready to issue orders. His action, which any magistrate might have taken on either of the preceding days, put an end to the riot.

Among the prisoners committed to Newgate was a young man named Bosavern Penlez, who had been arrested by the watch in Carey Street, with a bundle of women's clothes in his possession. These were identified as belonging to the wife of Peter Wood, whose house had been pillaged by the mob. It was clear that the accused had taken advantage of the riot to commit a robbery. Now the Riot Act was very rarely enforced, and Penlez was prosecuted under that Act. Therefore when he and another man named John Wilson were sentenced to death at the August session of the Old Bailey people were indignant. Wilson was reprieved, but the utmost efforts of his sympathizers failed to obtain mercy for Penlez, who was executed at Tyburn on October 11, 1749. Though dead he was not forgotten. Pamphlets and broadsheets poured from the press, and Fielding was moved to write a pamphlet in defence of the government under the title of "A True State of the Case of Bosavern Penlez." It was not convincing because Penlez had never been tried fór theft and the Riot Act had not been read.

By the end of 1749 most of the constables used by Fielding to maintain order were due to retire after their twelve months' service. He persuaded the best of them to continue in office for another year, probably giving them some small remuneration. The point is important, because these constables were the germ of the Bow Street police force and the forerunners of professional police in England. By the end of 1750 Fielding had eighty constables under his command, and he drew up a list of rules for their guidance. But Fielding had neither sufficient money nor places to keep his body of constables together indefinitely, and within a year it had to be disbanded.

Despite all Fielding's efforts, the condition of the streets of London was not much improved. Fielding had submitted to the Lord Chancellor a draft bill "for the better preventing of street robberies"; it was not adopted, but the riots of 1749 frightened the government into action, and a commission was appointed to revise the law. The Acts that followed (the Gin Act of 1751 and the Robbery Act) were passed, but since there were no police to enforce the law, all this legislation proved ineffective. People could not be induced to come forward as witnesses or prosecutors. Alarmed at the situation and at five murders committed in quick succession, the Duke of Newcastle consulted Fielding. In four days he prepared a plan for putting down the gangs that infested the slums of London. He stipulated for a sum of £600, but received only £400. Nevertheless with this meagre allowance he broke up one large gang by instituting "thief-takers"—the predecessors of the Criminal Investigation Department of Scotland Yard. They were "men of tried courage, householders, picked from among the peace-officers, moreover the moment anyone of them commits an act either of cruelty or injustice he is immediately discharged by the magistrate, from the office of thief-taker, and never admitted again."

These thief-takers seem to have been successful from the first. They broke up two important gangs, and in the space of three months no less than nine "gangsters" were executed at the cost of the life of one thief-taker. Besides these, several notorious highwaymen, among whom were Parry and Fleming, "who had struck terror into all the squares about St. James's," were brought to justice.

In the beginning of 1754, Sir Henry's health had become so bad that he resigned his office to his brother John, who had long been his assistant. Sir John Fielding, who was knighted in 1760, held office until his death in 1780. The defect in his eyesight was overcome by a compensating acuteness of hearing; it was said that he could recognize many of the habitual criminals of London by their voices alone. His original and witty personality used to attract audiences to listen to his examinations of prisoners, and the figure of the blind magistrate, with a bandage over his eyes and a switch in his hand to wave before him when he left the bench, came to be as familiar to persons of social importance as it was to the poor wretches who were brought before him. His celebrity amongst his contemporaries is attested by the frequency with which his name occurs in contemporary literature.

During Sir John's long tenure of office, the system instituted by his brother was expanded: the £400 which Henry had received was continued as an annual grant for the main-tenance of the professional thief-takers, who thus became a permanent force known as the Patrol. The jurisdiction of Bow Street had no limits. When seven other police offices were established in 1792 under the financial supervision of a receiver of police, the Bow Street patrol became, as it were, a state force which might serve in any part of the country, much as the Special Branch of Scotland Yard does now.

The six officers attached to Bow Street became known later as "Bow Street runners." Their salaries were £1.1.0 a week, raised in 1821 to £1.5.0—even at that time a very in-sufficient wage for men who were required to be financially honest. From the beginning of the nineteenth century there was in fact an organized armed police under the control of the magistrates. From the report of the select committee on police twelve months before Peel introduced his bill estab-lishing the Metropolitan Police, we gather that the idea of dividing the Metropolis into police divisions had already been adopted. "Occurrence" books were kept; weekly inspec-tions were held; the men were paid weekly; there was a police surgeon. The force amounted to one inspector, seven-teen conductors, and eighty-two patrols. They wore uniform —a red waistcoat which earned them the nickname of "Robin Redbreasts." The "runners" wore no uniform.

It was to Sir John Fielding that the public owed an effective weapon against the highwaymen who took toll of the mail coaches and post chaises on the roads within twenty miles of London. He enlisted some twenty gentlemen with country houses within twenty miles of London to subscribe two guineas to a common pool; to dispatch a messenger on horseback to him with written particulars of any crime com-mitted in his area, including, if possible, an accurate descrip-tion of the thief and the horse he was riding, together with the name of the victim, because private persons were afraid to come forward as prosecutors, and thus no proceedings could be taken against the criminal. On his way to London the messenger was to warn all publicans, stable helpers, and turnpike keepers against harbouring the fugitive, supplying him with a horse, or letting him pass. He was to return with a note from the magistrate showing that he had performed his task, and for this he was to be paid out of the pool. The information and description was to be published in the *Public Advertiser* at the cost of the pool. Even if the highwayman got safe to London he had to run the gauntlet of the thief-takers. The highwaymen were boastful young men and were generally tempted to vaunt their exploits in one of the taverns frequented by criminals of their type, and the thief-takers, who frequented the same places of entertainment, came to hear of them.

The outcome was the "Mounted Patrol," which in three months put down highway robbery. Unfortunately for the public, soon after Fielding's death the Mounted Patrol was allowed to fall into disuse, and immediately highwaymen took to the road again. It was not until 1806 that the grants for the thief-takers and the Horse Patrol were amalgamated and increased to £1,000 a year.

Though far more courageous and energetic than his compeers, Sir John Fielding shared the common view of his time on the demoralizing effects of pleasure on the lower classes, whose appetite for it he regarded as a fruitful source of crime. He was active in suppressing places of amusement; he requested mistresses of servants to send him anonymous letters about the amusements of their household staffs, "for so the most delicate lady may with safety give notice to the justice of any hop, gaming-house, etc., where her servants waste their time, lose their money and debauch their morals." He tried to put down gaming in public houses and to cleanse the streets of nuisances such as "beggars, the insolence of coachmen, carmen, hawkers, etc.; carters riding on their carts, obstructions by carriages or goods, and lastly street walkers." At any rate he was so successful that gangs of thieves left London disguised as gypsies to escape him.

CHAPTER IV

Bow Street Experiments

IT WAS TOWARDS THE END of Sir John Fielding's life that the Gordon riots took place. They were a standing testimony to the lesson which he had been teaching for years— the necessity of reorganizing the police. The immediate cause of the Gordon riots was the Relief Act of 1778, abolishing the disabilities to which Roman Catholics were subjected. A league called the Protestant Association, under the presidency of Lord George Gordon, was formed to procure the repeal of the act.

On June 2, 1780, sixty thousand "good protestants" assembled on the south side of the river and marched upon Westminster, waving banners and singing hymns. They arrived in Palace Yard just before three o'clock. Bishops and peers entering the House of Lords were assaulted. The Bishop of Lincoln was dragged from his carriage and half strangled, and a number of lay peers were roughly handled; Lord North's hat was snatched off and cut in pieces which were sold for a shilling each. The mob forced its way into the lobby, and members were imprisoned until nine o'clock when a body of Horse Guards and Foot Guards appeared.

There followed attacks upon the chapels of foreign embassies. That of the Sardinian minister was attacked, and attempts were made on those of the Bavarian and the Portuguese ministers, but the Bow Street magistrate obtained a hundred bayonets of the Guards which scattered the mob.

After his escape from the House of Lords, Lord Stormont ordered the Bow Street magistrates "to take immediately every legal method to keep the public peace," and that "a sufficient number of justices, constables and peace officers attend tomorrow to secure to the Lords and members a free access to and regress from both Houses of Parliament."

In spite of every effort the riots continued for over a week, and were not got under control until twelve thousand troops were quartered in London and had blocked the three bridges over the Thames. It was a sinister object lesson of the danger the capital was running through the parsimony of Parliament. It is difficult to estimate the strength of the civil forces. Sixteen years later it consisted of only one thousand peace officers of whom 149 were paid to give their whole time to the service. There were besides about two thousand watchmen, mostly beyond work. The rioters were favoured by the apparent disloyalty of Kennet, the lord mayor, and most of the aldermen. Mr. de Castro, a contemporary writer, tells us:

Until it became patent that the Metropolis was at the mercy of the rioters, their methods were countenanced (to use no harsher term) by the aldermen of the city, whose dislike of George III knew no bounds.

The next day thirteen prisoners arrested the night before were brought up at Bow Street before justices Addington and Wright, who committed all but one (who was admitted to bail) to Clerkenwell prison. The evidence against them was slender: probably some of them at least were harmless spectators who had been forced into the chapels as places of safety. The riots continued over the week-end. The Catholic chapel at Moorfields was destroyed. On the Monday the pulpit and furniture looted from the Sardinian minister's chapel were burned; the houses of men who had given evidence at Bow Street were attacked and set on fire. Five hundred rioters were threatening Lambeth Palace; others assembled outside the Houses of Parliament and afterwards burned the house of Justice Hyde, who had read the Riot Act in Parliament Square. Rioters paraded the streets armed with cutlasses and clubs; Lord Mansfield's house was burned because he had recently summed up in favour of a Roman Catholic prisoner who was acquitted.

The constables for Westminster were for the most part local tradesmen selected by a leet jury and formally appointed by the annual Court of Burgesses. They numbered eighty, and their principal duties were attendance at the Houses of Parliament and supervision of the night watchmen, but one may judge their efficiency from the fact that when the mob had invaded Palace Yard only six could be found!

The same evening the mob set the new prison of Newgate on fire and released a large number of the prisoners; another party attacked the Bow Street police office. It was more than an object lesson to the government of the urgent need of police; it was a revelation, for the rioters were allowed to pursue their outrages from 9 P.M. to 3 A.M., and the ground floor was entirely gutted. Sir Henry Fielding's son, who was present, declared that ten constables only would have sufficed to stop the rioting in Bow Street.

On the following day the rioting grew worse. Swollen by the prisoners released from Newgate, the mob attacked the Sessions House and the Old Bailey, burned the Fleet and the King's Bench prisons to the ground, and made an attempt upon the Bank of England. The regular troops were insufficient in number to cope with the riot, and the militia were called out. Although a few houses were burned on Thursday, the troops were now shooting to kill, and before evening the streets were quiet and empty. On Friday, Lord George Gordon was arrested and the riot was over.

London had been in the hands of the rioters for a week. The great objection to employing troops as police was that they were unwilling to act unless a magistrate was present to authorize military action. In the subsequent inquiry it was disclosed that only a few magistrates attended to do their duty, the great majority pleading that, if they did,

View of the **PUBLIC OFFICE** Bow Street, with Sir John Fielding presiding, & a Prisoner under examination

SIR JOHN FIELDING

THE half-blind magistrate who founded the Mounted Patrol for the suppression of highwaymen around London, presiding at Bow Street. By the late eighteenth century, Bow Street, with its "Bow Street runners," had become a sort of early Scotland Yard.

their houses would have been burned down. Probably Sir John Fielding was physically unfit to discharge his duty. He was ill in Brompton when the magistrate's court in Bow Street was sacked.

The Gordon riots might easily have been quelled at the outset if the military had made use of their arms, but the authorities remained for nearly a week under the mistaken impression that soldiers could not fire on the mob without an order from a magistrate, and no magistrate could be found with sufficient courage to give such an order. King George himself referred the point to the Attorney-General, who gave a considered opinion that they could, and as soon as the soldiers began to fire the riot collapsed.

The magistrates and the police had now to face a storm of indignation from all sides, and it was believed that Parliament and the public were now ripe for making drastic reforms. But the London and Westminster Police Bill, which was an anticipation of the Metropolitan Police Act of 1829, was thrown out by the influence of the lord mayor and aldermen on the ground that it would mean "the entire subversion of the chartered rights of the greatest city in the world"—a view that obtains even to this day in confirming to the City of London its own police force. This *"imperium in imperio"* works quite smoothly because there has always been a perfect understanding between the heads of the two forces.

After the Gordon riots Sir John Fielding retired, and in 1782 Sir Sampson Wright succeeded him as chief magistrate at Bow Street. In 1786 he founded the *Hue and Cry*—the forerunner of the *Police Gazette*—a four-page biweekly paper entirely devoted to police matters, accounts of crimes committed, descriptions of stolen goods and of suspected or escaped thieves. The back page was devoted to a list of deserters from the army and navy, with their descriptions.

In the year 1801 London was startled by the appearance of a new crime—the stealing and killing of dogs for the sake of their skins. Robert Townsend, one of the patrol, having received information that stolen dogs were concealed in the house of a woman named Sellwood, demanded admittance and found in a back room a pile of dead dogs and under the floor many more in a putrid state. Further inquiry showed that dog stealers were in the habit of taking small houses, and when they had collected as many carcases as the house would contain, they absconded without paying any rent. Further inquiry showed that Sellwood and Pollett were members of a gang.

On information received, Townsend visited the house of Anne Carter in Blackfriars Road and found ample evidence that she, too, was practising the trade. On the premises were two terrier bitches smeared with a preparation which attracted dogs and lured them to the house. While Townsend was there the father of the boy Pollett called at the house and was also taken into custody.

This crime of dog-stealing for the skin would today cause even more indignation than it did in 1801. Reprobation of cruelty to animals had yet to be born. Melville Lee thus describes the "sport" of bullock-baiting which flourished in Hackney and Bethnal Green in the early years of the century:

A fee having been paid to a cattle-drover, an animal was selected from his herd, peas were put into its ears, sticks pointed with iron were driven into its body, and the poor beast, mad with pain and rage, was hunted through the streets with a yelling mob of men, women and dogs behind it. The weavers left their looms to join in the pursuit and passers-by continually augmented the crowd until the exhausted victim could no longer be goaded into any show of resistance or movement, when it was left to die where it fell, or when sufficiently recovered, to be removed to some butcher's slaughter-house.

The Bow Street magistrate, Sir Richard Ford, was called upon to deal with an alleged breach of the combination law. Three journeymen bootmakers were brought up at Bow Street and charged with a number of others of forming a combination against their masters to exact an increase of wages. The court was crowded with employers. It was proved that meetings had been held and that men who expressed themselves satisfied with their wages had been threatened with personal violence. The three journeymen bootmakers had addressed letters to their employers asking for arbitration, and, what added to the crime, though they had signed individually, they had employed the plural pronouns "us" and "we."

The men's defence was that they could not maintain themselves on their wages; that they had taken legal advice, which was to the effect that individually they could refuse to work. The magistrates held that to persuade others to refuse to work was an offence against the Combination Laws, but they added that if it could be proved that two or more masters had combined, a similar legal remedy was open to the men. We have moved far in labour matters since 1802.

About the same time (September 1801) Bow Street had to deal with a case that had thrown the Church of St. Martin in the Fields into consternation. The curate was ill, and a young man officiated in his stead for a whole month, calling himself Lord Eldon's nephew, buying vestments, marrying over one hundred couples, administering the sacrament, christening several babies and burying twelve. He had obtained his canonicals on credit. The impostor was twenty-three years old, an eloquent preacher, and a dignified and devout clergyman, but the magistrates found him to be half-witted. The absent rector had to re-solemnize all the ceremonies he had performed.

It is strange to read that the pillory was in use as late as 1810. The theory of exposing convicted criminals in the pillory for an hour was, no doubt, to invest the right-thinking citizen with the power of punishment. In practice, however, at any rate in these later days, it was resorted to only when it was known that the crime had outraged public opinion, and it was then tantamount to public torture, ending sometimes in death. A house of ill fame was raided; the men taken in the raid were sentenced to exposure in the pillory in the Haymarket. Before any of them reached the place of punishment they were pelted with filth and blinded with blows. We learn from the *Morning Herald* of the day that

Vigers, the miscreant placed in the pillory in Cornhill, is at present blind in consequence of the pelting he received. He was so much bruised and lacerated that he is not expected to survive.

In 1816 a serious scandal involving certain police officers was discovered. There had been an epidemic of burglaries. Rewards were offered, and on the arrest of the burglars it was found that the crimes had been prearranged by a member of the Horse Patrol, who was to share the reward with the burglars themselves. The guilty patrol went into hiding, but he was afterwards arrested and the case was proved against him. This led to further inquiries, and the magistrates found it necessary to clean up their staff. Five officers were convicted of these malpractices.

The most famous of the Bow Street runners was undoubtedly Townsend, who began life as a costermonger and ended it as a familiar character at Court as protector of the King and the royal family. He was, for those times, passably honest, though he was assiduous in calling upon his noble acquaintances at Christmas time. He was a Bow Street runner for thirty years and left a considerable fortune when he died. In his old age he became boastful and garrulous about his intimacy with the great. He used to boast that the King copied him in dress—the fact being that he paid attention to the King's tailor, from whom he would cunningly elicit advance information about the last suit ordered by the King, and would order the same, contriving that his suit should be delivered first.

After Townsend the most famous of the runners were Sayer,[1] Ruthven, and Vickery. Though they were attached to Bow Street and were paid a regular wage of a guinea a week and fourteen shillings while travelling, they were rather private detectives than official police. Any bank or business in the country could hire their services and reward

---

[1]Sayer, the Bow Street runner, said that Duck Lane, Gravel Lane, and Cock Lane in Westminster were infested with so dangerous a gang of criminals that the police must go there in parties of five or six for safety.

them if they were successful. Townsend was adept at procuring jobs to which special pay was attached. He and Sayer
had for twenty-five years done ten days' duty a quarter at
the Bank of England, and after the attack made upon the
King by Margaret Nicholson they received an allowance of
£200 a year in addition to their pay. Their knowledge of
thieves and their ways had been acquired by frequenting
"flash houses"—the meeting places of thieves and highwaymen who had stolen property to dispose of. Owing to this
inside knowledge they became a terror to the thieves. In
most respects they were rather what we should call private
detectives in these days.

When a committee was appointed to inquire into the
causes of the high figures of crime and the conduct of the
police and the magistrates, Townsend and Sayer gave evidence. Townsend was then an old man who was reputed to
have "made his pile"; his evidence was therefore likely to be
unprejudiced. He condemned the scale of pay and the practice of giving rewards to informants who brought about
the conviction of offenders. A prospective share in the reward, he said, put temptation in the way of the officer to
give evidence that would result either in condemning or
acquitting the prisoner; the officer would naturally do all in
his power to secure a conviction even when the evidence was
doubtful; he thought, however, that at the most an officer
received £50 a year from such rewards. This, undoubtedly,
was an understatement of the facts, for in the same year
Vaughan, one of the Bow Street runners, was convicted of
a very serious offence. Vaughan and two other runners had
conspired to induce a number of boys of thirteen to commit
a burglary and to arrest them in the act, thus earning for
themselves the £40 for what was not improperly called
"blood money." All the three men were found guilty and
sentenced to five years' imprisonment. Vaughan was subsequently charged in the same session with a robbery committed during the previous year and was sentenced to
transportation.

In practice any of the runners were at the beck and call

of private persons or firms in any part of the country, provided that their pay and travelling expenses were defrayed
and they could be spared. The rewards they earned when
they were successful amounted to a considerable sum, and
their knowledge of the ways and the whereabouts of the
professional criminals in London, gleaned from the talk of
criminals in the "flash houses" of the Metropolis, very often
brought them success with its accompanying monetary
rewards.

Even as late as 1822 a committee reported that, outside
the jurisdiction of the City of London and the establishment
of Bow Street, there were still separate parochial police
establishments consisting of a high constable, a beadle, and
petty constables and watchmen for the greater part of London, who were practically useless, because the constables
could not make arrests in any parish but their own without
a special warrant. Selected in rotation as they were, the
constables were indolent and did not take the trouble to
pursue criminals when once they were outside their own
parish boundary. The report of this committee which recommended that there should be one central police force for the
whole of the Metropolis, excluding the City, was the starting
point of the Metropolitan Police as we know its history.

CHAPTER V

The Cato Street Conspiracy

Not even the horror excited by the Ratcliffe Highway murders in 1812 could move the government to adopt a measure recommended alike by the Fieldings, by Colquhoun, the founder of the Thames River Police in 1798, and by the parliamentary committee which sat from 1816 to 1818. Samuel Romilly scarcely overstated the case when he said that the criminal law in England was written in blood. In 1810, Romilly, in advocating a reduction in the number of capital punishments, said:

> If it were possible that punishment as a consequence of guilt, could be reduced to an absolute certainty, a very slight penalty would be sufficient to prevent every species of crime except those which arise from sudden gusts of ungovernable passion. If the restoration of the property stolen and only a few weeks' or even but a few days' imprisonment were the unavoidable consequence of theft, no theft would ever be committed. No man would steal what he was sure he could not keep.

Thefts of property worth more than one shilling could be punished, like murder, with death, and the saying that one might as well be hanged for a sheep as for a lamb must have been on the lips of the young criminals reared in the stews of London where all the inhabitants were criminals. But at a moment when the statistics of crime had increased by 36 per cent, and the Solicitor-General had declared in the House of Commons that "no man could promise himself

security even in his bed," it was not to be expected that
Parliament should make concessions to the criminal gangs
that held London by the throat. The law-abiding were still
convinced that the way with criminals should be to terrorize
them into good behaviour by getting rid of them either by
executing them in public or by transporting them to the
antipodes, where they would trouble London no more.

One of the most harmful practices of the time was the
payment of "blood money" to informers and the police who
were reluctant to arrest a malefactor until he "weighed £40"
—that being the amount paid by the government. According
to Lee, £80,000 was paid in 1815, and the runner Townsend
testified that officers were tempted to turn the scale against
the wretched prisoner on his trial in the hope of winning
this reward.

The punishment of the Cato Street conspirators as late
as 1820 is a case in point.

On February 24, 1820, the *Morning Post* published the
following announcement:

> We received late last night information which we communicate to
> the public with the strongest feelings of horror. The existence of a
> treasonable conspiracy of the most atrocious character, has, we under-
> stand, been for some time known to the government. The first blow
> was to have been struck yesterday by the assassination of His
> Majesty's ministers when assembled at a Cabinet meeting.
>
> About seven o'clock in the evening, Mr. Birnie, the Magistrate,
> under the direction of the Secretary of State for the Home Depart-
> ment, proceeded to the rendezvous of the conspirators on the Edgware
> Road with a warrant to apprehend them. They were at that time
> upwards of twenty in number with Arthur Thistlewood at their head.

Arthur Thistlewood had been a lieutenant in the militia.
He was a man of middle age and had already once been
acquitted on a charge of high treason. Learning that the
entire Cabinet were to dine together at the Earl of Harrowby's house in Grosvenor Square, he had got together in haste
twenty-five persons to join him in a plot to assassinate every
person found in the house, and then to seize the Mansion
House and the Bank of England and proclaim a provisional

government. In the existing state of the police such a plot might have been successful in its initial stage. When all the ministers were assembled, one of the conspirators was to ring the bell at Lord Harrowby's house with an urgent letter, and while the footman left the hall with the letter, the others were to run in, armed with pikes, cutlasses, and hand grenades, leaving two of their number standing outside the door in military uniform to keep the curious at a distance.

Unfortunately for the conspirators they had not taken sufficient care to sift the character of their recruits. On the Tuesday before the intended dinner the Earl of Harrowby was riding in the park to attend a council at Carlton House with a servant when a man stopped him at Grosvenor Gate and handed him a letter addressed to Lord Castlereagh, saying that it was important to Lord Harrowby himself. Lord Harrowby met the same man by appointment on the following morning among the young plantations in Hyde Park and received from him details of the conspiracy. He had already heard some rumours of the plot.

The Cabinet dinner was cancelled, and guided by their informant the authorities proceeded to mature their plans for a raid on the meeting place—a dilapidated stable loft reached only by a ladder from the stable below, which was situated in Cato Street, John Street, off the Edgware Road.

At the hour appointed, a strong force of Bow Street runners, with a company of the Guards in reserve, entered the stable and seized the man posted to guard the ladder. The lights in the loft were immediately extinguished, and the raid had to be made in darkness. Headed by a Bow Street officer named Smithers, the officers ran up the ladder, crying, "We are peace officers. Lay down your arms." The answer was a volley of firearms from the darkness above. Smithers was killed by a sword thrust through the chest, but after this the resistance became half-hearted. The leaders, including Thistlewood, were busy escaping from a window by a rope ladder. When lights were brought, only nine men were found, including a Negro, William Davidson, who was described as the only passably clean man among the gang. A

search of the loft disclosed a veritable armoury of weapons
—cutlasses and pikes newly sharpened and a tub containing
hand grenades about the size of oranges, together with a
bomb weighing fourteen pounds with fuse attached. There
was a good deal of resistance at first. The Negro Davidson
discharged a gun, fortunately missing his aim, but he was
quickly overpowered. Captain Fitzclarence,[1] who was in
command of the Guards, had his uniform torn into shreds.

A reward of £1,000 was offered for the capture of
Thistlewood, who was described as having been born in
Lincolnshire and apprenticed to an apothecary in Newark,
but in the course of the following morning six of the patrol,
headed by Bishop, found him in a room on the ground floor
of a house in Little Moorfields, where he had rented "half
a bed" which he was to share with the landlady's nephew.
She reluctantly surrendered the key, and when the officers
opened the door they saw a head gently raised from under
the blanket and recognized Thistlewood from his description. Presenting a pistol at him, Bishop said, "Mr. Thistlewood, I am a Bow Street officer; you are my prisoner." He
refused to speak on the way to the Home Office, and he
maintained silence when taken before Lord Sidmouth, the
Home Secretary.

True bills for high treason were found against Thistlewood and ten of his associates. They were removed to large
rooms in Newgate to await their trial at the Old Bailey
before a special commission on March 28. In the course of
the inquiry details of the conspirators' plans were given by
some of the minor characters. Adams stated that he had
thought that the day of the King's funeral at Windsor would
be a good opportunity. They might take the two pieces of
cannon and the six pieces in the artillery ground in Gray's
Inn Road and have London in their possession by morning,
for the Guards would be too tired to do anything on their
return from Windsor. If they had the cannon they might go
to Hyde Park and cut off communication with Windsor by
crossing the water and seizing the semaphore telegraph.

[1] A natural son of the Duke of Clarence, afterwards William IV.

This would give them time to set up a provisional government. "The present Royal Family had had the crown long enough," he said.

Another group of the prisoners preferred the assassination of the Cabinet ministers. "They were all so poor, they could not wait." Brunt, one of the leaders, said, "I'll be hanged if I don't believe, now, there is a God. I have often prayed that these thieves might be brought together in order to be destroyed together."

After the assassination, Harrison was to go to King's Street barracks and set the straw shed on fire with a fire ball. The rest were to go to the City Light Horse Barracks, Gray's Inn Lane, to reinforce those taking the cannon.

Some of the conspirators were not trusted very far. For example, Monument had instructions to go to Tyburn turnpike on the Wednesday night and he would then be told all about it. He was to say, "B.-U.-T.", and his friends would reply, "T.-O.-N."

On April 29 sentence was pronounced:

That you and each of you be taken from hence to the gaol from whence you came, and from thence that you be drawn upon a hurdle to a place of execution and be there hanged by the neck until you be dead, and that afterwards your heads shall be severed from your bodies and your bodies divided into four quarters to be disposed of as His Majesty shall think fit. And may God of His infinite goodness have mercy on your souls.

In its leader, the *Morning Post* describes Lord Chief Justice Abbott's address on passing the sentence as "finely pathetic and deeply affecting."

Thistlewood, on the contrary, described his trial as a mockery since he was not allowed to call Edwards, the government spy, as a witness. When he cited Brutus and Cassius as extolled to the skies for the murder of a tyrant he was taken up short by the judge, who said, "Prisoner, as long as your observations have been directed towards us, we heard you without interruption; but we cannot allow a person even in your situation to attempt to justify assassination."

Thistlewood, Ings, Brunt, Tidd, and Davidson received

the sentence of death; the six others, transportation for life. Newspapers of the time do not say where, but clearly it was to Australia. Transportation to the West Indies was instituted under Charles II; in 1718 to the colonies in North America; in 1776 temporarily to the hulks; in 1787 to the new penal colony in Australia. The last transportation was to Western Australia in 1867. It was reported that the six prisoners who escaped with transportation for life owed their escape from death to the intercession of Lord Harrowby. One of the prisoners, named Adams, had turned King's evidence. He said that he had been brought to Whitehall handcuffed to Thistlewood, who had advised him to say that he had been brought to Cato Street by Edwards; he had never seen Edwards. Thistlewood's counsel objected that Edwards, a Crown witness, had never been called. He lived in Fleet Street and was not an accomplice. Why was he not called? He would have told the jury how the case had been got up. Counsel cross-examined Adams closely and accused him of having altered his evidence. Ings, who had been by trade a butcher, pleaded that he was unemployed; that he had met Edwards, then calling himself Williams, who took him to the White Hart, where he gave him cheese and beer and promised him a job. He urged that Edwards should die on the same scaffold as himself. He would not have been in his present position but for Edwards. Admitting that the assassination of ministers might be disgraceful, yet those very ministers met and conspired to pass laws which in his opinion were blacker than assassination. He would rather die like a man than live like a slave.

Brunt, a shoemaker, threw out aspersions on Lord Castlereagh and Lord Sidmouth and asked whether conspiring to take away the lives of such men could be high treason. He claimed that Adams had entrapped him.

Gilchrist, one of those sentenced to transportation, was afterwards reprieved. He declared that he had met Adams for the first time at four o'clock on the day of the raid, and that when he entered the loft he knew nothing of the pur-

pose for which they had assembled. When he became aware
of it he wanted to leave but was threatened with death if
he did so, and on the first appearance of the police officers he
surrendered himself. "I have served my King and my country for twelve years and, oh, God, this is my recompense."

The Privy Council met on Saturday at the Palace in Pall
Mall. The King and all the ministers were present, together
with Lord Chief Justice Abbott; Lord Chief Baron Richard;
Chief Justice Dallas and the judges Richardson and Best,
who had tried the prisoners. After two hours' deliberation,
the council decided to make an early example of the conspirators and fixed the executions for Monday, May 1. The
governor of Newgate told the respited prisoners that they
owed their lives to the intercession of the very men against
whom their conspiracy was directed.

Preparations for the execution were made by enlarging
a platform outside the Debtors' Door at Newgate and
erecting a series of barriers thirty or forty yards distant
which were strongly manned by troops. The scaffold was
covered with black cloth, and sawdust was thickly spread.
Windows commanding the scaffold were let at exorbitant
prices; even the top of St. Sepulchre's Church was packed
with people, and the iron railing collapsed from the pressure
and gave way, carrying sixteen people down with it.

At twenty minutes to six, a company of Foot Guards left
the prison by the Felons' Door and were held in reserve.
A very large number of constables, reinforced by the firemen
employed by insurance offices, manned the barriers, which
were strengthened by posts. Beyond the outer barriers,
an immense crowd collected. At 7 A.M. four placards were
nailed to the boards, bearing the words, "The Riot Act has
been read; disperse immediately." But they were not exposed
to view. Shortly after seven, the executioner made his
appearance and set up a ladder to the beam. The coffins
were brought out and laid on the sawdust in front of the
drop. Sawdust was thrown into them. The block was brought
out and placed at the head of the first coffin. It was of an
unusual shape; instead of presenting a flat surface, the top

of it was quite sharp. Then the prison bell began to toll, and the assembled crowd uncovered. Mr. Cotton, the prison chaplain, found that none of the prisoners except the Negro Davidson would accept his ministratiòns. They claimed to be "Deists." Davidson asked for a Wesleyan minister, a man named Bennett, but "as this man was in a situation of life not well adapted to reveal the tenets of salvation to a dying man, it was thought more prudent that Davidson should, if he wished, have a regular clergyman of any persuasion he might think fit." On hearing this, "the rays of Christianity burst, as it were, through his dungeon's gloom," and he immediately requested the spiritual consolation of the Rev. Mr. Cotton. That gentleman visited him constantly. At five o'clock that morning he had administered the sacrament to Davidson and had offered it also to the other men. Brunt took the wine, but only in order to drink the King's health. The other men conversed freely with the officers and declared that this morning was the happiest of their lives.

The procession was now formed. The men were pinioned, and their irons were struck off. Headed by the sheriffs, the procession moved slowly through the dark passages to the scaffold outside the gate. Thistlewood followed the chaplain; Tidd walked behind him, and then came Ings, laughing immoderately; Brunt appeared, sullen, morose, and indifferent, and lastly came Davidson, praying loudly. Thistlewood was the first to ascend the scaffold. He gazed calmly at the multitude, holding an orange in his hand. As White, the executioner, was adjusting the rope, a man on the roof of a house shouted, "God Almighty bless you." Thistlewood nodded. Ings was sucking an orange given to him by the sheriff and screamed discordantly, "Oh, give me death or liberty." Brunt exclaimed, "Ay! to be sure. It is better to die free than to live slaves." It was now Tidd's turn. Ings seized his hand and with a burst of laughter said, "Come, my old cock-of-wax, keep up your spirits; all will soon be over." He bowed to the populace and nodded to someone at a window. He continued to suck his orange till the cap was drawn over his face.

Ings was still singing, "Give me death or liberty" when he was summoned to the scaffold. He shouted, "Remember me to King George the Fourth. I owe him no animosity." Brunt gave three cheers before the executionor adjusted the rope. When James Ings saw the coffins he shouted to the crowd, "Here we goes, my lads. Here's the last remains of James Ings." Tidd, who stood next to him, said, "Don't, Ings; we can die without making a noise." At the last moment he cried, "Let it be known that I die an enemy to all tyrants. Ha, ha! I see a good many of my friends are on the houses."

When all the ropes were adjusted the drop fell. In those days hanging meant strangulation; the drop was insufficient to break the vertebræ. In the case of Ings, the executioner shortened his struggles by hanging onto his legs. According to the sentence, the bodies were left hanging for half an hour, then the executioner returned and gave the signal for lifting them to the platform. Thistlewood was cut down and his body dragged to the first coffin; the cap and rope were removed from the neck, and the executioner informed the sheriffs that the moment had come for carrying out the next part of the sentence.

Up to that moment the vast crowd had been quiet and orderly and as far as could be judged had shown no sympathy with the condemned men, but now a grotesque figure wearing a mask and dressed in the habit of a sailor sprang through the trapdoor armed with a butcher's knife. He dragged the dead body of Thistlewood to the block and cut off his head. Shouts of execration rose from the crowd, which was more deeply moved by the indignity to the dead than it had been by the sufferings of the living. The time had gone by for terrorizing the mob by brutality, and this situation showed how far the government and the judges were out of touch with the spirit of the time.

The dripping head was seized by the executioner, who exhibited it to the crowd, crying three times, "This is the head of Arthur Thistlewood, a traitor." To a loud accompaniment of hisses and groans the other bodies were decapitated, and the heads and bodies were placed in the coffins and carried into the prison. The quartering of the bodies was omitted. There can be little doubt that this medieval vengeance and the fright administered to the ministers of the day prepared the way for the creation of a central police force for London.

In the following year occurred the riot at Queen Caroline's funeral.

Princess Caroline Amelia Elizabeth of Brunswick was born in 1768. She married the Prince Regent (George IV) in her early twenties, but almost from the first there was incompatibility of temper between the two, and soon after the birth of their daughter, Princess Charlotte Augusta, in 1796, they separated and she went to live in Blackheath.

In 1806 there was gossip about her, but when the matter was examined, she was acquitted of immorality though censured for indiscretion. In 1813 she wrote to the Prince Regent asking for the removal of the restrictions on her intercourse with her daughter, but her prayer was unsuccessful. In the following year she left the country and went to Italy, where she seems again to have behaved indiscreetly with a young Italian of humble origin, and an attempt was made to dissolve her marriage with the Regent on these grounds, but it was abandoned. She rejected all suggestions that she should remain abroad and relinquish all title to the British throne in return for a fixed annuity, and on the Prince Regent's accession to the throne in 1820, she returned to England at once to claim her rights. Though she was allowed to use the title of Queen while she was in England, orders were given that she should not be recognized as Queen of England in any foreign court or be prayed for in the Liturgy.

On the day of the King's coronation at Westminster, she was refused admission to Westminster Hall. She went thence to the Abbey, thinking that she might be allowed to watch the proceedings from Poets' Corner. Lord Hood conducted her to the door, but as she was not provided with a ticket of admission the doorkeeper refused her leave to pass. There was some rude laughter at her discomfiture from a few bystanders, but when she returned to her coach with dignity, there were cries of, "Shame! the Queen! the Queen!" In the following August she contracted peritonitis and died on August 7, 1821, at the age of fifty-three at Brandenburgh House, Hammersmith.

The transition from the feeling for a princess of foreign blood, who had done little to win the affection of her adopted people, to becoming at her death a victim and a martyr was due to the unpopularity of George IV and his court, and it was perhaps natural that her funeral should have been made the occasion of a popular demonstration.

The government had enjoined due observances of respect at the funeral. The theatres were to be closed; the Court was to go into mourning. The funeral arrangements were entrusted to Mr. Bailey of Mount Street. The mourning coaches set out at 4:30 A.M., "Preceded by thirteen mourning coaches and six, a hearse and eight horses, with the usual funeral trappings," and arrived at Brandenburgh House between five and six. Minute guns were fired from the bank of the Thames, opposite the house. There was a warm altercation between Dr. Lushington, one of the executors, and Mr. Bailey, the undertaker, about the removal of the body. Mr. Wilde, another of the executors, presented Mr. Bailey with a written protest before the removal of the body was carried out. On the royal hearse was an imperial crown and the letters, "C. R." The procession moved slowly, the rain falling in torrents, until the head of the cavalcade reached Kensington Church. There, a body of men, twenty deep, formed across the street, to oppose the advance. A severe conflict here took place between them and the police, and several on both sides were hurt. The populace tore up the pavement and threw down trees which they laid across the road. Apparently the object of the mob was that the procession should go through the gate at Hyde Park Corner to the city.

After a severe struggle the procession was diverted to Cumberland Gate, where a serious riot occurred. Stones were flying in every direction, and the Horse Guards fired upon the mob, killing two men. This infuriated the crowd, who hooted continually but kept at a wise distance from the soldiers, and the procession was able to get clear of London without further hindrance. In consequence of this action the Life Guards earned the nickname of "The Piccadilly Butchers," and the Duke of Wellington urged the government to lose no time in forming either a police force or a military corps or both, of a different nature from the regular military force. The Duke had been seriously concerned about the spirit of unrest that was growing in the army and felt strongly that police duties ought not to be entrusted to troops.

In the course of the night at Colchester the executors, in compliance with a codicil in the dead Queen's will, affixed to the coffin a plate inscribed:

Here lies Caroline of Brunswick, the injured Queen of England.

Despite the protests of the executors this plate was immediately removed by those charged with the conduct of the funeral.

The procession reached Harwich at five o'clock on the Thursday afternoon. A boat from H.M.S. *Glasgow* was ready at the landing stage, and the coffin was immediately embarked. A few minutes later the squadron sailed for Stade.

The final service was held in the cathedral church of St. Blaise at Brunswick. With much ceremony the coffin was deposited in the family vault. Among the English present was Alderman Ward, who had made himself conspicuous during the execution of the Cato Street conspirators.

Two years before the institution of the Metropolitan Police at Scotland Yard occurred the robbery of the mailbags from Paris. The case is worthy of notice if only to show how even in these early days of international postal communications the sanctity of the mails was maintained.

At six o'clock on Monday morning, January 29, 1827, the Dover mail pulled up before the General Post Office in Lombard Street, and the mail porters pulled from the receptacle for letters in the rear of the coach the mail portmanteau. Immediately afterwards a clerk rushed out of a side door, crying, "Hold hard for God's sake! The mail has been robbed!"

He had unbuckled the straps of the square portmanteau in the presence of the porters and had thrown the two compartments open when he saw a long knife cut in each, large enough to allow the enclosed bags to be drawn out. Several of these also were cut. The Paris letter bill had been untouched. It read:

No. 203. Direction Générale des Postes de France. Départ de Paris pour Londres, ce Vendredi, 26 Janvier, 1827. Le contenu de votre dernière Dépêche du 24me a été exactement distribué et ultérieurement expédié pour sa destination: l'Administration vous demande le même soin pour le contenu de la présent du reçu de laquelle vous voudrez bien lui donner avis.

There followed a list of the bags and their weights from France, Italy, Spain, Portugal, Switzerland, Germany, and Turkey. The Italian bag, the heaviest and therefore probably the most valuable, was missing.

When the return Dover mail left the Elephant and Castle that night it had for one of its inside passengers the solicitor to the General Post Office, a man especially entrusted with the investigation of delicate matters connected with the postal service. He took up his quarters at the Ship Hotel at Dover to await the postmaster from Calais and the captain of the *Henri Quatre,* the French packet by which the mail had been brought over. After a consultation these gentlemen satisfied themselves that the mail had arrived intact at Dover. This particular mail had been so unusually heavy that it had excited the suspicion of a Dover customs officer, who insisted upon accompanying it to the packet agent's office and inspecting its contents. The portmanteau was unbuckled in the presence of this officer, of Sir Thomas Coates, the packet agent, and of three other persons, who were satisfied that the bags were then in a perfect state.

Therefore the robbery had been committed somewhere between Dover and London.

The Post Office solicitor proceeded to cover every
stopping place of the coach on its way to London, and at
Canterbury he received what he believed to be very important information. On the night of the robbery there had been
four inside and three outside passengers from Dover to
London; one of the "outsides" for Chatham; another for
Canterbury or as much farther towards London as he
pleased; the third "outside" was booked to Canterbury only.
When the coach reached the Fountain Inn, Canterbury, the
outside passenger who was booked as far towards London
as he pleased got down and paid his fare, stating that he
would go no farther; the passenger booked for Canterbury
left the coach at the same time, and the two walked away
together. One of the mail-coach proprietors who lived in
Canterbury happened to be looking at the coach when he saw
two men, dressed as if they had just been upon a journey,
crossing the street. They stood consulting together for a
few moments, and then, when they were fifty yards away, a
third man joined them. They conversed for about a minute
and then separated, two of them going down the street in
the direction of London; the third entered the coach office,
booked himself for London, mounted the coach, and left
with it.

Shortly after the mail left, two strangers, coming from
the direction the coach had taken, entered the Rose Hotel
and ordered a chaise to London. On being asked whether
they would change horses at Ospringe or Sittingbourne, they
said it was immaterial so long as they got to London quickly.
They had a small bag with them. They ordered brandy and
water in the sitting room and shut the door. Fifteen minutes
later the waiter, looking in to tell them the chaise was ready,
saw twenty or thirty letters and a number of small packets
lying on the table. The men were feeling the letters and
holding them before a candle. They showed some confusion,
crammed the letters into their pockets, paid their bill, and
at once set off in the chaise for London. Further inquiries

showed that they had been set down between six and seven on the Monday morning near a watchbox in the Kent Road; that they paid the postboy and walked off towards Surrey Square.

So many people had seen them at the Rose Hotel and at places along the road that a description of them was drawn up and communicated to Bow Street, where the description of one of them was found to fit one Tom Partridge, who had been implicated in several of the mail-coach robberies that had recently been reported. A warrant was obtained partly on the personal description, partly on hints from police informants that Partridge had been concerned in this particular robbery.

Many weeks passed before Tom Partridge was arrested. At Bow Street he was positively identified as one of the men who had booked an outside seat at Dover and as one of the men who had been seen examining letters at the Rose Hotel in Canterbury. On this evidence he was committed for trial. He had strongly denied his guilt and had applied for bail, but this was refused; he had to stay in gaol from March until August.

On August 21, 1827, the prisoner appeared for the first time in the dock at the Maidstone Assizes. The courthouse was packed, for it was known that a large number of French witnesses would give evidence through an interpreter and that the prisoner intended to bring forward irrefutable proofs of his innocence.

The prisoner proved to be a man of middle size, with a queer, humorous face, lighted by twinkling blue eyes. He appeared to be enjoying the interest he was exciting as he leaned over the front of the dock, toying with the herbs which were supposed to protect the court from gaol fever. The case for the prosecution, resting as it did entirely on circumstantial evidence, was soon dispatched and the prisoner was called upon for his defence. He produced a paper and asked that it might be read aloud. This was done by an officer of the court. The prisoner denied that he was guilty, stating that in the month of January he was travelling with a friend named Trotter on business in the counties of Somerset and Devon; that on the Monday of his alleged crime he arrived at the George Inn, Glastonbury; that they left the same day, and went to an inn in Somerton and thence in the landlord's gig to Yeovil; that, taking a fancy to the horse, he sent back word to the landlord that if he had a mind to sell it, he would meet him at the George on the following Thursday; that on the Thursday he bought the horse for twelve guineas, tried it on Friday morning, and left it with the landlord; that he and Trotter left Glastonbury at half-past eleven by the Exeter coach on the 27th to Tiverton, where they put up at the Three Tuns Hotel, leaving on Monday the 29th by the Bristol coach to Bridgwater.

Then, being called upon for evidence of this watertight alibi, he called a dozen witnesses to prove every detail in his statement. After the final witness had been heard, the judge asked the Crown counsel whether he desired to press the case. Counsel turned to consult the Post Office solicitor, but members of the jury intervened to say that they were satisfied that a mistake had been made. Whereupon a verdict of acquittal was recorded, and Mr. Tom Partridge bowed to the judge and walked smiling out of the dock.

Some two years after the trial the Post Office solicitor was walking along Bishopgate Street on his way to a coach when a man jostled against him as he went into a public house. It was Tom Partridge. He had often thought of Tom Partridge, puzzling his brain for a solution of the mystery; and now, having a few minutes to spare, he crossed the street to look at the public house into which Tom had vanished. At that moment Tom Partridge emerged, looked up at a window, and shouted, "Hi!" Whereupon from an upper window appeared the head and shoulders of another Tom, the replica of the original Tom. There were two Tom Partridges—one standing on the street and the other looking out of the third-floor window.

Next morning found the solicitor closeted with the officer in charge of Post Office criminal cases, and shortly afterwards a confidential messenger was dispatched with a letter

addressed to a Mr. William Barker, otherwise Conkey
Barker, otherwise Bill the Nobbler. That evening Mr. La
Trappe of the General Post Office sat waiting in his private
house in Brunswick Square. As the clock struck eight the
servant came in to announce a visitor, who was dressed in
stable clothes and smelt strongly of horses.

"Sit down, Barker," said Mr. La Trappe, pointing to a
chair. "I want a little information from you. It can't hurt
anyone, as the affair is dead and buried. Do you remember
the robbery of the Dover mail?"

"I should think so," replied Barker, grinning.

"Ah! We tried a man named Tom Partridge for it, but
he was acquitted on an alibi. He did it, of course?"

"Why, of course he did."

"That man has a double who was travelling in Somerset
and Devon at the same time, and the double worked the
oracle for him?"

"How did you find that out?"

"Never mind how I found it out. What I want to know is,
who is the double?"

"Tom Partridge's brother—old Sam, one year older
than Tom and as like him as two peas. Old Sam had been out
in Ameriky all his life, and when he first came back everybody was talking about his likeness to Tom; you couldn't
know them apart. Fiddy, the fence, thought that something
might be made of it, and he planned the whole job—the
cream, the tins, and the horse what he bought. Tom's got
that horse now to drive in his shay on Sundays."

"One more question, Barker. How was the robbery done?
The contents of the mail portmanteau couldn't have been
cut without unbuckling the straps, and they couldn't have
done that on the top of the coach."

"Ah, that was the best game of the lot. The job was done
while the portmanteau was lying in the agent's office in
Dover. It lay there from three o'clock in the afternoon till
between seven and eight in the evening. Tom Partridge and
his mate, they opened the door with a skeleton key. There
was no one there, and they had plenty of time to work it."

"And Tom's mate—who was he?"

"Ah! That I can't say. I never heard tell of *his* name," said Barker, looking at the ceiling.

A year later, this frank gentleman, Mr. William Barker, was condemned to death for horse-stealing. Just before his execution he sent for Mr. La Trappe and confessed that *he* had been Tom Partridge's mate in the robbery of the Dover mail. Mr. La Trappe thanked him, but he could do nothing more for him.

PART III

THE ESTABLISHMENT
OF SCOTLAND YARD

CHAPTER VI

The Public Opposition

In 1822 SIR ROBERT PEEL became Home Secretary. His first act was to appoint a committee under his own chairmanship. It sat for three months, and despite his advocacy of a police force directly under the control of the government it reported that it was impossible "to reconcile any effective system of police with that perfect freedom of action and exemption from interference" which was "one of the great privileges and blessings of society in this country." Peel entirely disagreed, but he concentrated his first term of office to reforms in the criminal law which had been long overdue. He attacked the old obsession that severity of punishment was the best preventive of crime and urged that the best preventive was certainty of arrest and punishment.

In his second term of office as Home Secretary he pressed successfully for a second committee which would obtain the necessary parliamentary backing for his great reform. The committee found that the alarming increase of crime was to be attributed to the cheapness of gin, unemployment, the neglect of children, juvenile gambling, and lack of vigour and consistency in the police. It took evidence on the practice of "compromising" for the restitution of stolen property which was regularly negotiated by lawyers and police officers, especially the Bow Street runners, and even by banks. It exposed the evils of "flash houses" such as the Brown Bear in Bow Street as harbouring places for criminals. The existence of such taverns was defended by the Bow Street runners on the ground that without them they would not know where to find criminals who were ripe for arrest. Finally the committee recommended the establishment of a police office under the Home Secretary, with a general control over all the police establishments of London. As Peel wrote to the Duke of Wellington, his intention was to "teach people that liberty does not consist in having your house robbed by organized gangs of thieves."

On April 15, 1829, Peel introduced his bill. He gave a comparative statement of the volume of crime in the metropolis and the rest of the country, from which it appeared that the committals in London and Middlesex during 1828 were one in 378 of the population as against one in 822 for the rest of England and Wales. The committals in London and Middlesex during the year 1821 were 2,480 out of a population of 1,167,000, and in 1828, 3,568 out of a population of 1,349,000. Here then there was an increase of crime in seven years of no less than 41 per cent in a population which had grown by only 15.5 per cent.

The committals for the same seven years in England and Wales were 11.5 per cent, while the increase of population had been 28 per cent. He argued from these and other figures that the increase of crime in London had arisen from the defective organization of the police, and he proposed that the parochial authorities should no longer be the sole guardians of life and property—a system which was expensive and inefficient, to the knowledge of everybody—whereas by concentrating the police in a single force efficiency and economy would be achieved. He said that frequently one side of a street was in one parish and the other in another parish, and if a parish watchman saw a crime being committed on the opposite side of the street he was powerless to interfere. Thus in practice much property was left entirely unprotected.

He proposed therefore to establish a central board of police under the control of three magistrates; to relieve the parishes of the rate levied for watchmen and to substitute a police rate which would amount to less. This would not only diminish the expenses of public prosecution, but would tend to prevent crime and to mitigate the severities of the criminal code, none of which could be done unless they had sufficient means to prevent crime.

He did not believe that distress was so great an incentive to crime as many had stated. Idleness and profligacy mainly led to its commission; and when so much was said, and properly said, of the liberty of the subject in this country, some care should at the same time be taken of the property of the subject when the individual had not the means of protecting himself.[1]

Leave was unanimously given for the introduction of the bill. The editorial comment in the *Times* and the *Morning Post* was to the effect that all the world was agreed that the change was necessary and that the only criticism possible was that the government should have made the change long before. As for the bill itself, the *Times* considered its chief merit to be that it left the way open for future improvements and was frankly experimental. It viewed with anxiety the extra patronage that the Crown would enjoy and suggested that the parochial authorities should still exercise the right of appointment and the Crown the right of dismissal for incompetence; that in any case the police should lose the power of voting for candidates for the House of Commons. The *Standard* put the other side of the question. It was

to take from the people of this metropolis all control over the armed police, transferring the authority which they now possess over a body capable of being so formidable . . . to the Home Office—the Quarter Guard, as we may call it, of our metropolitan camp. . . . Nobody doubts, we suppose, that it will be a sharply and severely efficient police that the Duke of Wellington proposes to confer on the country. There was a time, however, when Englishmen thought that the advantage of a military police might be bought too dear, but all that has been changed.

---

[1] Peel's speech in the House of Commons.

It goes on to print correspondence hostile to the bill and foretells that it must soon become

an Irish brigade, and to prove that it must we have only to cite the fact that every decent Englishman, even to the degree of a day-labourer, enrolled in the body, is already retiring from it. . . . Its ranks must of necessity be filled by those who take the lowest wages, and perform the lowest drudgery of the Metropolis, viz.: the Popish labourers imported from Ireland. . . . The Metropolis and all that it contains is to be in the hands of a body of Popish Irish spies, subject to no civil control and at the command of His Grace, the Duke of Wellington.

On September 29 the *Standard* replied to an attack by the *Morning Chronicle:*

The *Morning Chronicle* replies this day in an article of some length to the few lines which we offered yesterday upon the subject of the new police, or *gens d'armerie,* or Irish Brigade, or "legion of intelligence," or by whatever name the novelty is to be called. Our contemporary, which seems to like the police project as much as we dislike it, and probably for the same reason—that it is wholly re-pugnant to the spirit of English law and to the theory of free govern-ment—divides our objections into two classes for the purpose of answering them, and then proceeds to argue, first, that the body is not by its constitution a body of spies, and secondly that it is not likely to become a mere Irish brigade.

Now, upon the head of espionage little need be said. The low con-stable—the fellow of the rank of a low day-labourer—is instructed that he is to make himself acquainted with the inhabitants of every house within his beat, and that his prospects of promotion depend upon the extent and accuracy of his information in this particular. Now, for what is this information wanted but to enable somebody to exercise a surveillance over our domestic habits and private conversation; and *is not this espionage?* And how is this information to be obtained in the first instance but by pumping of servants, collecting of gossip at chandlers' shops, eavesdropping, etc.—and *is not that espionage?* . . . Within six months after it shall be at work whatever passes at any dinner-table in London . . . may be known at the Home Office before the words are half an hour uttered. . . .

That there was much public disquiet about the bill is shown by the following passage in a leading article in the *Times* of April 23:

We have received many letters on the subject of Mr. Peel's Police Bill, but they are so voluminous and some of them so intemperate that insertion cannot be given to them.

A case is reported in Lambeth as having happened yesterday, which proves, if any proof were needed, the absolute want of a central and controlling power in the Metropolitan police. Here were a gang of robbers pursued by one set of watchmen and actually suffered to escape by another set who would not stir a foot beyond their own boundary line to cross and turn the flying villains. It is impossible, without a spirited and cordial coöperation, to afford protection to property or to punish crime.

The *Times* went on to quote another case that had been before the court on the preceding day—that of the watchman Beazley. This man had been a brothelkeeper and had been suspended by the magistrate for general misconduct as a watchman, but had been reinstated by the parish authorities almost immediately. On the preceding night he had arrested a young man on the charge of ringing a doorbell, shouting, and creating a disturbance. On taking him to the cells he had struck him a violent blow from behind, felling him, and had then left him for half an hour, bleeding and unconscious on the floor. On the question of the magistrate whether he had seen the prisoner ring the bell, he had to admit that he had not—that he had arrested him on suspicion. The gaoler deposed that Beasley had long been unfit for his position as watchman. On this the magistrate again suspended him and sent him to the Sessions on a charge of assault.

On May 26, 1829, the Metropolitan Police Bill was read a third time in the teeth of opposition from Mr. John Bright, and passed. On June 6 the Duke of Wellington moved its adoption in the House of Lords and it became law. The long battle between common sense and false notions of liberty was won.

Not the least of Peel's difficulties was the selection of the men who were to control the new force, for he knew that if he appointed any prominent man the cry of jobbery would be raised against him. On the other hand his scheme might be wrecked if he appointed nonentities who would be incapable of maintaining a high standard of discipline, for every dereliction of duty would be seized upon by the opposition to inflame the popular prejudice against the new force. He wrote to the Duke of Wellington:

The chief danger will be if it is made a job; if gentlemen's servants and so forth are placed in the higher offices. I must frame regulations to guard against this as effectually as I can.

He began by ruling out all candidates who might apply for the new appointments and kept the selection in his own hands. His first choice was Colonel Rowan (afterwards Sir Charles Rowan, K.C.B.) who had fought under Wellington in the Peninsula and at Waterloo. On his retirement he had become a police magistrate in Ireland, and it was there that Peel, when Chief Secretary for Ireland, had been made aware of his ability. Richard Mayne, his second choice, was a young barrister on the northern circuit and the son of an Irish judge. Seeing that the two men had equal powers and each had access to the Home Secretary without consulting the other, it is a remarkable tribute to Peel's choice that they should have worked amicably together for twenty years. Rowan was in charge of the discipline; Mayne drew up the general instructions to the force in words that have stood the test of time for more than a century:

The primary object of an efficient police is the prevention of crime; the next that of detection and punishment. The protection of life and property, the preservation of public tranquillity, and the absence of crime will alone prove whether those efforts have been successful and whether the objects for which the police were appointed have been attained.

Both commissioners were sworn in as justices to maintain the tradition that the police are judicial functionaries acting under magistrates. The practice still continues. The commissioner and all the assistant commissioners are sworn in as magistrates.

The example of these two men embodied the modern conception of the police as a citizen body; servants, not masters, of the public, courteous and helpful. In the '30's

A VIEW OF OLD SCOTLAND YARD
Engraved in 1776

A PRISON SHIP AT DEPTFORD
ONE of the dreaded prison hulks, from an engraving made in 1826.

and '40's inspectors and sergeants were detached as instructors to the new forces which were being established in the counties and cities in England and Wales, and some were sent overseas to the colonies on like missions. Thus the principles of the commissioners were carried far and wide over the British Empire.

A high compliment was paid to Rowan and Mayne by the parliamentary committee of 1833–34:

On many critical occasions and in very difficult circumstances, the sound discretion they have exercised, the straightforward and honourable course they have pursued, whenever their conduct has been questioned by the public, calls for the strongest expression of approbation on the part of your Committee.

While the new force was being constituted, the *Times* continued to give instances of the working of the old system in its police news—for example:

Two young men of gentlemanly appearance (one of whom gave his name as "Young Hell") were brought up at Bow Street on a charge of disorderly conduct. They had refused to pay their coachman the fare he demanded for driving them to the opera house, and there they were refused admittance and roughly hustled to the watchhouse in the Strand. The night watchman was too drunk to write down the charge. The magistrate ordered these young bloods to compensate the coachmen and the constables for their part in the affray and refused to acknowledge the night watchman any longer as a constable.

In the same issue it recorded that James Weatherstone, a patrol, was charged with stealing a turbot from Billingsgate and was sentenced to seven years' penal servitude.

On July 16 the whole of the Dismounted Police patrol were mustered in the Treasury passage and were inspected by the newly appointed police commissioners, who appeared to be pleased with their appearance.

On August 12 about eight hundred men had been recruited. They were divided into four classes—a superintendent, inspectors at £100 a year, sergeants at three shillings and sixpence a day, and police constables at three shillings a day. They were to wear a plain uniform supplied at contract price and were not to be less than five feet seven inches in height. It was decided that they should take up their duties on September 7 and in the meantime that they should be regularly drilled by sergeants from the Guards. For the purpose of examining persons arrested during the night, an office was taken in Great Scotland Yard with an entrance in Whitehall Place. It was thus that the headquarters of the Metropolitan Police came to be known as "Scotland Yard," even after they were moved to their present position on the Thames Embankment nearly opposite the Home Office, when the official designation of their headquarters became "New Scotland Yard." Old Scotland Yard stands on the site of a palace built during the reign of the Saxon kings for the reception of the kings of Scotland or other august visitors.[1]

On September 24 the first police instructions were issued. They included a provision that the men should pay the contractors ready money for their uniforms, or apply to the commissioners to have deductions made from their pay until their uniforms were paid for; that no liquor should be accepted from publicans without paying for it at the time; and that each constable should bear on his uniform the letter indicating his division and a number.

To meet the strong public opinion that existed against militarizing the police, the uniform was made as simple as possible—a blue coat and trousers and a top hat. One of the fables about this headgear which was circulated at the time has found its way into a modern book:

These top hats, however, were no ordinary top hats, but were made in a special way and performed a function of their own. They were made with a strong metal frame which would stand the weight of the wearer and were often used to stand on when it became necessary to look over a high wall, and were occasionally used as seats when the

---

[1] It was not the first time that police had been housed in Scotland Yard. John Evelyn, the diarist, had been one of the "police commissioners" appointed in 1622 to control the lighting, scavenging, etc., in the streets, and licensing the newly introduced hackney coaches.

policeman wearied of his beat and, unobserved by authority, desired to snatch a rest.[1]

The government was moving tentatively; it hesitated to extend the powers of the force to the whole of London until it had been tried. We find even the *Morning Post*—a strong supporter of the scheme—deprecating the idea that it should be applied to the City by a change in its charter, since it would "have argued a contemptuous disregard for chartered rights—such as we trust the British Parliament will never display—to have forced upon the City a system yet untried." More than a century has passed, and the City of London still has its own police force which works in close and amicable relations with Scotland Yard, though the latter has engulfed in its police jurisdiction the huge area of Greater London. The *Morning Post* sounds one note of warning; it hopes "that a wise jealousy for the security of personal freedom will always forbid arrests in anticipation of apprehended or merely conjectural offences."

The *Times,* on the other hand, places first in the duties of the new police the *prevention* of crime and thinks that if occasionally an individual policeman should err on the side of overzeal, no great harm will have been done.

On October 16 we find a leading article in the *Times* commenting on the number of parochial meetings that have been held to protest against the Metropolitan Police:

We shall be glad to see the question of the police brought forward and abuses remedied if any are proved to exist, but it would give us sincere concern to find the system itself abandoned.

A little while later, on November 4, we find the following:

We have not room for more than a brief expression of our abhorrence of the unjust and cruel spirit which the mob are constantly displaying against the New Police. It behoves all honest men to discourage this malignant feeling by all means in their power. The system may have defects; let them be fairly stated and examined; we have no

---

[1]*The History of the Criminal Investigation Department,* by Margaret Prothero.

doubt that the respectable persons who have the direction of this useful branch of public service will attend to all rational suggestions; but in the name of common sense and common humanity we call upon Englishmen to abstain from outrageous violence against their fellow-countrymen who are merely acting in the faithful discharge of the duties imposed upon them.

The fact was that the police had been seized upon by the Opposition as a stick with which to beat the government. It was quite easy for hostile propagandists to work up a case against any innovation and so convert a reform into a political party quarrel. On December 1 Earl Grosvenor presented a petition for the repeal of the Metropolitan Police Act from his constituents in St. George's, Middlesex. He said that he himself could not support the petition.

It was a year of riot and unrest. King George IV had died on June 26. A General Election was pending; the Reform Bill was shortly to be introduced; the "National Political Union," a new body, was busy fomenting trouble all over the country; there were riots everywhere on one excuse or another, not because of the general trade depression so much as from the kind of sympathetic unrest which was affecting all European countries in 1830. A minor instance of the general insubordination is recorded on October 9, when some youths were put in the stocks at Surfleet. The crowd brought tankards of ale to them, and when they themselves had imbibed freely, they broke away the stocks and released the culprits.

In April the weavers in Lancashire destroyed their machine looms; not a single loom was left standing in Blackburn or within six miles round it. Cavalry were called out; the Riot Act was read; lives were lost. The riots lasted from Monday to Wednesday and were followed by similar riots in Manchester and Wigan; not less than a thousand power looms were destroyed at a loss of £30,000.

The spirit of unrest had spread to the prisons. In September 1823, Sir J. C. Hippisley had published the result of his observations on the treadmill. He inspected the men as they descended in rotation for their five minutes' rest after fifteen minutes on the wheel. "Every one of them was perspiring, some in a dripping sweat." Examining them privately, he found that they suffered pain in the legs and feet. In those days women also were employed on the treadmill. The matron said that her charges sometimes fainted and often "had not a dry thread belonging to them." The finest physiques were worn down after a few weeks' work and she, the matron, had to ask for a few days' relaxation. The most unsatisfactory aspect of the treadmill was that it was doing no useful work; as in the case of Appold's hard-labour machine ("the crank"), it was grinding the air, and yet the treadmill was still working in most of the prisons as late as 1896. It is fair to say that in its later years it was used for pumping water.

In May 1827 there was a serious riot in Bodmin gaol. The prisoners refused in a body to climb the treadmill or do any kind of hard labour. Two of the visiting magistrates were summoned; they remonstrated with the rioters, but in vain; the mutineers broke up the railings round the wheel and prepared for resistance. The staff of the Cornwall militia was brought in and drawn up in the prison yard; the mutineers tried to wrest their muskets from the militiamen, whereupon some of them were knocked down with the butt ends of the muskets, and five of the most refractory were lodged in separate cells.

The ringleader of the mutiny, a man named Sowden, who was serving a sentence for a violent assault on the constables of Camborne, was ordered by the magistrates to ascend the wheel. He refused. Then and there the magistrates sentenced him to corporal punishment (which they had power to do) in the presence of the other rioters, who were ordered in their turn to ascend the wheel under pain of a like punishment. On this they yielded and promised obedience for the future. One of their demands was to be given a clean shirt every day.

In this state of unrest all over the country as well as in London it was at once the worst and the best moment for introducing a new form of authority—the worst, because in the irritable state of the public nerves it was questionable whether the government was strong enough to stem the tide of public opposition; the best because without some centralized police force the disorders in London might well let loose something approaching civil war. It must be remembered that the Metropolitan Police Act entailed a new and unfamiliar form of taxation on the ratepayers, which meant that property owners as well as the criminal classes were in strong opposition to the scheme and ready to believe any calumny about their loss of liberty which the opposition press was circulating day after day. Nevertheless the commissioners went quietly about their business of making bricks without straw, quite undaunted by the storm of opposition.

It is a remarkable fact that the general instructions issued by the commissioners under the Metropolitan Police Act and sanctioned by the Home Secretary were so well drafted that in the main they have remained unchanged for more than a century. They begin:

The following general instructions for the different ranks of the police force are not to be understood as containing rules of conduct applicable to every variety of circumstance that may occur in the performance of their duty; something must necessarily be left to the intelligence and discretion of individuals, and according to the degree in which they show themselves possessed of these qualities and to their zeal, activity and judgment on all occasions, will be their claim to future promotion and reward.

It should be understood at the outset that the principal object to be attained is *the prevention of crime.* To this great end every effort of the police is to be directed. The security of personal property, the preservation of the public tranquillity . . . will thus be better effected than by the detection and punishment of the offender after he has succeeded in committing the crime. . . .

When in any division offences are frequently committed there must be reason to suspect that the police is not in that division properly conducted. The absence of crime will be considered the best proof of the complete efficiency of the police. In divisions where this security and good order have been effected the officers and men belonging to it may feel assured that such good conduct will be noticed by rewards and promotion.

This preamble reflects the minds of men who knew little of the underworld of London. It was the product of the office table and not of men of practical police experience. In piloting his bill through the House of Commons Sir Robert Peel had always laid stress upon prevention of crime as the principal object of his new police. It sounded well in theory, but in practice there were obvious difficulties. Was crime to be prevented by the sudden appearance of a policeman at the crucial moment? Or was the policeman who met a thief well known to him to murmur, "I've got my eye on you" as he passed him? Was he to take a thief into custody when he saw him loitering outside a jeweller's shop, and if so what charge was he to bring against him? In the light of experience statute law came to the aid of the police in the Prevention of Crime Act (1908), which constituted loitering with intent to commit a felony a crime in itself.

Nor was it fair to the police to make distinction between divisions in the matter of the amount of crime committed in each, since in divisions consisting almost entirely of slums inhabited by the poorest people in London it was self-evident that more crime would be committed there than in the divisions of the West End.

At first the Metropolitan Police district was divided into five divisions of eight sections each and each section into eight beats. Each division was to have a station or watchhouse which was to be the office of its superintendent with inspectors, sergeants, and constables under him. The division was to consist of sixteen parties, each party consisting of a sergeant and nine men. Four sergeants' parties constituted the command of an inspector. The equivalent of a division was to perform duty in the immediate neighbourhood of the commissioner's office.

Most of the police orders of those days point to the determination of the commissioners not to furnish their critics with material for agitation against the new force. Nevertheless the agitation continued, though there were signs that it was dying down everywhere but in the opposition press. It required a tragedy to bring Londoners to their senses.

About midnight on August 17, 1830, a constable named Long, who was on duty in the Gray's Inn Road, noticed three suspicious-looking men loitering about the pavement. Telling a colleague to be on the alert, he followed them, picking up on his way a man named Peter Milligan who accompanied him. They came upon the men at the entrance to the cemetery. Constable Long crossed the road and said to the men, "What have you been after?" whereupon one of them plunged a shoemaker's knife into his body while the others held him by the arms. The blade of the knife remained in the wound. The men made off, closely followed by a crowd shouting, "Stop thief!" and two men were caught and handed over to the police. The unfortunate constable died almost immediately; on the scene of the murder were found a number of housebreaking tools. Of the two men arrested, one who gave his name as Smith, but whose real name was Sapwell, was positively identified by several witnesses; he was found guilty and sentenced to death, protesting his innocence to the last.

But the real interest for us in the tragic business lies in its sidelights. It was natural that the Bow Street magistrates should subscribe a sum for Long's widow, but it might well have been otherwise with the professional criminals; yet when a policeman encountered a well-known housebreaker personally known to him and began to question him the man became indignant. "I would never work with a cove who'd draw a knife," he said; "nor would anyone of my family." And putting his hand into his pocket, he drew out a sovereign for the benefit of Long's family.

On the same day two officers from G Division entered a house in Old Street where a gang of burglars were collected. One of them, addressing the sergeant, said, "Waddington, if you want us, any of us, you shall find some difficulty in taking us into custody, for we shall give you a turn-up first, let what will follow." But when they found that the object of the visit was to obtain information about the murder, they expressed their abhorrence of so cold-blooded a crime. Although they did not deny that they lived by plunder, murder was a crime they detested. They immediately made a collection among themselves and handed £1 to the officers for Long's widow. Many other sympathizers sent small sums to the *Times* and the *Morning Post* with the same object.

The witnesses for the prosecution were all of the same class as the accused. One of them—Mary Ann Griffiths, who had seen the blow struck and swore that she had never lost sight of the prisoner until he was taken into custody—admitted that she made her living by walking the streets. Her evidence was not shaken by the most trenchant cross-examination. The fact emerged that among the criminal class in London at the time the murder of a police officer was regarded as "hitting below the belt."

On the morning of his execution, Sapwell had a short conversation with the sheriff, who asked him whether he had anything to say before he quitted the world. He replied, "When I appear before my Maker and He asks me, 'What have you done and who sent you here?' what shall I say?" The sheriff replied, "You have been tried by a jury of your countrymen and convicted of an atrocious crime. It is for that you are condemned to die." "Very well," replied the prisoner, "then He will say, 'You have been wrongfully convicted and you ought not to have come here; however, walk in.'"

An enormous crowd attended to witness the execution. Every window and roof within sight of the scaffold was occupied by people who had assembled before daybreak, but there was no sign of sympathy with the condemned man, and the crowd dispersed in silence. In accordance with the sentence the body was given to the surgeons for dissection before it was handed over to the wife for interment.

CHAPTER VII

The Duke of Wellington's Mistake

Duration THE LATE SUMMER OF 1830, the police were called in to deal with some curious cases. In August a fire broke out at the shop of a pawnbroker in Berwick Street, Soho, which consumed not only the shop but its entire stock of pledges belonging to the poor of a densely inhabited district. Before the site was handed over to the builders, an auction of the half-burned pledges dug out of the rubbish was held, and since it was supposed that no one but Jewish dealers would attend, all others were excluded, including the poor people to whom the pledges belonged.

There was at the time no marked anti-Semitic feeling among the poor in London, but the patent injustice of excluding owners of the pledges from the sale fired the mob. The auction had scarcely begun when the place was surrounded by hundreds of people of both sexes waiting for the Jews to come out with their purchases. No sooner did the first Jew make his appearance than he was set upon by the crowd, chiefly by the women, and despoiled of what he had bought. The news was carried inside; a panic seized the Jews, who burst out of the ruined shop and ran for their lives, with the Christians yelling behind them. Some made their escape, but others took shelter in the first open house that presented itself. In one house in Wardour Street a regular siege was opened by the pursuers, who demanded the surrender of half a dozen fugitive Jews. The women attacked the house with fury, smashing the windows with stones and plastering the walls with mud and filth. The garrison consisted of a single woman, who poured down buckets of water and less agreeable contents on the heads of her assailants and succeeded in withstanding the attack and saving the Jews until the arrival of a party of police which dispersed the crowd.

A human cormorant, named Dando, who made a practice of defrauding restaurant keepers by neglecting to pay for what he ate, seems to have been too much for the police courts of those days. He was arrested on the complaint of one Mason, who kept an oyster stall, that he had eaten no less than eleven dozen oysters as well as bread and butter and had walked away whistling a lively air. On being stopped he said, "I must have victuals, and if I have not got the money, why, those must suffer who have."

His defence was that he had just been discharged from jail for a similar offence and was very hungry. The magistrate decided that he must be summoned before a Court of Requests. But the prosecutor knew a better way. "I should like," he said, "to give him a good sound thrashing with this cane, and if I thought I should be justified, I should do it before he escapes out of this neighbourhood." To this the magistrate replied that he should discharge the prisoner and that he must not meet with any obstruction on leaving the office. He was proceeding to give the prisoner a lecture on his conduct when the oysterman slipped unobtrusively out of court and, having obtained the loan of a bucket of water, lay in wait for Dando at the door, emptied the bucket over him, and thrashed him with his cane, to the great amusement of the crowd, who cared nothing for the niceties of the law and approved of summary justice.

In September a case reported in the newspapers produced an unfavourable impression in the public mind. James Cole, a constable of A Division, charged a hotel porter with stealing a handkerchief from a gentleman's pocket. He swore that the victim of the theft had given his name as Hippesley, with an address in the Temple. On inquiry it was found that

no such person was known in the Temple, and three witnesses were called to prove that they saw the arrest made;
that there was no gentleman near the prisoner at the time;
and that they had distinctly seen the policeman pull the
handkerchief out of his own pocket just before making
the charge. On this the jury returned a verdict of not guilty.

A few days later two constables were indicted for rob-
bing a drunken man whom they had been asked to escort
safely home. They were each sentenced to seven years'
transportation.

The first hint we have of a breach with Sir Robert Peel's
principle of using the police almost exclusively for the prevention of crime is found in September 1830, when a number of Metropolitan Police were put into plain clothes to
deal with the gangs of thieves and pickpockets who frequented Bartholomew Fair. These thieves knew most of the
City police officers by sight and thought that any of the
new police who might attend the fair would be in uniform.
They were disagreeably deceived when men, who were apparently ordinary members of the crowd, pounced on them.
One young thief was arrested in the act of putting his hand
into the pocket of a policeman. In consequence of this excursion into detective work within the sacred confines of the
City of London, large numbers of young thieves appeared
next morning before one of the aldermen, who expressed
his views so strongly on the subject that on the following
day of the fair no member of the new force made an appearance.

The month of September was unfortunate for the popularity of the new force. On the 15th a respectable young
couple who were in a box at Vauxhall Gardens for the first
time in their lives were accosted by Sergeant Mace, who
accused them of being well-known bad characters in the
Gardens and insisted on searching them in the presence of
the crowd that had gathered round. If they did not like it,
he had said, he would lock them up. They lodged a formal
complaint with the superintendent, who, on inquiry, found
that their characters were irreproachable. They demanded

a public apology from the sergeant, but the magistrate declined to interfere. On this they carried their complaint to the commissioners, and the incident obtained much publicity.

The undiscovered murderer of Mrs. Whillett, who kept a marine dealer's shop in Lambeth, had not added to the reputation of the police. The brutality of the murder had caused much indignation, for the poor old woman had been beaten to death, and the object of the crime had not been robbery, for her valuables had been untouched by her assailant. The police had arrested a young man named Witham and had kept him a week in custody, because it was discovered that the dead woman had secretly married him, and his coat had been found covering the body; but in spite of every effort on the part of the police no further evidence was forthcoming, and Witham was discharged.

In November 1830 an unfortunate error of judgment was committed by the government of the day, of which the Duke of Wellington was Prime Minister. King William IV, who was far more popular than his predecessor, had celebrated his sixty-fifth birthday on the 21st of August and had promised to enter the city in state on November 9. Great preparations were made to receive him, but after the decoration of the route had been made the lord-mayor-elect, Alderman Key, took upon himself, behind the backs of his fellow aldermen, to address a letter to the Duke of Wellington stating that he had received information of a design "to make an attack on Your Grace's person on your approach to the hall." On this the Cabinet held a meeting and advised the King to cancel his engagement.

The *Times*, commenting on this change of plan, said very properly that a meditated outrage on the Prime Minister, whether it was authentic or not, should not have "become the groundwork of a Cabinet remonstrance to His Majesty," and pointed out that King William was "a most popular and beloved monarch, whose presence never fails to delight his faithful subjects." The *Times* went on to say that the police protection for the procession was fully adequate and that "the postponement of the royal visit has been an inconsiderate and ill-judged act, proceeding evidently from imperfect and erroneous information."

There was deep indignation in the City, and even some measure of panic. Citizens went out to buy arms; consols fell 3 per cent in one and a half hours. There was more to come.

In the evening a meeting was held at the Rotunda in Blackfriars Road, at which Henry Hunt, the Reform agitator, presided. The hall was packed, and at half-past eleven at night, when the chairman had retired, a man mounted the platform waving a tricolour flag with the word "Reform" painted on it. "Now for the West End!" he shouted. It was a preconcerted signal, for the whole body formed in the street in ranks and proceeded to follow the banner. At that time they were about a thousand strong, and as they went they shouted, "Reform!" "Down with the police!" "Down with the Raw Lobsters!" "No Peel!" "No Wellington!" As they passed through Fleet Street and the Strand their numbers swelled. The Adelphi Theatre was closing, but the shouts of the mob were heard in time, and the doors were shut until it had passed. By this time a horde of bad characters had joined the crowd and were shouting abuse of the police. They passed first into Downing Street, forming in a line before the house of Lord Bathurst. A man in the house came out upon the balcony with a pistol in each hand, declaring that he would fire upon the first man who attempted to enter the house. There were yells and groans and cries of, "Go it! Go it!" but when another man came out on the balcony and relieved the first man of his pistols the crowd cheered him.

Meanwhile a strong body of the A Division police arrived from Scotland Yard and barred the way to the House of Commons. They were joined by volunteers, and the disturbance grew into a riot. In the skirmish many received injuries and the banner was captured. Reinforcements from B and E divisions now arrived, and the mob took to flight in every direction. Three of its leaders were arrested and taken to the Westminster watchhouse. Guards were mounted at the Horse Guards, and strong bodies of the police patrolled the streets.

There was no further disturbance that night, but in the afternoon of the following day six men dressed as country labourers were brought in and charged with inciting the mob to acts of violence. A witness deposed to having seen a mob of nearly two thousand people moving towards the Strand led by the prisoner Wiblin, who was remarkable for his height and athletic form. He was reading from a printed paper and kept on turning round to harangue his followers with violent gestures. Having passed through Temple Bar, he waved his hat and shouted, "Now, my boys, down with the police!" The crowd cheered him. There was great alarm, and the shopkeepers put up their shutters. When opposite to Somerset House, Wiblin called a halt and turned up New Church Court, followed by the mob. In Russell Street, Covent Garden, they encountered a party of police, headed by two sergeants, who succeeded in arresting the six prisoners in spite of a fusillade of mud and stones and shouts of, "Down with the police!" "Down with Peel's gang!" Wiblin was especially active. Before entering the station house in custody he shouted, "Are ye Englishmen? Are ye men, thus to suffer us to be taken quietly into this place?" But the mob made no attempt at a rescue.

When brought before the magistrate next morning, Wiblin, who seemed to be a remarkably intelligent though uneducated man, denied that he had led the mob; he had merely read a newspaper to some of his "brothers among the people," which he supposed he had a right to do.

Several independent witnesses, however, gave evidence against him and a man named William Elder, who was fined £5 and detained for further inquiry. One of the witnesses said that the mob was shouting, "Down with Wellington!" "Down with the new police!" "Down with the Ministers!" and "Reform for ever!" The police arrangements were so well organized that the Duke of Wellington was able to leave the House of Lords unmolested, and in the meantime the mob that had been collected at Apsley House was dispersed by the police. About one hundred persons received injuries in the mêlée, but there were no serious casualties. The *Morning Post* when commenting on the riot said:

> The Police, both individually and as a body, merit the highest tribute of praise for their conduct, and have established a claim to the gratitude of the whole city.

One of the results of the riot was that the police stations were crowded with householders who came to offer their services as special constables. Sir Richard Birnie, the Bow Street magistrate, in trying a number of charges of assaulting the police during the riot, exclaimed, "I wish there were a war, except for the sake of the country, that we might get rid of some of these fellows!"

The combined effect of the King's speech, the decision to cancel the King's visit to the City of London on account of a rumour that a personal attack would be made on the Duke of Wellington and the riot which followed it, was to bring about the fall of the government. On a motion to refer the Civil List to a select committee the government was beaten by a majority of twenty-nine. It was the personal unpopularity of the Duke of Wellington, no doubt, which turned the scale. Admirable as he had been as a commander in the field, he, like most soldiers, was out of his element in democratic politics. The views of those who disliked him are set forth by the *Standard* of November 9, 1830:

> He [the Duke of Wellington] will not on one side permit his Sovereign to enjoy a triumphant popularity which he cannot share; on the other, he may not allow that sovereign to hear and see the living testimony to the odiousness of his ministry which His Grace meets everywhere.

The real cause of complaint against the Duke was the belief that he was opposed to reform. It is not so easy to understand why the police were linked in the public mind with the Duke of Wellington, except that Sir Robert Peel was a member of his Cabinet. Hear the *Standard* again:

The ministry are unpopular, as they deserve to be; the police are unpopular and we should despair of the spirit of Englishmen if an establishment so repugnant to the fundamental principle of the Constitution were not unpopular.

In the King's speech, which created so unfavourable an impression, His Majesty was made to say:

I am determined to exert to the utmost of my power all the means which the law and the constitution have placed at my disposal for the punishment of sedition and for the prompt suppression of outrage and disorder.

Here is a specimen of the inflammatory placards distributed at this period:

LIBERTY OR DEATH! ENGLISHMEN! BRITONS!! AND HONEST MEN!!! The time has at length arrived. All London meets on Tuesday. COME ARMED! We assure you from ocular demonstration that 6000 cutlasses have been removed from the Tower for the use of PEEL'S BLOODY GANG. Remember the cursed speech from the Throne! These damned police are now to be armed. Englishmen, will you put up with this?

In truth, the state of the country called for firm handling. Scarcely a night passed in the Home Counties without some daring act of incendiarism. In Norfolk agricultural machinery such as threshing machines was wantonly destroyed. In Carlisle the Duke of Wellington and Sir Robert Peel were burned in effigy; and yet there was a marked division of opinion about the police. On December 11 an attempt was made to murder Superintendent Thomas, who was stabbed by a man in the dress of a waterman and was saved by the accident that one of his waistcoats was double-folded. Two nights later a constable on duty at Milwall was met by four sailors who seized him and dropped him into the Thames, twelve feet below. The tide was out; he fell into the mud, striking his head against the gunwale of a boat and cutting his right cheek. The men made off unrecognized.

On December 14 Sir Robert Peel presented petitions from Hampstead and Deptford, praying that the new police might not be withdrawn; a day later a petition from St.

Mary's, Lambeth, prayed Parliament to repeal the Metropolitan Police Act. These conflicting petitions became common. Opposition journals such as the *Standard* suggested a middle course—that the true remedy

for the unpopularity of the police and its insufficiency would be to take it out of the hands of the government—to restore the appointment and direction of the officers to the magistracy or the parochial authorities, or, if it seems better, to extend the organization to district boards appointed by the householders.

But, as we learn from a large number of meetings and petitions, the real grievance against the police was its expense. The police rate in the first year was considerably higher than had been estimated when the act was passed—much higher in fact than the rate for the old, inefficient watchmen. There is something very modern in the attitude of householders in the suburbs of London, who sat up day and night at their windows to count how many times a policeman passed them. It did not occur to them that the very fact of the existence of the force had so intimidated robbers that they kept away and therefore more frequent visits were unnecessary. All they could see was the increase in their rates, and some of the petitions declared that the officers in their parishes were too numerous for their needs.

There can be no question, however, that the Metropolitan police were justifying themselves by their courage and efficiency at a time of disorder verging on anarchy, and though, judged from our present experience, they fell far short of an ideal civil force such as London has today, notably in the absence of a Criminal Investigation Department, yet there was little danger of a return to the old, bad system.

This chapter should not be concluded without a reference to the last of the pirates hanged in public at Execution Dock on December 17, 1830. The adventures of these two men deserve to live. George James Davis, *alias* George Huntley, and William Watts, *alias* Charles Williams, had been convicts transported to Botany Bay. In consequence of their refractory conduct they were with sixteen others ordered to be conveyed to Macquarrie Harbour. This was before Tasmania was used for the purpose of confining refractory men. They were embarked in the *Cyprus,* the vessel employed for this purpose, when they mutinied and succeeded in seizing the ship and confining the soldiers and the crew in their convict quarters. On reaching an uninhabited island, they set the soldiers and crew on shore and made sail for Japan. Strange to relate, they actually succeeded in reaching their destination, but the Japanese authorities made them so unwelcome that they abandoned their vessel and continued their voyage in an open boat. Only four, of whom Huntley and Williams were two, survived that voyage, and as soon as they reached China they were arrested by the British authorities and sent home to England for trial on the capital charge of piracy on the high seas. The four survivors were convicted and sentenced to death, but two were respited.

It is not surprising to find that the heroes of this odyssey of adventure met their fate without flinching. They left Newgate in a cart and reached Execution Dock at 9:30. Huntley jumped out of the cart without assistance and walked very fast to the scaffold with Williams close behind him. When the ropes were adjusted about their necks, Williams addressed the crowd and said that they had been far worse treated than the people they had set ashore on an uninhabited island, for they had given them plenty of provisions. Then they shook hands and the drop fell. The *Morning Post* reporter records that "they struggled a long time before the vital spark was extinct."

Ten years had passed since a pirate had been hanged at Execution Dock, and this was the last recorded instance.

In examining the sentences passed on prisoners at this period, it is impossible not to notice the startling contrast between the treatment of offences against property and offences against the person. Whereas a forty-shilling fine with the alternative of two months' imprisonment was imposed for gross cruelty to a child, or for beating a wife, death or a long term of transportation was considered the proper penalty for housebreaking. On April 17, 1831, leave was asked to introduce a bill to abolish capital punishment for housebreaking. The member who introduced the motion said, "The criminal laws of this country have been described by Mirabeau as requiring blood and a pound of flesh for every offence." The Solicitor-General objected that "murder, burglary and arson were crimes that endangered human life." Cobbett spoke in favour of the motion. He spoke of French and American methods of treating crime and suggested as an amendment "that all criminal enactments since the accession of King George III should be taken in a bunch and flung into the fire."

"Oh Gracious God!" exclaimed the Solicitor-General; "to think of going to America for an amendment of the laws of England!"

Leave was given to introduce the bill.

The fact was that in the early years of the nineteenth century England was to all intents still in the atmosphere of the eighteenth, though some of the old ideas were already in the melting pot. Rank was held in the highest reverence; the rights of labour were entirely unrecognized; there were no trade unions; no railways or telegraphs or telephones; few people travelled about the country except the rich; the people knew nothing of events that happened outside their own country; the great majority of the country people could neither read nor write; discipline in the family, the navy, and the army was maintained by corporal punishment; the factories were choked with goods that could not be sold; the greater part of the cities were living in poverty and filth; the streets were filled with prostitutes and drunken men and women; the children were growing up like young savages in a state of inconceivable ignorance and neglect; three million pounds were estimated to be spent annually in gin.

The Reform Act of 1832 took some years to change this state of things, and yet, though the ship of state seemed more than once about to founder, the people contrived to live not uncheerfully. London at that time was a small city; its boundaries on the north and west reached only to the Regent's Canal and Edgware Road; the southern boundary was the river and a narrow strip of houses in the borough.

At the opening of the nineteenth century a hundred and sixty offences were recognized as punishable with death. Between 1805 and 1818 there were said to have been two hundred executions for forgery alone, but the statistics at this period were unreliable. It is difficult now to realize that in the lifetime of our grandparents a man might be hanged if he appeared in disguise in a public road; if he cut down young trees; if he shot rabbits; if he poached game at night; if he returned to England from transportation before the end of his sentence; if, being a gypsy, he remained in the same place for twelve months. It was even a capital offence to break down the embankment of a fishpond and let the fish escape; to cut down a fruit tree in a garden or orchard; to steal a handkerchief of above the value of one shilling from another man's pocket. Yet under the same code it was no offence to receive cash or specie, bank notes or bills, knowing them to be stolen, inasmuch as specie, notes, and bills were not considered as coming under the head of goods and chattels. A notorious receiver of stolen goods could be convicted and punished severely for buying a bottle or a pewter pot; but if he received twenty thousand pounds in cash, bank notes, or bills, he escaped with impunity. It was estimated in 1798 that there were in London more than three thousand receivers of stolen goods, whereas twenty years earlier there had been under three hundred.

The thefts of government property lying in the Thames were estimated at half a million pounds a year, and it was believed that these stores were resold to the public boards three or four times over.

The case of coiners and utterers of base money was quite as scandalous. Colquhoun wrote:

Scarcely a waggon or a coach departs from the Metropolis which does not carry boxes and parcels of base coin to the camps, seaports and manufacturing towns.

In fact the false coinage in circulation in 1800 was estimated to be gaining ground upon the products of the Mint. The coiners did not stop short at the coinage of the realm; in London and Birmingham French louis d'or, half Johannas, as well as Belgian, German, and Spanish dollars of perfect workmanship were being turned out in quantities. There was even a spurious mint for the coins of India which were made of blanched copper tempered to show the cracks in the edges which are always to be found in the genuine pagoda. After being double-gilt they cost the maker three halfpence each; they trickled through Jewish dealers into India, where they passed at the full value of eight shillings. The gold sequins of Turkey were also extensively counterfeited. At the beginning of the nineteenth century there were more than 650 names in the register of the solicitor to the Royal Mint, and yet the evil continued unabated. Two persons could coin from £200 to £300 in base silver in six days. The law relating to counterfeit coining had been passed a century earlier; the penalty was slight—there was no capital sentence for coining.

The sanguinary code of penalties for other offences defeated its own object, since everyone, from the judge downwards, disapproved of its severity in respect of the minor offences. The professional criminal had immediate recourse to some disreputable attorney who knew every trick in the game of defeating the ends of justice; accomplices were hired to swear an alibi; honest witnesses were cajoled, threatened, or bribed to go back on their evidence sworn before the committing magistrate. Prosecutors were intimidated by the expense, or, softened by appeals to their humanity, they neglected to employ counsel[1] or produce witnesses. The grand jury would throw out the bill, and the professional criminal was released to continue his depredations, whereas the unfortunate novice in crime, knowing nothing of the procedure, was often convicted. The scale was further loaded against him, for he was not allowed to give evidence in his own behalf, and it was not until the year 1836 that counsel for a prisoner accused of felony was permitted to address the jury on behalf of his client.

The registers of the Central Criminal Court afford a lamentable proof of the trying of criminals without a public prosecutor. During the last seven years of the eighteenth century no less than 4,262 prisoners, against whom the grand jury had found "true bills," were let loose upon the public by acquittals. That was not the end of the evils. No sooner was a criminal convicted than the sympathy of the humanitarians was his. Petitions for pardon were drawn up and presented; the unfortunate relations were bled by fraudulent sympathizers to support petitions to save the felon from the gallows, or even from transportation, and to make matters worse, the needs of the navy and the army were brought into play. Common thieves received full pardons on the condition of joining either service. They deserted almost immediately, to resume their old way of

---

[1] An advocate.

life, and all the work of bringing them to justice had to be begun over again.

The criminal code of that period seemed to have been founded on the maxim of Draco, who lived in the seventh century before Christ and justified his severities on the plea that he punished all crimes with death because small crimes deserved it and he could find no higher punishment for the greatest.

The history of the gradual softening of the criminal code in Great Britain is very curious. During the first quarter of the nineteenth century the protest against the infliction of death for minor felonies was at its height, but it failed to force the government to adopt the logical course of abolishing the evil by legislation. The judges were still compelled by law to pass the death sentence, but by tacit consent it became the practice in all cases, save that of murder, to order the sentence "to be recorded," which had the effect of a reprieve. The process had been going on for more than forty years before the establishment of the Metropolitan Police at Scotland Yard. Blackstone wrote in his *Commentaries* (1765):

The injured, through compassion, will sometimes forget their oaths and either acquit the guilty or mitigate the nature of the offence; and judges, through compassion, will respite one-half of the convicts and recommend them to Royal mercy. . . . All laws which appear not to be consonant with the dictates of truth and justice, the feelings of humanity, and the indelible rights of mankind, should be abrogated and repealed.

Sir Samuel Romilly, who attacked this bloodthirsty code in his *Observations on the Criminal Law of England* (1810), was interpreting the growing feeling among thinking men which was leading juries to refuse to convict persons guilty of trifling offences that carried the death penalty. As Sir Walter Besant observed, "The value of human life was slowly rising"; but it was not until 1861 that all these blots were finally erased from the Statute Book. The stocks were abolished in 1827 when the treadwheel was introduced; hanging in chains, in 1834; the dissection of murderers' bodies was not actually abolished by law until 1861, but it was made optional in 1832.

The Central Criminal Court, which holds its sessions at the Old Bailey, was founded in 1834. Even after the creation of Scotland Yard had deprived the magistrates of Bow Street police court of their control of the police, Bow Street remained the premier police court as it is now.

Angelo, the Italian fencing master, who wrote of London as he saw it in the last quarter of the eighteenth century, wrote of public executions as follows:

Generally an execution day at Tyburn was considered by various classes as a public holiday. The malefactors, being exposed thus publicly through the main street for three miles, it was supposed, would tend to morality by deterring many who were witnesses of the agony of the miserable culprits from the perpetration of those vices that had brought them to their pitiable fate. This, however, was at length discovered to be a mistaken policy, for these cruel spectacles drew thousands from their lawful occupations, and emptied the manufactories and workshops.

At an early hour on the morning of an execution thousands of mechanics and others who on the previous night had agreed upon *making a day of it,* met at their proposed stations. It was common throughout the whole metropolis for master coachmakers, framemakers, tailors, shoemakers and others who had engaged to complete orders within a given time, to bear in mind to observe to their customers, "That will be a hanging day and my men will not be at work." There were also various grades of amateurs of these sights, both high and low, whose ardour in the pursuit excited them to know and to see the whole appertaining to the scene from the first examination of the prisoner at Sir John Fielding's office in Bow Street to his exit at "fatal Tyburn Tree." Foote, speaking of some prominent characters of this class, designated them "The Hanging Committee." . . .

Those of the lower grade who were most eager for these sights, early in the morning surrounded the felon's gate at Newgate to see the malefactors brought forth, and who received nosegays at St. Sepulchre's. Others appeared at various stations and fell into the ranks according to convenience; hence, the crowd accumulating on the cavalcade reaching St. Giles', the throng was occasionally so great as to entirely fill Oxford Street from house to house on both sides of the way, when the pressure became tremendous within half a mile of Tyburn. The Old Bailey, Newgate Street, from St. Sepulchre's

Church, Snow Hill and Holborn, as high as Furnival's Inn, were filled with one dense mass of spectators.

Nothing can be conceived more impressing than the solemn manner in which the unhappy criminals were received by the multitude. . . . The two Perreaus, Dr. Dodd and Ryland, in consequence of their previous respectability, were indulged with mourning coaches. A hearse containing the coffin also formed part of the procession.[1]

---

[1]The procession to Tyburn was abandoned in 1783, and the use of the drop to accelerate death by hanging was introduced. The pillory was abolished in 1816 for all offences except perjury. Flogging in public was abolished in the following year.

The Tyburn ticket was a certificate granted by a judge or a justice to the person who captured and prosecuted a felon to conviction. It freed the holder from liability to serve as a constable; it was transferable, and therefore it had a pecuniary value, generally of £10 or more, though one was known to have fetched as much as £40.

CHAPTER IX

Early Years

WHILE THE METROPOLITAN POLICE were gradually wearing down opposition, a new organization had become urgently necessary in the provinces. Many London criminals had migrated to towns where trade was on the increase and marauders were allowed a freer hand than in London. Travellers on the highroads had to run the gauntlet of robbers; in few places were there convenient detention cells for prisoners on remand; in Sussex the magistrates had to hire a man to be handcuffed to the prisoner day and night in a public house.

A royal commission of which Colonel Rowan was a member was appointed in 1839 to inquire into the whole matter. It recommended the establishment immediately of a paid rural constabulary throughout England and Wales, organized on the lines of the Metropolitan Police. A Permissive Act was passed, leaving it to the magistrates in each county to raise and equip a paid police. It produced a very meagre result. The government followed this by an Act making the service voluntary on a majority vote of the magistrates, but this, too, proved to be a failure. By 1842, however, the county magistrates were glad to accept the services of police officers, trained in London, to supervise the local constables.

Peel had always hoped to form organizations modelled on the Metropolitan Police, and he selected Cheshire, a county with high criminal statistics, as a place for the experiment. A beginning was made, but on far too small a scale. The county of Essex, however, had taken advantage of the Permissive Act by utilizing the services of McHardy, a retired naval captain, and authorizing him to recruit a force of constables. He used some of these men as assistant relieving officers for vagrants, which had the advantage of reducing vagrancy and giving the police a first-hand knowledge of this difficult class. Other counties followed suit, but it was not until 1856 that the whole of England and Wales was covered. The co-operation which followed greatly increased the efficiency of all police bodies.

It had never been Peel's plan to establish a national police controlled from Scotland Yard. The jurisdiction of the police commissioners had already been extended farther than had been anticipated, for in 1860 Scotland Yard had already been put in police charge of the Royal dockyards at Portsmouth, Devonport, Chatham, and Pembroke Dock. This arrangement came to an end only in 1934 on the ground of economy.

In 1856 a law was passed to compel all counties and boroughs in England and Wales to appoint paid police forces and to furnish the Home Secretary with annual statistics of crime. Constabulary inspectors went round the country and reported upon their efficiency. Thus Sir Robert Peel's dream of thirty years earlier was fulfilled. Officers from the Metropolitan force were often sent on loan or permanence to these provincial forces.

One of the most notable triumphs of the two commissioners lay in their handling of riots. Before 1830 there had been only two methods of dealing with a riotous mob —the first to leave it severely alone, and the second to allow a regiment of cavalry to trample it into submission. The general laws that sway men when assembled together in a mob—described by an American writer as the "volcanic forces which lie smouldering in all ignorant masses"—have been very accurately summed up by Melville Lee. He says that the gathering of a mob without any definite object, and often at great inconvenience to the individuals who compose it, is due to the gregarious instinct. It is quite normal up to a point when entirely new forces begin to act.

When this moment arrives all self-control is repudiated; decent and orderly men become desperadoes; cowards are inspired by a senseless bravado; the calm reason of common sense gives place to the insanity of licence, and unless the demoralising tendency is checked, a crowd rapidly sinks to the level of its most degraded constituent. The explanation of these phenomena is probably to be found in an excessive spirit of emulation, aroused under conditions of excitement, which makes a man feel that the responsibility for his actions is no longer to be borne by himself but will be shared by the multitude in which he has merged his identity. It is the business of the police to exhaust every art in a sustained effort to prevent the ferment from reaching the critical stage and to watch the crowd so narrowly that the first symptom of violence may instantly be suppressed. This can best be accomplished by local constables who are acquainted with the persons and names of individuals, while it is of even greater moment that the constabularly should not be the first to give offence, or to contribute to a breach of the peace by the use of exasperating language or aggressive action.

The policeman has a harder task than a soldier before the enemy; he has to strive for peace while actually engaged in conflict. The plan of the officer in charge must be easy to understand and must leave the lawbreakers at a strategical disadvantage. Nothing is so fatal as vacillation, for partial success leads on the mob to the commission of fresh excesses; partial repression only aggravates it.

The same writer speaks of the importance of keeping a crowd moving in a definite direction rather than dissipating the strength of the police in attempts to arrest leaders, for such attempts may "degenerate into a series of disconnected single combats, not uniformly favourable to authority."

He goes on to refer to the tact of the modern London policeman, which, in his opinion, is more responsible for keeping good order than the London crowd's alleged good humour. This has developed gradually, as the police and the public get to understand one another better.

James Munro, who was commissioner for two years in 1888, wrote:

Weak in number as the Force is, it would be found in practice altogether inadequate were it not strengthened to an extent unknown, I believe, elsewhere, by the relations that exist between the police and public, and by the thorough recognition on the part of the citizens at large of the police as their friends and protectors. The police touch all classes of the public at many points beyond the performance of their sterner duties as representatives of the law, and they touch them in a friendly way. . . . The police, in short, are not the representatives of an arbitrary and despotic power, directed against the rights or obtrusively interfering with the pleasures of law-abiding citizens; they are simply a disciplined body of men, specially engaged in protecting "masses" as well as "classes" from any infringement of their rights on the part of those who are not law-abiding.

It would be hard to gauge police efficiency by figures, but the records of commitments in the census years are some guide. The following table of indictable offences tried at assizes and quarter sessions merits examination:

Census Years	Population	No. of Commitments	Proportion per 100,000
1841	15,914,148	27,760	174.6
1851	17,927,609	27,960	156.2
1861	20,066,224	18,326	91.3
1871	22,712,266	16,269	71.6
1881	25,974,239	14,704	56.6
1891	29,002,525	11,605	40.0

When Queen Victoria came to the throne in 1837, 43,000 of her subjects were convicts; in 1901 they numbered less than 6,000 though the population had nearly doubled.

Throughout the year of 1831 all minds were occupied with the Reform Bill which was to take away the right of representation from fifty-six decayed or rotten boroughs and to distribute the 143 seats thus gained to counties or large towns which as yet had sent no members to Parliament; to establish a £10 householder qualification for voting in boroughs and extending the county franchise to leaseholders and copyholders. The bill was laid before

the House of Commons in 1831, and the Ministry was defeated. An appeal was made to the country; the new House
of Commons at once passed the bill, but it was rejected by
the House of Lords. This rejection produced agitation
and disorder throughout the country to so alarming an extent that the peers took fright and when the bill was again
introduced the Lords who opposed withdrew from the
House and allowed it to become law.

The elections in those early days of reform were contested not only with the tongue, for on February 21 we read
in the Birmingham *Gazette* as an ordinary item of election
news that a poor man named Cheney, living in Warwick,
"died on Thursday last in consequence of wounds he received from bludgeons during the late contested election
for the borough."

The intense unrest fostered by agitators when the Reform Bill had been thrown out by the House of Lords was
shown by disorders all over the country. The riots at Bristol were the worst of these manifestations. They broke out
when the recorder, Sir Charles Wetherell, drove through
the streets to the Guildhall. He was hooted and stoned,
and when he rose to speak in the Guildhall his voice was
rendered inaudible by coughing. Meanwhile in the streets
outside a posse of constables were trying to arrest those who
had thrown missiles at his carriage. The mob had now increased to nearly ten thousand people, and a mêlée ensued.
By four o'clock the police had restored order but were
foolishly allowed to retire to get refreshment, whereupon
the riots broke out afresh; the windows and doors of the
Mansion House were smashed; troops were called out to
prevent the mob from burning down the building. Colonel
Brereton, who was in command, tried to pacify the rioters
by soft speech and was even cheered; it was not the way to
deal with serious disorder when the speaker had force at his
back, as the citizens of Bristol were soon to know.

The following day was Sunday. The rioters had had
time to sketch out their plan of action. During the morning
they attacked the gaol, smashed in the great doors, and re-

leased the prisoners, first stripping off their prison clothes and pushing them out into the streets almost naked. A piece of black cloth was tied to the weathercock over the porter's lodge as a signal for burning down the prison. The treadmill was completely gutted and the governor's house damaged. During these proceedings a party of the Guards arrived. They were loudly cheered by the mob; they acknowledged the salute by taking off their caps before wheeling round and departing.

The mob then divided; some to set fire to toll houses and others to burn down the Gloucester county prison, the bridewell, and the bishop's palace, the bishop being absent at the time. The other party burnt down the custom house and forty-two private houses in Bristol. A good many of the mob received injuries during the riot. There were a hundred casualties; twelve dead from burns, shots, sword cuts, and excessive drinking. The authorities were wise enough to bring back a detachment of troops which had been roughly handled by the mob on the previous day. These promptly cleared the streets.

There was a discussion in the House of Commons, and the government promised to appoint a special commission to inquire into the handling of the riots by the authorities during the recess. The special commission began its sittings at Bristol on January 2, 1832, and continued them until the 14th. Besides a number of prisoners charged with thefts during the riots, twenty-four persons were capitally indicted for arson at the gaol, the bridewell, the bishop's palace, and the dwelling houses. Twenty-one were found guilty, but all except four of these escaped with their lives. Of these four, one was proved to have led the destruction of the gaol; one, of the bridewell; and the other two, of dwelling houses. A second special commission was sitting at Nottingham, where the riots had been as severe as in Bristol. The rioters had burned down Nottingham Castle, and a silk mill, and had attacked and attempted to burn Colwick Hall, and this had caused the death of the occupant of the house. Twelve rioters were brought to trial, and six of them were convicted, in addition to the three concerned in the attack on Colwick Hall. The evidence was insufficient to convict two persons who were indicted for burning down the castle. Of the nine convicted, five were condemned to death, but the sentence was carried out against only three of them.

The reformers and their newspapers made immense efforts to save the lives of the men sentenced to death by the special commissions. Meetings were held all over the country; resolutions were passed, and petitions to the King and Parliament were drawn up, urging mercy on the ground that the crimes were committed merely owing to political excitement and anxiety to prove that there had been no reaction in public opinion with regard to the Reform Bill. A meeting of the "National Political Union of Working People" was held in Manchester to protest against the executions. One of the speakers declared that the men of Bristol would not be satisfied until they had "hung the rascal, Sir C. Wetherell, and that if the King did not grant the petition the people must legislate and act for themselves."

The petition assured the King that the petitioners viewed "with horror and alarm" the infliction of death or transportation on persons who had been driven to desperation by the conduct of Sir C. Wetherell and the Duke of Newcastle, and by the rejection of the Reform Bill, and that justice would not be done until these individuals who had been the cause of the rioting were awarded the same sentences as the rioters.

A tragic episode arising out of the riots was the court-martial of Colonel Brereton, who had been in command of the troops during the riots. The charges were that he had shown weakness and vacillation in dealing with the rioters. The charges were abundantly proved, but before the court assembled on the fifth day it was announced that the proceedings were at an end, for Colonel Brereton had shot himself.

The Bristol reformers tried to throw the blame for the riots upon the lack of energy and discretion shown by the magistrates and demanded that they should be brought to trial. To this the ministers consented. The Attorney-General was instructed to prosecute, though it was known that the real object of the prosecution was "to render the Corporation and the Magistracy odious"; but when Mr. Pinney, the mayor, was brought to trial the jury not only found him not guilty, but commended him for his "great firmness and propriety."

On February 1 three out of the five rioters condemned to death were executed upon a scaffold erected in front of the gaol, two having received a respite. The execution was delayed until the arrival of the London mail in case it should bring a reprieve, but there was none, and at 11:40 Beck, Armstrong, and Hearson were brought out to the scaffold and pinioned. Hearson had joined fervently in the prayers that morning, but on seeing the vast crowd which had assembled six hours before, he danced and waved his cap. A man on the roof opposite applauded him, but Armstrong remonstrated: "None of that, George; it's not sense. I say that I am innocent because I am so, but I'll have none of that." Just before the drop fell there were loud cries of "Murder! Blood!" from the crowd.

There were curious incidents in connection with the riots. Three men were tried at Taunton for beginning to demolish the White Hart Inn at Bath. Captain Wilkins of the yeomanry had been riding to Bristol on duty connected with the riots there, on October 30, 1831, when he was set upon by a mob of three hundred, who threw stones and mud at him and compelled him to take refuge in the White Hart. A police officer joined him there and stood by his side while he addressed the mob, saying that as a soldier he had to obey orders. Thereupon an attack was made upon the inn by several hundred rioters, the inn being defended by Wilkins, Hall, and the inn servants. There was a conflict lasting twenty minutes, the attacking party shouting, "Bread!" and "Reform!" and "We have been starving long enough."

Hall succeeded in making his way to the town hall and brought back with him a small body of special constables which gradually grew into a force of some hundreds. The mob was in the act of piling faggots and furniture against the doors. Many arrests were made, but many of these were rescued by the rioters; those who remained to be tried were found guilty.

I have already had occasion to mention a body called the "National Political Union of Working People," which had been growing with impunity for months past. In the middle of May 1833 the society advertised a meeting for the purpose of forming a national convention. The meeting was to be held behind the prison in Coldbath Fields. The government had been increasingly uneasy about this society, and they instructed the police to break up the meeting at the first symptom of rioting. Some three hundred members of the National Union and a rough crowd, making a total of a thousand persons, met near Calthorpe Street, carrying banners, one, the American Stars and Stripes, and others inscribed, "Death or Liberty."

The police were present in force, but the majority of the men of C and E divisions were kept out of sight in stables. According to an eyewitness, Stallwood, at the inquest, a caravan was to be used as a platform, but the driver took fright on seeing the mob and drove away, leaving a young man named Lee to mount a paling to make his speech. He proposed a man named Mee as chairman. The speeches seem to have been quite moderate, though, according to a constable, when Police Constable Culley was stabbed to death, Richard Lee was heard to say, "Serve the King so." However this may have been, the sight of police reinforcements enraged the mob, who attacked the constables with truncheons weighted with lead. It was at that moment that Culley was stabbed by a man named James Cortman, a journeyman baker, and Superintendent Baker narrowly escaped the same fate.

According to Stallwood, a prejudiced witness, the mob made no resistance when the police advanced to disperse it after the murder of Culley; he said that the police knocked down men, women, and children without distinction, and that the ground was covered with bodies. He himself expostulated with the police from the balcony of his house, and Superintendent Thomas called him a scoundrel for his pains.

This inquest was memorable on account of the prejudice displayed by the jury, who subjected Superintendent Baker to a violent cross-examination until the coroner observed that they seemed to be trying him as a felon instead of examining him as a witness. They asked Stallwood whether in his opinion fifty of the old police would not have managed the affair better, and Stallwood assented.

The inquest was resumed on the following day, and the jury displayed the same spirit of prejudice. The witnesses for and against the police gave violently exaggerated and contradictory evidence. One of the witnesses, Major Fitzgerald de Roes, who had been attached to Colonel Rowan to summon military assistance from the Horse Guards if needed, said that he saw no women in the crowd and that the incident lasted only five minutes. He was grossly insulted by the jury, and the inquest was again adjourned.

Meanwhile Lee was brought up at Bow Street, and the thirty-three prisoners arrested on various charges in connection with the riot were committed to the Court of King's Bench. The inquest continued on May 18 and May 21, and the jury continued to be as recalcitrant as ever, finally bringing in a verdict of "justifiable homicide." The coroner declined to accept it unless the word "justifiable" were struck out. This the jury refused to do, and they were discharged. As soon as the crowd outside the court got wind of the verdict there was loud cheering for ten minutes. This verdict was so flagrantly at variance with the evidence that the Crown applied to the Court of King's Bench and the inquest was quashed.

The whole question was ventilated in Parliament, and a committee was appointed to inquire into the conduct of the police. It was shown that they had acted strictly in accordance with their instructions and that if anyone was responsible for what had happened it was the Home Secretary, Lord Melbourne, and that he had tried to escape responsibility by throwing the blame upon the commissioner, Colonel Rowan. This finding was opportune, for it aroused the sympathy of the public and allayed the indignation that had been aroused at the inquest. After all the only serious casualty had been that of the murdered policeman, Culley, whose murderer was not convicted.

CHAPTER X

The Institution of a
Criminal Investigation Department

For the first thirteen years of its existence Scotland Yard was condemned to work without the help of a detective force. Up to the year 1839 a few of the old Bow Street runners still survived and were ready to work for anyone, either in London or the provinces, who was ready to pay their expenses, but in that year the last of the survivors retired, and the uniformed force of what was still called the New Police were expected to deal efficiently with all classes of crime. From time to time the commissioners had authorized the employment of a few men in plain clothes, but the results in these cases were so unhappy that the institution of a plain-clothes force was retarded.

The National Political Union had been giving increasing anxiety to the government, and the commissioners were asked to send someone to its meetings and to report whether it was really conspiring against the government. Obviously this could be done only by directing a policeman in plain clothes to become a member of the body. Unfortunately, the officer chosen—a policeman named Popay who was burning with zeal and longing to win promotion—fell easily to the temptation to become what the French call an *"agent double,"* or rather an *"agent provocateur"*; that is to say, he became a recognized leader of the union, and, probably with the intention of providing himself with material against other leaders, he himself made inflammatory speeches. He had entered the union under an assumed name, representing himself to be a struggling artist, in sympathy with the French revolutionaries and their methods of realizing freedom and liberty. He went so far in his speeches as to incite his fellow members to arm and overthrow the government.

All might have gone well with him but for an accident. It chanced that a fellow member of the union entered the police station at a moment when Popay was making an entry in the charge book. For a moment he hesitated, doubting the evidence of his own eyes, but then, feeling sure of his man, he challenged him. Having no convincing lie ready, Popay stammered out the absurd excuse that he was helping a police friend over his accounts, but the indignant member of the union sought out the superintendent and denounced Popay as a red-hot revolutionary. The union was ablaze with indignation and set wild stories afloat in Camberwell, their headquarters, that the district was flooded with police in every kind of disguise, and that no man's life was safe. A petition, signed by hundreds of respectable persons, was presented to Parliament, protesting against the use of policemen in plain clothes to act as spies. A committee was appointed; Popay's conduct was severely censured, and he was dismissed from the force. But the incident left an unpleasant impression behind it, and no police were employed in plain clothes for the next two years. It needed some startling case, in which the public clamoured for action, to revive the question of instituting a force of detectives.

This occurred in 1842. On April 6 a middle-aged Irish coachman, named Daniel Good, who was employed by a Mr. Shiell, of Granard Lodge, Roehampton, called in a chaise, on a pawnbroker in Wandsworth and bought a pair of black knee breeches. He was seen by the shop boy to hide a pair of trousers under the skirt of his coat and conceal them with the breeches in the chaise. The pawnbroker charged him with the theft, but he drove off, with a constable in pursuit. He was followed to his employer's stable, where he lived. The policeman arrested him and proceeded to search the chaise and the stables, but Good put his back against one of the stable doors and refused to allow anyone

to pass through it. A neighbour, summoned by the policeman
and the shopboy, mounted guard over Good while the search
was proceeding, Good meanwhile offering to return to the
pawnbroker and pay for the stolen trousers.

Suddenly the policeman, who was moving trusses of hay
in the inner stable, exclaimed, "My God! What's this?"
Good fled from the stable and locked them in, and finding
it impossible to force the door, they stayed where they were
and examined what had been found under the truss of hay.
It was the trunk of a dead woman. They succeeded at last in
breaking down the door and sent the shopboy to summon
more police. Good had taken advantage of their plight to
make his escape; the police tracked the fugitive's footprints
across a field in the direction of Putney, but could trace them
no further.

The surgeon's assistant who was summoned found that
the body had been dismembered by a sharp instrument and
the bones broken or sawn through. He adjudged the woman
to have been about twenty-five and apparently pregnant. A
horrible smell drew them to the harness room, where they
found the charred remains of the head and limbs, and an
axe and saw stained with blood.

Good had been seen the previous evening at Roehampton
Club with a young woman whom he seemed to be courting.
His employer did not give him a good character. He had
had sundry affairs with women and at the moment was
engaged to marry a young woman named Susan Butcher,
who lived at Woolwich. His little son had been living with
an aunt in Manchester Square, and there he had taken
refuge after his flight from the stable, but he had gone off in
a cab the same evening. Noticing his nervousness and pallor,
the cabman asked him whether he was ill; he replied that he
was getting over a bout of drinking with friends. He told
the aunt's landlady that his wife was going to a situation at
a place four miles from Roehampton, and he disposed of
her mangle and bedding. Some of her garments which she
had worn on the preceding Sunday, Good gave to his fiancée,
Susan Butcher.

It has always been observed that the public interest in a crime depends less upon the horror of the crime or the prominence of the victim than upon the successful escape of the perpetrator. It was so in this case. Good was at large after having been under arrest; there was a hue and cry all over the country. People who had been vociferous in opposing the establishment of the New Police were now accusing them of inefficiency. For two weeks people spoke of little else, and for the first time there was talk of instituting a detective branch in plain clothes.

And yet, considering the defective communications at the time, the uniformed police did not do badly. On the 18th, twelve days after the escape, Thomas Rose, a former policeman at Wandsworth, recognized Good in the person of a bricklayer working on some new cottages at Tunbridge. He had arrived in a fish van four days before and had applied for work. He was found to be a good workman, abrupt and reserved with his work mates. He told the woman at his lodgings that he had been a hawker and dealer in rabbit skins. She noticed that he slept badly and became very nervous when anyone knocked at his door.

The ex-policeman informed the police, who arrested him and took him before a magistrate. He denied his identity, but it was observed that he had combed his hair to cover a bald spot which might have helped to identify him. He was taken to Bow Street and examined by Mr. Halls, the magistrate, still disputing his identity, but he was committed for trial at the Old Bailey. Only when his ten-year-old son appeared as a witness against him did he break down. The court was crowded to excess, chiefly by women, "even young ladies," records the chronicler.

Besides the judge, Lord Denman, on the bench, were the Duke of Sussex, the Chevalier Bunsen, and other distinguished people. Good passionately protested his innocence. He had admitted his identity long before the trial. He said, "Susan Butcher was the cause of it all," and added that his reputed wife had cut her own throat and that a friend had advised him to conceal the body.

In summing up, the judge warned the jury against building too much on circumstantial evidence, but added that the medical evidence had clearly proved that the woman's throat had been cut. The jury returned a verdict of guilty, and Good was executed at Newgate.

It is doubtful whether a Criminal Investigation Department would have hastened Good's recapture at all, or would have been any more competent in marshalling the evidence for the prosecution, but the opportunity given in the change in public opinion was not to be missed. A few days after Good's execution it was announced that a Criminal Investigation Department consisting of two inspectors and six sergeants was to be attached to Scotland Yard for the investigation of crimes committed in the Metropolitan area. It was a beginning, and it must be confessed not a very successful beginning, chiefly because the men were not specially trained, were not sufficiently numerous, and were attached only to headquarters. Some of the magistrates compared their work unfavourably with that of the old Bow Street runners.

On the other hand these detectives began to work immediately a case had been reported to them. Since they were established public servants they had no temptation to delay until their expenses were guaranteed to them, as was the practice of the Bow Street runners. Gradually the department grew and some small measure of training was introduced. It was at any rate a departure from the old idea of Sir Robert Peel that his police should prevent crime rather than content themselves with arresting criminals, for unless a uniformed policeman actually saw a crime committed, he could do no more than report the circumstances to his superintendent.

Many useful things can be taught in a detective class, but no class teaching can ever cover every eventuality if the pupil is not already born with natural intuition.

The author has described elsewhere[1] how a mystery was solved in a few minutes by Detective-Inspector Crutchett,

---

[1] *Queer People*, by Sir Basil Thomson.

the inspector of the detective class, during the first year of
the Great War. An urgent request was received from a chief
constable in the Midlands for help from Scotland Yard.
The family of a doctor in good practice had been upset by
receiving a series of outrageous letters and postcards, bearing the signature of a lady's maid who had lately gone to
another situation. While she had been with them she had
been a quiet and respectable person, and yet her letters
could only have been written by a woman of vicious and
depraved character. They came in various ways; sometimes
pushed under the front door; sometimes thrown in through
an open window; and though the front door had been kept
under police observation and no one had been seen to come
to it, they were dropped into the letter box at intervals of
three hours.

And then the house itself became bewitched. The mistress
would put down her bunch of keys on the kitchen dresser for
a moment, and a wicked fairy whisked them away. The cook
would put a pound of butter into the larder; it vanished.
The housemaid lost her pen and ink, the doctor his comb;
the house was ransacked from top to bottom, and nothing
was recovered. It is a most harassing thing for a doctor in a
busy practice to come home to a house which has been bewitched. I asked for a list of the officers who were available;
practically all the most suitable for an inquiry of this kind
were engaged upon Admiralty and War Office inquiries. One
only remained: Detective-Inspector Crutchett. There was
nothing to go upon except the bundle of anonymous letters,
which certainly bore out the description which the chief constable had given of them.

When I had given the inspector a brief account of the
circumstances, he asked for the bundle of letters and took
the next train to the Midlands. I thought that the case would
take him at least four days to unravel; it took him a shade
over two hours. When my messenger came in to announce
him next day, my heart sank. Obviously he must have failed,
and with his failure went some of the prestige of Scotland
Yard.

"Well," I said, "I suppose that you could make nothing of it?"

"Oh, yes, sir; we've quite cleared it up."

"What did you do?"

"Well, sir, on the way down in the train I read through all those letters and made a note of every word that had been wrongly spelt. There were seventeen of them. Then I made up a piece of dictation which included all the seventeen words. I'm afraid that it was great nonsense, but I told the doctor the object of the dictation, and he called together the entire household and put them round the dining-room table—himself, his wife, the children, and the five servants —and I served out paper and pens to all of them. They seemed to enter into the spirit of the game. I dictated slowly. At the end of twenty minutes the pens ceased scratching, and the copies were handed in.

"They didn't take me long to run through, and in a very few minutes I was able to dismiss them all except the mistress and the between-maid, a child of fifteen or sixteen. I got them to take me up to her sleeping quarters, and I asked her to point out her box. At first she said that she had lost the key, but when I said that we should have to break it open she found it in her pocket. At the top of the box I found paper and envelopes exactly like those used for the anonymous letters, and after a little pressing the child began to cry and made a clean breast of it."

She disliked the lady's maid who had gone to another situation. What gave her joy was to see the entire household in a flutter. She had begun with the letters, and when these seemed to be losing their effect, she became the wicked fairy with the keys and the butter pats. Some people are surprised to think that children of sixteen can be depraved enough to write horrible letters, but experience has shown that this is quite a common aspect of adolescent lying.

AT FOUR P.M. ON January 20, 1843, there occurred a murder which resulted in a change in the procedure of the criminal courts in the United Kingdom. Mr. Edward Drummond, Sir Robert Peel's private secretary and a nephew of the chairman of Drummond's bank, was returning from a visit to the bank when he was shot in the leg. James Silver, a police constable, happened to be going from Whitehall to Charing Cross when he saw a gentleman staggering on the pavement with his hand to his side, and a man a few paces distant with a pistol in his hand. With great promptitude he tripped him up and disarmed him before taking him to the police station in Gardiner's Lane. There the man gave his name as McNaghten.

It was hoped that the victim of the shooting would recover. The Queen and Prince Albert were deeply concerned and called for constant reports on Mr. Drummond's condition, but after the bullet was extracted it was found that there were internal injuries, to which the patient succumbed on the following day.

The case is interesting to us as an illustration of the way in which criminals were handled by the police in those early days. Inspector Tierney cautioned the prisoner, and then had several conversations with him in his cell, putting leading questions to him about the riots in Glasgow and the weavers in Paisley, in both of which places the prisoner said he had been.

On the following morning the inspector asked McNaghten what reason he had to give the magistrates for his crime. He said that he would give a short explanation. To this the inspector observed, "You might have stated anything you thought proper to me last night, after the caution I gave you."

McNaghten then said that he was persecuted by the Tories. The inspector remarked, "I suppose you are aware of the identity of the gentleman you shot at?" McNaghten replied, "It was Sir Robert Peel, wasn't it?" At first the inspector said, "No," and then changed his reply to, "We don't exactly know who the gentleman is yet." The prisoner then asked that their conversation should not be repeated in court, but to this Inspector Tierney replied that he could make no promise; he had duly cautioned the prisoner.

The trial was a long one. A host of witnesses were called to prove the unbalanced behaviour of the prisoner for a long time past. Mental experts were called to give their opinions on the prisoner's responsibility, but they were all at one in considering McNaghten to be insane. The jury retired and returned a verdict of "Not guilty, on the grounds of insanity." Accordingly, the prisoner was technically discharged, but he was removed to an asylum for permanent confinement.

The case had excited enormous public interest, and there was a strong feeling that the verdict was wrong, as well as the judge's direction to the jury. The case was raised in the House of Lords, and was referred by the peers to the judges, with the result that ever since that date, when a jury considers a prisoner to be insane and not responsible for his action, the form of the verdict should be "Guilty, but insane," and the sentence should be, "To be detained during His Majesty's pleasure," which means detention in a criminal lunatic asylum where the cases are regularly brought up for revision after a patient has completed a detention, in the case of murder, of twenty years, that being the length of sentence served by a convicted murderer whose life has been spared.

The McNaghten case is interesting to us in another aspect. The prisoner was, it is true, cautioned that anything he might say could be used in evidence at his trial, and the inspector then proceeded to question him. Great Britain is the only country in the world, I believe, where the police are forbidden to question accused persons after they have decided to prosecute them. The restriction was made in the interest of fair play to the accused, but it is apt to prove a fatal bar to the administration of justice. When it came to the examination of suspected spies during the Great War, it was found impossible to prepare cases for the Central Criminal Court unless some latitude was allowed to the police.

A spy generally carried with him mysterious documents, either in cipher or code; he had sent telegrams ostensibly ordering goods and he had to be asked for whom these goods were intended. He would name some Dutch firm known to the police as a receiving address for spy communications. It was obvious that in a time of war the old restrictions might become a source of danger to the country. Accordingly representations were made to the judges, who discussed the question and agreed that in espionage cases the police should be free to put questions to an accused person provided that the usual preliminary caution was administered and recorded in the depositions. After the Armistice the old restrictions were resumed, and in 1928 a royal commission under the chairmanship of Lord Lee of Fareham considered suggestions for placarding every police cell with the words, "Questioning by the police not allowed." Happily, so foolish a restriction was not adopted in the report of the royal commission.

THE SALT HILL MURDER

The murder that was committed at Salt Hill near Slough on January 2, 1845, created a deep sensation at the time, because the murderer, John Tawell, was a Quaker, a married man of comfortable means, who had formerly been a chemist; but to the historian of Scotland Yard it is of interest as having been the first, or almost the first, criminal case in which that new marvel, the electric telegraph, was used by the police.

Just as in the Crippen case, recorded later in this volume, in which wireless telegraphy was used for the first time, almost every scientific discovery has been turned to account by detective science—photography, electro-block printing, X-rays, classification of fingerprints, microscopy, telephony, telegraphy, and wireless, without counting the ingenious apparatus used for the detection of forgeries and tampering with documents.

The details of the crime were squalid enough. John Tawell had had relations with his former servant, Mrs. Sarah Hart, who lived with her children near Slough. One of her neighbours, hearing stifled moans coming from her cottage, went to see what was the matter and met Tawell coming down the garden path, agitated and trembling. She found the woman lying on the floor apparently dying. On the table were glasses and a bottle, but an examination of these showed no trace of poison. Nevertheless, an analysis of the contents of the stomach showed the presence of prussic acid.

As the prisoner's behaviour appeared suspicious, the "person who conducts the electric telegraph" was informed, and "a signal was made to the station in London," with the result that when Tawell, who was known to be making for the City, arrived at Paddington, he was met by a policeman "with a plain coat over his police dress" who kept him under observation on the omnibus as far as the house of a Quaker who lived near Cannon Street. He took no action that day, but on the morrow, no further news coming from Slough, he took another officer to the house and arrested Tawell, bringing him back to Slough and handing him over to the superintendent of the Eton police.

The prisoner affected to discuss the matter fully with

Superintendent Perkins, explaining that Mrs. Hart had herself taken the poison. "She was a good servant, but a very bad woman." He declared that she poured something from a phial into her stout, and then lay down on the rug; he then left her.

It was proved that the prisoner had bought two drachms of prussic acid "for an external injury." His statement was inconsistent. He said that Mrs. Hart had poured something from a phial into her glass, but no trace of the poison was found in any of the vessels examined, nor was there any trace of poison in two phials found in the cupboard.

The prisoner's defence was that though he had in early life offended against the moral laws, he had since atoned for his lapse from virtue by a life of industry and kindness. There were long, technical arguments on the poisoning. One suggestion was that the neighbour who had come in and administered water to the dying woman had caused her to choke. After a three days' trial the jury found the prisoner guilty. He was executed at Aylesbury. His respectability, his profession, and his firm and unshrinking bearing, both before and after conviction, aroused intense interest in him, and a reprieve had been generally expected. Before his execution he wrote a full confession. He was hanged in his Quaker's dress.

THE HAMPSTEAD MURDER

THE FIRST MENTION of "the detective force" in a criminal case is to be found in the contemporary account of the Hampstead murder in 1845. At about 7:30 in the evening of Friday, February 21, a baker named Hilton heard cries coming from a field near Belsize Lane. The cries continued for three or four minutes. He informed Police Constable Baldock, who was patrolling in the neighbourhood. The constable found the body of a man lying against the blank wall surrounding Belsize House. Sergeant Fletcher, whom he had brought with him, went for a stretcher, and in his absence a young man strolled up, singing, and said, "Hallo, policeman! What's wrong?" Baldock replied, "I think that it's a man who has cut his throat."

The young man stooped to feel the dead man's pulse and said, "It's a nasty job, policeman." He added that for some years he had taken this route from town and had never been molested, but his parents had always warned him not to go this way at night. He remarked that the policeman had a cold job before him and offered him brandy, which Baldock refused, though he accepted a shilling.

The young man remained until the stretcher arrived and followed the little procession as far as Belsize Lane. Later he was seen by a witness, returning home to Portland Town at a run. At that time he had given his name as Thomas Henry Hocker and his age as twenty-two.

Meanwhile the police had found a witness, a young woman, who made her deposition in tears; she testified that Hocker had dropped in to see her and her friend about nine o'clock. He was wearing a mackintosh and explained that there was a little blood on his shirt; that he had been tipsy and had had a fall. He showed them a silver watch and a ring which he said he had just bought.

The news of the murder in the Lane was already known, and Hocker discussed it quite naturally with his family. A little later his brother came in, and they sang duets together. When Detective-Inspector Shackell called and questioned him about the watch, he said at first that he had just re-deemed it from a pawnbroker, but when his brother pointed out that one of the hands failed to move round, he became confused and said that the watch had been given to him by a Mr. Delarue, with whom it was afterwards known he had been acquainted. By this time the body of the man found in the Lane had been identified as that of James Delarue, a music professor living in Hampstead.

Hocker's brother deposed that the young man had brought money home with him; that he appeared to be in rather a dishevelled state. Thomas Hocker accounted for this by saying that he had been "romping" with his young woman, Sarah Cox, and her brother, but when these two persons were questioned they denied the story indignantly.

Hocker was detained and his clothing was examined. It was found to be extensively stained with human blood, and even the mackintosh was spotted. After he was charged with murder he was put in charge of a police constable, James Euston, in Marylebone police station. He was given coffee and toast. An hour later he kicked at his cell door to attract the attention of the gaoler. He said that he had gone to Swiss Cottage, a short distance away, on the evening of the murder, about fifteen minutes after it was believed to have occurred, and he asked that the waiter who had served him with rum and water might be sent for to give evidence on his behalf.

At the time of the murder the victim, Delarue, had in

his pocket a letter, written in blue ink and signed "Caroline," making an appointment with him at the spot where his body was found. Blue ink of exactly the same tint was found in the prisoner's room. The letter was addressed to "Mr. Cooper," the name for the victim used by the prisoner in corresponding with him.

When Hocker was tried at the Central Criminal Court before Mr. Justice Coleridge, the prosecuting counsel dwelt upon the strange fact that the murderer should have returned to the side of his victim. "It would be inexplicable," he said, "except for the fact that criminals have done such things before."

The judge gave the prisoner leave to speak. It seemed to be the opportunity he had been waiting for. He asked the judge's leave to fetch some notes of what he intended to say, and was out of court for a few minutes. He returned with some sheets of manuscript, but with entire self-possession he waited with folded arms until there was complete silence; then with an air of insufferable self-conceit he began to read.

It was the kind of fantastic story that belonged to the early days of the cinema scenario, the story of his rivalry with Delarue in the affections of a "genteel young lady" at Hampstead (name not given) and how Delarue had seduced the poor young thing. And so he, Thomas Henry Hocker, had stepped in as her champion, had forged the young lady's name to make an assignation with Delarue, at which the young lady's brother was to be present. He had accompanied the brother to the Swiss Tavern, where he waited while the brother went on alone to "the fatal spot"; hearing cries of "Murder!" he hastened to the place and found his rival lying dead. Since it was he who had made the assignation he felt that he was responsible for the tragedy, and he "sought out a slaughter house in Hampstead and there disfigured his clothes in a pool of blood."

There was much more of this rhodomontade to which the court had to listen, but the jury made short work of it. After ten minutes' deliberation they found the prisoner guilty. He was executed on April 28, and there the spirit of bravado deserted him. He had practically to be carried to the scaffold.

A commentator of the time said that he had "exhibited a very extraordinary degree of audacity and of misdirected talent; by pretended revelations he had several times sent the officers of justice on vain searches and had even succeeded in raising doubts as to the justice of his sentence ... a greater compound of wickedness, falsehood and conceit never graced the annals of Newgate."

Since the establishment of rural police on the confines of the Metropolitan area to deal with the desperate gangs that infested the shores of the Thames, there had been so many threats of retaliation that it was decided to remove the threatened men to Metropolitan police stations and send other Metropolitan police officers to take their places.

Among these was a constable named George Clarke, who was given a beat at the Four Wants on Monday, June 29, 1846. He was posted by Sergeant Parsons, but when that officer went his round early the next morning he could not find him. Dagenham Waters and other ponds in the vicinity of the village were dragged, but it was not until late on Friday evening that Clarke's body, shockingly mutilated, was found lying in a potato field belonging to a Mr. Collier. His broken staff and his cutlass were found in the hedge; his head was unrecognizable; he had been thrown so violently to the ground that in spite of the dry weather the body had left an imprint where it fell. A forefinger had been cut off; a wound in the throat had nearly severed the head from the body; the right hand was grasping a quantity of wheat; the struggle must have been desperate.

The most experienced officers of the London police were sent for, but in spite of their utmost diligence and the large rewards that were advertised, no clue to the murderers was ever obtained. In the course of the investigation, however, it transpired that Sergeant Parsons and other members of the squad had given a false account of their proceedings on the night of the murder, either to cover some neglect of duty or for a graver reason. They were all taken into custody on suspicion, and the suspicion pressed more heavily against Sergeant Parsons than against his subordinates. No doubt it was hoped that detention might lead some of them to make admissions, but as no further evidence was obtained they were discharged from custody and dismissed from the force. The case had excited a painful public interest.

This murder was committed on the site of what is now the great Ford Motor factory on the Essex coast of the Thames.

BURKING HORSES

In 1847 a new form of crime made its appearance. For some weeks farmers had been suffering severe loss by the death of valuable horses which they had left safe and sound at night and found lifeless next morning. Some new form of epidemic was feared.

A man named Bentley, described as a knacker, was in the habit of purchasing carcases, which he sold in the London market, probably as food for the poor. On January 4, 1847, a farm labourer named Mason heard a horse moaning as if in pain. He followed the sound and in the dim light saw Bentley bending over the horse. Having a stick in his hand, he struck him over the head, but the man ran off and Mason could not secure him. The horse was dead but still warm. Mason communicated with the police, who handled the case very cleverly. They found that Bentley had lately had a number of transactions with purchasers of dead animals in London, and on examining his head they found the mark of Mason's stick. His method was to choke the nostrils of the unfortunate beasts with haybands and to tie up their jaws with ropes, which, of course, he removed as soon as they were dead. It was, in fact, an adaptation of the crimes of Burke and Hare, who murdered people and sold their bodies to the medical schools in Edinburgh. Bentley was very properly sentenced to fifteen years' transportation.

THE REVOLUTIONS OF 1848

The wave of political unrest which beset every European country in 1848, a year of revolutions, was not likely to leave Great Britain and Ireland untouched. One may imagine that when the news of the disturbances in Paris on March 6 reached London, it was not only the commissioners of the Metropolitan Police who were uneasy, but every citizen in the Metropolis. The deposition of King Louis Philippe and the restoration of the Republic was the match that set alight the powder magazine in Germany and elsewhere in central Europe.

England had her own troubles. There were the Chartists and the unemployed, and on Monday, March 6, an open-air meeting had been called by Charles Cochrane, a parliamentary candidate, to assemble in Trafalgar Square and Charing Cross to protest, not, as in other capitals, against the form of government, but against the income tax. Now, the Act 57 George III C 19 expressly forbids any open-air meeting to petition the legislature within a mile of Westminster Hall when Parliament is sitting, and it was the duty of the police commissioners to enforce it. They advised Mr. Cochrane that his meeting was illegal, and on Monday he issued notices to this effect and attempted to prevent the meeting. It was too late. A huge crowd had assembled, and the announcement was received with indignation. By one o'clock ten thousand people were gathered in the Square.

At first the mob was playful, if that word can be used for horse play such as pushing people into the fountain and "bonneting" them from behind. Then the inevitable orators made their appearance and attempted to draw morals from the revolution in Paris. People were still pouring into the Square, and when the orators had exhausted their breath, the mob had increased to fifteen thousand, among whom gangs of pickpockets were busy plying their trade.

The police were overwhelmed by numbers. Having vainly tried to hold back the crowd with their staves, they had to retreat to their station in Scotland Yard. The mob tore down the wooden fence round the Nelson Column and used the timber as weapons. With large reinforcements the police re-entered the Square and attacked the crowd at various points, though without dispersing it. The fighting continued until nightfall. There were shouts of *"Vive la République!"* and about eight o'clock a lad wearing epaulettes led a party down Pall Mall "for the Palace," breaking the lamps as they went. At Buckingham Palace the Guard turned out and at sight of the bayonets the mob sheered off and returned to its starting point in Trafalgar Square. The general intention had been wanton mischief, but on the way a baker's shop and a public house were beset and rations of bread and ale were exacted. Several of the ring-leaders were arrested; among them the youthful hero of the epaulettes, who burst into tears.

By midnight quiet was restored, but for some days after-wards the disturbances were renewed by a few hundreds of ragamuffin boys bent upon smashing the shop windows. The exasperation of the shopkeepers and their assistants would certainly have led to reprisals on the boys with any weapon that came to hand, but the rioters realized their unpopular-ity in time and disappeared without any resort to force. The nuisance had one useful effect: it roused the London citizens to meet the more formidable dangers of April 10.

There were sympathetic disturbances in Manchester, where the police had much trouble, and in Newcastle, Edin-burgh, Glasgow, and other places, but the general effect of these was to arouse a spirit of revolt against mob law, and a disposition to help the police.

A Chartist meeting planned to take place on Kennington Common on March 13 failed to justify the fears that had been expressed. Apart from the spectators, who held aloof, there was a crowd of young roughs from the slums. They were put to flight by a downpour of rain, but not before they had sacked a pawnbroker's shop. Great preparations had been made by the police; over two thousand were posted round the common and twelve hundred more were posted to control the bridges, besides reserves in the police stations and military reserves in readiness. The looters were very severely dealt with. Fifteen lads of between thirteen and twenty were tried for looting the pawnbroker's shop; four were acquitted, but two were sentenced to fourteen years' transportation and the rest to seven years'.

Two days after the trial—on April 10—the great Chartist meeting was to take place, its object being to present to Parliament a monster petition with five million signatures. The government was in some anxiety in view of what had happened in other parts of Europe, though they felt sure that the leaders were not at all desirous of producing a national convulsion. The danger was that the rank and file might snap their fingers at their leaders. The government took no chances. A notice, signed by the commissioners of police, and quoting an act of Charles II against disorders fomented by persons on the pretence of presenting petitions to Parliament, and prescribing that the number presenting a petition must not exceed ten, was posted. Knowing that it was intended to be a mass presentation and that persons presenting it had been advised to carry firearms, the commissioners forbade the meeting and called upon all well-disposed persons to co-operate in protecting the public peace. The petition might be presented in the constitutional way, but there was to be no organized procession.

Preparations were made on a lavish scale; 170,000 special constables were sworn in, and the force of police held in readiness on the Common and at the bridgeheads was imposing.

The Chartists assembled at various points and passed across Blackfriars and London bridges in a continuous line, the largest unit numbering six thousand. The most striking was that of the national convention, numbering about twelve hundred men. Messrs. O'Connor and E. Jones were carried in a great car drawn by six horses, together with the ten who were to present the petition. Behind them came a car drawn by four horses and containing the monster petition with appropriate Chartist banners and devices. One of these bore the words, "And Guizot laughed immoderately."

The attendance was disappointing. At the most it was calculated that there were twenty-three thousand present. When the two cars had taken up their position, a police inspector of gigantic stature and good-natured aspect was seen pressing through the crowd towards Mr. O'Connor's vehicle. He told O'Connor that the commissioners desired to speak to him for a few moments near the Horns Tavern. O'Connor alighted with his friend McGrath and followed the inspector, who strode through the mob as if it had been standing corn. As they passed, a cry went up that the leaders were deserting, and a rush was made for O'Connor and McGrath. They turned very white, and at one moment they came near to fainting. But they were protected and arrived safely at their rendezvous with the police commissioners, who made it clear that a peaceful meeting would not be interfered with if O'Connor would give his word that it should remain peaceable; but that a return in procession would be stopped, by force if necessary. O'Connor gave the undertaking, shaking hands with Mr. Mayne in pledge, and then returned to his place in the car.

This resolute attitude on the part of the police had the effect of stopping all the intended proceedings. There was a squabble among the leaders, and a few hot-headed members of the crowd delivered violent speeches, but the meeting gradually broke up; the banners were rolled round their staves, and the monster petition was consigned to the humbler conveyance of three cabs, chartered to carry it to the House of Commons. For a time there was some skirmishing at the bridge head, and a few men had to be carried on stretchers to a dressing station, but by three o'clock all was quiet, and the mob had melted away.

The events of the day produced a great effect, not only in Great Britain, but throughout Europe. The foreign comments were that a dangerous assemblage had been put down, not by troops, nor even by police, but by the people themselves—by the almost unanimous determination of all classes that such disorders should not be permitted.

When the petition came to be examined, it was found that it had not been signed by anything like five million people. The number did not exceed one and a half millions, and a large number of these signatures were faked. The Duke of Wellington's name, for example, was signed seventeen times, and the same liberties had been taken with the names of Colonel Sibthorpe (a leading member of Parliament), Lord John Russell, Sir Robert Peel, Queen Victoria, and Prince Albert. A large number of the supposed signatures consisted of "obscene words, cant phrases and gross ribaldry." Moreover, the presentation led to a personal squabble between two of the Chartist leaders which covered them with ridicule.

This was not the last of the Chartist agitation, for on April 24 there was another demonstration in Leicester Square against the Poor Law. A procession of fifty thousand persons was to present a memorial to Sir George Grey, the Home Secretary. Mr. Cochrane, the late member for Westminster, drove into Leicester Square with a van adorned with daubs purporting to illustrate scenes in a workhouse. Not only were they badly drawn, but some of them offended against decency. The police kept the crowd moving, and Cochrane, finding that his plans were frustrated, drove down by-streets to the Home Office, only to find that Sir George Grey was out. The petition had to be left with the clerks.

Nevertheless Chartists in England and Scotland were arming, and the danger of an upheaval was not quite at an end. There was, however, a rush of volunteers to be sworn in as special constables.

On May 31 the conviction of John Mitchell in Dublin caused an explosion of rage among the disaffected in London. The Chartist and Confederate clubs collected followers from all parts of the Metropolis and set out for Finsbury Square, and thence in procession to Smithfield and Trafalgar Square. Here an imposing body of police dispersed them. On the following night a meeting was held on Clerkenwell Green, and the police interfered to stop inflammatory speeches. They pressed forward on the speakers in a compact mass with mounted constables at its head. It was then, perhaps for the first time, that the value of mounted police in suppressing riotous assemblies was realized.

All through that week there were disorderly meetings, not only in London but in the provinces, but all came to nothing.

On June 3 another attempt was made to incite the mob at Clerkenwell and Paddington. One hundred mounted police were employed to disperse the crowds when they were in the act of assembling, and a considerable force of pensioners and troops were held in reserve. By two o'clock there was no sign of a demonstration, and the police were able to picnic in the fields. At that hour McDougal, one of the Chartist leaders, sought out the magistrate, Mr. Arnold, and asked him whether the government really intended to stop the Chartist meetings. The reply was given emphatically—"Yes, sir"—and the leader disappeared. An hour later the weather took charge of the proceedings. A terrific thunderstorm broke over the fields, and by 4 P.M. not a soul was to be seen but the police sheltering under the hedges.

The government now felt that the Chartists had been given rope enough. Knowing that they had public opinion behind them in suppressing the nuisance, they took into custody a number of representative leaders—Jones, a barrister, Fussell, Williams, Sharpe, and Vernon—and committed them for trial on bail. The men guilty of outrages were sentenced to varying terms of hard labour; one of these had struck a constable with an iron bar. On August 11 a round-up of leading Chartists in London and the provinces was begun.

A constable named Bright, who had been mistaken for an officer who had given evidence against McDougal at his trial, had been murdered by the mob before he could be rescued. Pikes and other weapons were secured in great quantity at Bradford.

In London the final blow was struck. Three hundred armed police were concentrated at the Tower police station. They marched suddenly to the Angel Tavern in Blackfriars, where they surprised a committee of fourteen Chartists. There was some attempt at resistance, but the inspector in charge cried, "If any man offers the least resistance, I will run him through. A large force surrounds the house." The Chartists were marched to the police station in Tower Street and searched. They were found to be in possession of pistols, loaded to the muzzle, three-cornered daggers, spearheads, and swords hidden under the seats they had occupied at the inn. Some of them were wearing iron breastplates, and others had gunpowder, shot, and tow balls for incendiary purposes. One man had seventy-five rounds of ball cartridges. It was believed that an armed procession had been planned for midnight and that if the police interfered public buildings would have been fired.

It is doubtful whether the plot would have had any success, for troops were under arms at every vulnerable point —Buckingham Palace, the Tower of London, the Mint, the Bank of England, and the various barracks also were under arms. Scotland Yard was in continual communication with the City force and with the military. That was the end of the Chartists.

THE ABOLITION OF TRANSPORTATION

AT THE BEGINNING OF THE YEAR 1850 the detective police found themselves faced with a new form of crime. Chloroform had recently come into prominence as an anesthetic, and there was an epidemic of robberies in consequence. On the 10th of January two notorious women used it to render a Mr. Jewett, a solicitor in the Whitechapel Road, unconscious. He woke to find himself stripped of his clothing and valuables, lying on a filthy bed in a wretched lodging. His health suffered severely in consequence. He recovered sufficiently to be able to identify his assailants, who were sentenced to seven years' penal servitude.

On June 29 Sir Robert Peel, the founder of the Metropolitan Police, sustained a fatal accident on his return from an audience with the Queen at Buckingham Palace. On his way up Constitution Hill the horse he was riding threw him, and he fell sideways on his left shoulder. He was sixty-two. Two gentlemen who saw the accident raised him to a sitting posture, and Dr. Foucart, who happened to be passing, asked him whether he was much hurt. "Yes," he said, "I am very much hurt," and then he lapsed into unconsciousness. He was taken home in a carriage. Sir James Clarke, the Queen's physician, met the carriage and got in beside him. When they arrived at his house in Whitehall Gardens, he was conscious. He said that he felt very much better, and was able to walk into the house, but he fainted in Dr. Foucart's arms and was laid on a sofa in his dining room. It was found that his clavicle and several ribs were fractured, and that one of them had pierced the lung. He lived for three days in much pain, and passed away on July 2 in the presence of his friends.

A commentator of the time wrote:

It is impossible to exaggerate the feelings of profound emotion with which the intelligence of Sir Robert's death was received throughout the country. All remembrance of the political offences of his earlier career were forgotten; nothing was remembered but his great practical reforms and the power of mind and strength of purpose which made him the leading statesman in Europe and the master mind of English policy.

In the House of Commons a rare tribute of respect was paid to his memory. On learning of his death the House immediately adjourned without transacting any further business. The French Assembly, as a testimony of their appreciation, voted unanimously to enter a record of the fact of his death and their sympathetic regret on the official minutes of the Chamber. Lord John Russell proposed a public monument in Westminster Abbey, and this was agreed to. The burial took place in the quiet churchyard of Drayton Bassett, quite simply, amid the respectful grief of thousands who attended the funeral and the universal sorrow of the nation.

Sir Robert Peel was born at Bury in Lancashire. His grandfather was a calico printer, who, after the invention of the spinning jenny, took to cotton-spinning and grew wealthy. His father, who was the third son, carried on the business. He entered Parliament as the supporter of Pitt and contributed munificently towards Pitt's war policy. He was rewarded with a baronetcy in 1800.

Sir Robert was educated at Harrow and Christchurch, Oxford, where he obtained first-class honours, both in classics and mathematics. He entered at Lincoln's Inn, but was elected to Parliament at the age of twenty-one. He made his mark in the House by his close attention to Parliamentary duties and by a style of speaking which owed its force to knowledge of the subject, to clear exposition, close reasoning, and tact in dealing with a parliamentary audience. He inherited his father's Tory politics.

Having become Secretary for Ireland in 1812, he was violently abused by O'Connell, and was ill advised enough to challenge him to a duel—an affair that covered them both with ridicule.

His domestic life was singularly happy. He had five sons and two daughters. Three of his sons distinguished themselves in public life; the youngest, Arthur, was considered one of the best speakers in the House of Commons. He was created a viscount on his retirement in 1895. His son was the First Commissioner of Works in Baldwin's second ministry in 1924.

Peel had lived long enough to see his creation, the Metropolitan Police, wear down the public opposition that assailed it in its infancy and become a national institution. After its first twenty years it had become part of the fabric of the nation, and it is perhaps not too much to say that the Metropolitan Police was in some measure to be credited with the tranquillity in which Great Britain passed through the fateful year of revolution in 1848.

The year 1850 marked a radical change in the disposal of criminals and therefore a change of great importance to the police. The advocates for transportation had had all the arguments on their side for many years. They argued that crime was largely due to unwholesome upbringing in the overcrowded slums of great cities; that the wide and healthy territories of Australia and Tasmania were lying empty for lack of emigrants and that convicts, of whom many were not inherently vicious, made admirable colonists. In theory, of course, this was true, but the first obstacle to realization of the ideal was that the great majority of these men had been city-bred and that they would never take kindly to life on the soil, especially the soil of an undeveloped and primitive country. Undoubtedly, a few of

SIR ROBERT PEEL

It was Sir Robert Peel who in 1829 secured the passing of the
Metropolitan Police Bill which laid the firm foundations of the
modern London police system. For many years his police, with top
hats and blue coats and trousers, were known as "Peelers."

these men did reform and did become prosperous when they had earned their ticket of leave,[1] but it was among them and their families that the agitation against transportation first began. Throughout the early years of the century there had been in Australia an insistent cry that the mother country should "consume her own smoke," and the highly coloured narratives of returned convicts that found their way into the press in the British Isles were producing strong propaganda against transportation there. From time to time cases, for the most part exaggerated, found a prominent place in the newspapers.

The callousness about human suffering that marked the early years of the nineteenth century had by the middle of the century given place to a morbid humanitarianism. Undoubtedly it was time, for it was argued by those responsible for the government of the hulks, the convict ships, and the transportation colonies that it was impossible to maintain even a semblance of discipline unless men could be sentenced to floggings of a hundred lashes. That was the ordinary penalty for attempts to escape from the colony.

A general awakening to the criminal problem is to be found in the general report in 1842 of the magistrates for Westminster:

It is still greatly to be deplored that some humane plan has not yet been devised by which a beneficial restraint might be exercised towards prisoners awaiting trial so that the innocent and novices in crime might be separated from hardened offenders.

A report in this same year from the inspectors in Millbank prison stated that the Secretary of State had appropriated that prison as a depot for the reception of all convicts under sentence or order of transportation in Great Britain instead of their being sent to the hulks. Inspectors were in future carefully to examine prisoners and their

---

[1] By good conduct every convict could earn a remission of one fourth of his sentence on what was called ticket of leave. This did not entitle him to leave the colony before the expiration of his sentence, but he had all the privileges of a free colonist.

papers and make recommendations to the Home Secretary from time to time as to their disposal.

In the same report we learn what was the general rule approved by Lord Stanley as to convict discipline in the Penal Colonies. There were four stages:

1. Detention at Norfolk Island.
2. The probationary gang.
3. Probationary passes.
4. Tickets of leave.

This is followed by an apology for the then existing system of transportation:

> Experience has proved that the practice of commuting sentences of transportation to periods of imprisonment in England is unsound in principle and injurious in its effects; and that the uncertainty which attends its execution forms one of those chances of escape from punishment on which offenders invariably calculate. The convict too, on his liberation, is unable to obtain, or unfitted to pursue an honest employment, and returns too often into society only to pollute its morals and disturb its peace.

One could ask no more from official apologists for a decaying system. They were the same in 1842 as doubtless they are now.

It was not until August 1853 that Lord Palmerston, the Home Secretary, announced that the Australians were in revolt at seeing their country turned into a dumping ground for British malefactors. Transportation was thenceforth to be limited to Western Australia, and the transportees were to be employed on public works in Great Britain and then released on a ticket of leave that could be revoked. The country had been paying little short of £200,000 a year for the transport of its convicts to Australia, and it was estimated that the charge for providing accommodation for them in England would result in an annual saving of expense.

It was objected that the ticket-of-leave system would break down through the new principle of subjecting a new class of free men to having their liberty abridged by the will of a Secretary of State. This objection was met by

Lord Palmerston by the argument that the ticket of leave would introduce an element of hope and that the fear of forfeiting it would teach criminals habits of self-control. With anyone acquainted with the mentality of convicts—especially that of the professional criminal—this kind of idealized parliamentary talk raises a smile. It was not then realized that a great gulf is fixed between the habitual and the accidental criminal—a gulf which still exists. For example, a murderer who acts in a fit of ungovernable rage very seldom reverts to crime, whereas the habitual thief rarely adopts an honest way of living, for the earnings of honesty, lacking as they do the spirit of adventure, are too humdrum to be tempting.

Probably, as is usual in such cases, the truth lay midway between the two schools of thought, but the local agitation in Australia against receiving any more convict drafts turned the scale, and the mother country had to provide in haste the machinery for "consuming her own smoke." There was a growing accumulation of men and women sentenced to penal servitude in hulks lying in the Thames and in the various ports, but these became grossly overcrowded. In 1850 the first convict prison was opened. For thirty-five years a war prison, built to accommodate the prisoners of the Napoleonic wars, had been lying derelict on Dartmoor, about fifteen hundred feet above the sea. The old granite buildings were rapidly converted into cellular blocks by partitions of corrugated iron, and men were moved up from the hulks as rapidly as the accommodation could be provided. Similar arrangements were made at Portland, Parkhurst, and other prisons, and in 1850 the necessary legislation was passed. It is right to say here that none of the sombre forecasts made by the advocates of transportation came to pass. As time went on, attempts were made to classify the convicts in accordance with their characters, and their aftercare was greatly developed. It cannot be said that the convict prisons were reformatories, but the results that could be cited, particularly among the younger men convicted for crimes of violence, were not far short of the cases that could be cited in favor of reformatories.

There was something to be said for transportation if it had been properly managed, but the system as it was then carried out, beginning with the convict hulk and the voyage out to Australia in an overcrowded ship, the free use of the lash to subdue the spirit of refractory prisoners, the iron discipline of the penal settlement of Tasmania, gave ample material for the sensational journalist to use in condemning the system. The real evils of transportation lay in the indiscriminate association of the bad men and the less degraded, which ground them all to the same pattern. While the mother country was ridding herself of the worst of her citizens she was creating at home bitter resentment against her government, which inevitably deprived her of any sense of loyalty and pride of nationality in the masses of the people.

In one respect the change from transportation to penal servitude was an advantage to Scotland Yard. A branch was formed at headquarters called the Convict Supervision Office and manned by specially selected detectives. Under the law every convict was entitled to earn a ticket of leave after he had served three quarters of his sentence, and during the remaining quarter he was required to report himself to the Convict Supervision Office once a month and give an account of how he was living. He was required also to notify it of any change of address, and this notification was verified. In special cases the requirement to report was specially remitted by the Home Secretary, but on the whole it was a very salutary provision.

As might be expected, the ill-disposed among the ticket-of-leave holders objected very strongly to reporting themselves, and when they were subsequently arrested for a fresh offence they would plead that it was impossible to earn an honest livelihood with the police dogging their footsteps and whispering to their employers that they were discharged convicts. These allegations have always been entirely without foundation. The men selected for the Convict

Supervision Office are as keenly interested in seeing that their charges "make good" as any philanthropist, though, no doubt, they could indicate in advance far better than the philanthropist which of their charges would revert to evil courses. One advantage enjoyed by the Convict Supervision officers is that they can have a private interview with a convict about to be discharged and have a heart-to-heart talk with him. Very few convicts resent this interview.

Much has been written about the horrors of transportation; much that is true and more that has been exaggerated. But there remains always the fact that the day was at hand when the colonies would rebel against the system. The fact was that all the severities and the cruelties of the British penal system may be traced to fear. Children were allowed to grow up in slum rabbit warrens without education and without a decent example. From an early age they drifted naturally into crime. The police system was purposely left medieval because the ratepayers feared the expense of paying for a disciplined force. The one preoccupation of the justiciary was to get rid of the criminal, and if that could not be done by the gallows it must be done by transportation.

There were, of course, numerous instances of convicts who by exemplary conduct in the colonies qualified themselves for a ticket of leave and eventually made good. We are not allowed by the opponents of transportation to hear of these. All has to be painted in the darkest colours in order to produce the effect sought—the abolition of transportation, which began in 1849.

A remarkable case was dealt with at the Liverpool Assizes in March 1843. One George Robinson was brought up at Liverpool for sentence for having illegally returned from transportation. He made a remarkable statement which was never refuted. He said that he had been convicted of highway robbery in 1820 at the age of eighteen and sentenced to transportation. He did not dispute the justice of his sentence. Some time after his arrival in Port Jackson he made an attempt to escape by a brig which was lying in the harbour. She was driven ashore by bad weather, and he was handed over to the authorities to receive one hundred lashes. He was sent by them to the penal settlement, first at Hunter's River and afterwards at Macquarrie Harbour. For twelve months he never had the irons off his legs.

Then he joined other convicts in an attempt to escape. Three days later they were attacked by natives. They were afraid to go back, knowing that they would receive a hundred lashes and be sent to work with the worst gang in the colony, so they wandered about the Blue Mountains for two months, naked, until their privations forced them to make for the coast. Natives acted as their guides, but when they drew near Port Philip, another tribe captured them and surrendered them to the authorities. They were taken to Coal River, naked as they were, but the blankets that were lent to them there had to be left behind when they were embarked for Sydney.

At Sydney they were supplied with clothing by public charity, though one man had nothing but a pair of trousers for six months. They were sentenced to one hundred lashes, but the doctor declined to pass them as physically fit for the punishment.

Robinson again made his escape by stealing a whaleboat. With some companions, he contrived a sail out of the shirts of the party and ran down the coast for nine days. Provisions failing them, they put in at Hobart Town, where they were caught by the authorities and sent back to Macquarrie Harbour. This time they were sent to the depot for the worst offenders. He drew a horrible picture of this depot, where he remained for seven years before being sent to Hobart Town. There he succeeded in stowing away on a vessel for twenty-one days. The captain gave him up at St. Helena, and he was taken back to the Cape and thence to Robben Island, off the coast, where he worked for seven months with twenty-five-pound irons on his legs. He was then sent back to Macquarrie Harbour. For his brave conduct during a gale he was recommended for "merciful consideration" and was allowed to obtain a ticket of leave three years later.

Still longing for home, he made his escape in an American whaler and cruised in her for months. Knowing that the captain intended to give him up when he arrived in Australia, he took advantage of a chance call in New Zealand and threw himself on the mercy of the Maoris, who treated him well. He then boarded a vessel bound for Boston, worked his passage to Quebec and thence to Greenock and Liverpool. He had since been living in Manchester and earning an honest livelihood. He protested that since his original sentence he had never offended against the law, and he submitted his sufferings and his good conduct to the merciful consideration of the authorities.

Mr. Baron Park, the judge, pointed out that he had no discretion in the matter. A sentence of transportation could not be modified because the convict had been able to escape. His duty was to order the prisoner to be transported again for the term of his natural life. The prisoner bowed respectfully and was removed from the bar.

We are told by an eyewitness that the physical appearance of the man went far in supporting the truth of his story. His features were drawn by suffering, "and there was something very moving in the manner in which he received the sentence that was again to consign him to the horrors he had been describing."

IN MAY 1850 Sir Charles Rowan retired from the post of commissioner, and died in May 1852, at the age of seventy. He had had a distinguished military career, both in Spain and at Waterloo, where he commanded a wing of the 52nd Regiment and was wounded. He was the fifth son of an Irish squire, Robert Rowan, of North Lodge, Carrickfergus. He had been selected by Sir Robert Peel to be joint commissioner with Sir Richard Mayne, and these two Irishmen had contrived between them to live down the public prejudice against the Metropolitan Police for twenty-one of the most difficult years in the history of the force without, so far as we know, a hint of misunderstanding between them.

Sir Charles Rowan was succeeded by Captain Hay, who for ten years had been visiting superintendent of the Metropolitan Police. Like Rowan he had taken part in the Peninsula War and in the battle of Waterloo. Unfortunately, though it had been intended that he should be subordinate to Mayne, their exact relations had not been defined, and he was not a loyal colleague. For example, without informing Mayne, he submitted a scheme for police duties to the Home Secretary, and when public feeling ran high against the police for mismanagement on the occasion of the Duke of Wellington's funeral he communicated to the newspapers a paragraph informing the public that his colleague had been responsible. The relations between the two became

142

strained, and when Hay died in 1855 Mayne was given sole control with two assistant commissioners to help him.

Rowan seems to have had little to do with the detectives in plain clothes appointed in consequence of the Daniel Good murder in 1842, and Sir Richard Mayne, in his fear of reawakening popular prejudice against officers in plain clothes, determined to keep all the men at headquarters and employ them under his own eye. Unfortunately they seem to have had little or no preliminary training as detectives, and consequently their work differed little from that of officers in uniform. None of them has left his mark on history. From 1842 to 1864 this handful of so-called "detectives" remained a branch of the Commissioner's Office—only from 8 to 15 strong in a force of 8,000 men.

The year 1851 was notable in the annals of the criminal courts, for it produced legislation to amend the law of evidence and to improve the administration of criminal justice. The Great Exhibition in Hyde Park, afterwards removed to its present position at Sydenham under the name of the Crystal Palace, drew crowds to London. The public was concerned chiefly with the burning question of Free Trade and Protection, which was hotly contested in rioting all over the country. We hear of the detectives from time to time, as, for example, on June 28, when they prevented a bank robbery in St. James's Square. Six weeks earlier two detectives had noticed an ex-convict named John Tyler loitering near one of the fountains. They kept him under observation and saw him join an old man named Cauty, a notorious receiver. They followed the two into St. James's Square and watched them enter the Westminster Bank. They remained there for about fifteen minutes, but there was no robbery on that occasion. Nevertheless, Inspector Lund warned the bank officials, and it was decided to place the money in security and to leave the cashbox containing marked notes in its usual place in the manager's office. The thieves fell into the trap and were caught in the act of carrying off the box. It was a departure from the injunction that the police should prevent the commission of crime, but it was very much what would have been done in these latter days. The two men were sentenced to seven years' transportation.

One of the first recorded instances of the police being called upon to render first aid occurred on June 16, when two "experienced aeronauts," Mr. and Mrs. Graham, went up in a balloon from Barry's hippodrome in Kensington. Before the balloon had attained any height it struck a flagstaff, tearing a hole in the silk. The aeronauts threw out sand ballast, which fell on the Crystal Palace, then still in Hyde Park. It drifted towards Colonel North's house in Arlington Street, knocked away the coping and the chimney pots, and broke through the roof. The police went to the rescue and found Mr. and Mrs. Graham lying senseless on the roof, suffering from serious injuries. They carried them to a neighbouring surgeon's house and then freed the balloon and took it to the station house. This was the kind of duty which in succeeding years served to increase the popularity of the force.

It was not surprising that towards the close of 1851 there was a popular outcry about the inequality of sentences. For example, on October 8, Sergeant Earthy of the Metropolitan Police took Constable Bayley with him to investigate a case of highway robbery in Acton. In one of the lanes they discovered two masked men. One of these shot the sergeant in the thigh. As he fell he saw the constable struggling with the prisoner, Harris, one of the two masked men, and very pluckily he attacked Harris and secured his pistol. The other, named Round, escaped at the time but was arrested on the following evening at Paddington Station for trying to pay for a railway ticket with a medal instead of a sovereign. On being arrested he asked whether the sergeant was dead, saying that if he was it was his own fault for knocking up his, Round's, hand. The two prisoners were condemned to death, but the sentence was commuted to transportation for life.

At the ensuing sessions in December there were terrible cases of cruelty to women and children. For example, a woman was convicted of having consistently ill-used her little daughter by burning her with a red-hot poker. She was sentenced to six months' imprisonment. A man killed his illegitimate child in the absence of its mother because it was crying, by beating out its brains against the floor. The sentence of death passed on him was commuted to transportation for life. At the same sessions a woman who had stolen £4.10.8½ from a lady's pocket was sentenced to transportation for ten years. In another case a man named John Stevens was awarded six months with hard labour for consistent ill-usage of his wife. She asked him for food, having fasted for two days and he beat her with a picking rod, a spiked tool used by weavers, and afterwards beat her into insensibility. These cases of inequality of sentences were taken up by the press. It was not the juries that were at fault, but the judges and the Home Secretary.

In November 1862 there was an outbreak of garrotting in the London streets. The method was quite simple. One ruffian would come up behind an unsuspecting wayfarer, put a hand over his shoulder and compress his throat while a confederate rifled his pockets. The unfortunate victim could not cry out. He was left writhing on the ground with his tongue protruding, and was quite unable to describe his assailants.

Robberies by the garrotte had now extended to the North. All through the early months of the year garrotters were busy in the neighbourhood of Hull, Sheffield, and Glasgow.

In June riots broke out in Stockport. They began with an attack by Roman Catholics on a Protestant school. The Protestants replied by attacking an alehouse frequented by Roman Catholics. They sacked the Catholic chapels and made a bonfire of the furniture and images; sixty-seven people were wounded and one was killed. Three days later troops arrived and put an end to the rioting. A great number of arrests were made, both of Irish Catholics and English Protestants. The magistrates selected ten of the most prominent rioters from each side; they were sentenced to various terms of imprisonment, but the Protestant who had killed an Irish rioter was transported for fifteen years.

The Metropolitan Police proved their usefulness in the crush at the funeral of the Duke of Wellington on November 10. Inadequate arrangements had been made by the commissioner for the lying-in-state. The day was wet and boisterous, but thousands of people waited their turn for admission for hours in the rain. When the public were admitted three people were crushed to death; women were knocked down; children were held in the air to escape suffocation; families were torn from one another; finally Superintendent Pearce, who had been in charge of the police at the Great Exhibition, stepped in and, thanks to his experience of organization, there was no further sacrifice of life. He summoned more police; he erected barriers with the aid of soldiers, and restored order.

The year 1853 was remarkable for its legislation. An Act was passed for rendering the forging of bank notes more difficult. Greater powers were given to the magistrates for dealing with assaults on women and children and for cutting down expense and delay in the administration of the criminal law. They were empowered to sentence prisoners up to six months, with or without hard labour, and relief was provided for the wife while her husband was in prison. Other useful provisions were made. The duties on soap were repealed, and vaccination was made compulsory.

On April 13, 1855, a discovery was made which seriously endangered public confidence in Scotland Yard detectives. A thirteen-year-old boy, John Reeves, had been sentenced to two years' imprisonment and had made charges against Charles King, a detective officer. The boy said that he had known King for three years and had met him first in Dean Street, Soho. King took him to the Serpentine, where people were skating, and pointed out a lady whom it would be easy to rob. The boy took her purse, and he and King then shared its contents, King hiding the purse in a hole in a hollow tree. They then went to a coffeeshop in Sloane

Street. The boy said that King told him not to attempt to steal from people crossing the bridge over the Serpentine because they would be on the alert. The boy picked another pocket, and a second boy, who was out with him, was caught in the act by the beadle, who seized him and would have secured him but for King, who put out his foot and tripped him.

On December 31, 1853, a park keeper had seen King and several others busy about an old tree in Hyde Park. He had searched it and had found an empty purse in a hole. He had informed the police, who had been watching King going about with these boys. Another police officer had seen King trip up the beadle and said that when the police went to arrest him he ran away. All this was given in evidence at the Central Criminal Court, and King was sentenced to transportation for fourteen years.

The scene for police activity had now changed to Hyde Park. In June the bill before Parliament for stopping Sunday trading was made the excuse for a mob to collect "to see how the aristocracy kept the Sabbath." They hung about the rides and drives, but beyond frightening a few horses they did little harm. A larger demonstration was planned for the first of July. The commissioners of police issued a notice that the demonstration would not be allowed. That was enough. A crowd nearly a mile long collected from the poorer suburbs and invaded the Park, where speeches were made and the police attempted to disperse the crowd, using their staves rather freely. One speaker narrowly escaped drowning. He attempted to swim the Serpentine and had to be rescued by a boat of the Royal Humane Society.

The riots in the Park were becoming alarming. Any well-known person who passed through it was hooted and in some cases assaulted. On July 8 the mob left the Park and assembled at the top of Grosvenor Place. Thence it marched into Belgrave Square and Eaton Square, smashing windows as it went. At one point it tried to set fire to the straw laid down before a sick person's house, but a timely arrival of the police caused a dispersal. A week later the disturbances had died down.

A number of people who had witnessed the scenes on July 1 were of opinion that the police had acted with unnecessary violence, and an inquiry was demanded. It was conducted in legal form, a solicitor being appointed to represent the public. There was ample evidence that individual policemen had lost their tempers and that Superintendent Hughes, without sufficient grounds, had ordered his men to use their staves and had failed to control the excesses of the men under his command. Moreover, it was found that the police cells in Vine Street had been grossly overcrowded. When another outbreak of rioting occurred in October it was noted that the police had taken the findings of the inquiry to heart. No violence was used on that occasion. The crowd was kept within the Park and kept moving by a considerable body of mounted police. The cold weather soon brought these demonstrations to a close.

A CASE THAT CREATED enormous public interest in December 1855 was the poisoning of a young racing man, John Cook, who was taken ill at the Raven Hotel, Shrewsbury, on the day after the Shrewsbury races. He had won money on Pole Star. His companion at the races, a Rugeley surgeon, a Mr. William Palmer, had given him a drink on their return to the hotel, but had declined to have one himself. Cook complained to a man named Fisher that the grog "burned his throat awfully" and that he was sure that Palmer had "dosed" him. A few minutes later he was violently sick; he repeated to another acquaintance, a man named Herring, that he had been "dosed." Herring expressed his surprise that Cook should have subsequently arranged to breakfast with Palmer, and Cook replied, "Ah! You don't know all." In some way he seemed to be in Palmer's power.

As he seemed to be feeling no better, Palmer carried him off to Rugeley and settled him in a hotel there; he and other doctors being in attendance. Cook complained of some pills which Palmer described as "morphine," and the other doctors advised him to change them as they seemed to be causing the patient severe pain and attacks of rigidity. Palmer then administered two pills which he said contained ammonia. Soon after taking them Cook was seized with violent pain and convulsions and died on December 20.

On hearing of his death, Cook's stepfather, a Mr. Stephens, who was much attached to him and was suspicious of Palmer, came to Rugeley and announced his intention of having a post-mortem examination. This was done by physicians from Guy's Hospital in London, who found in the body large quantities of antimony; they failed to find any strychnine, though they felt sure that it had been administered.

Immediately after Cook's death the chambermaid, unknown to Palmer, who thought that he was alone in the room, saw him thrust his hand under the dead man's pillow and feel in all his pockets. No trace could be found of Cook's betting book. The police inquiries very ably conducted by Detective-Sergeant Field revealed some startling evidence of former crimes. Palmer had for years been receiving large sums from life insurance offices for insuring persons who died soon after the policies were taken out. His own wife was one of these, and so was his brother; indeed a total of sixteen murders were attributed to him. That was not all. Just before the Rugeley case he had been arrested for forging a cheque in favour of a Mr. Padwick; it had been dishonoured. Palmer said that the signature was that of his late wife. He was transferred from the custody of the sheriff and detained at the suit of the Crown. The local feeling against Palmer was so strong that the case was removed from Stafford to the Central Criminal Court in London.

His trial, which laster fourteen days, began on May 4 1856, and was a *cause célèbre*. A vast crowd came to the Old Bailey to hear it, but no one was admitted without a ticket. The seats surrounding the Bench were crowded with members of both Houses. Charles Dickens was present. Some of the judges, even, were among the audience. As strychnine had not been found in the organs of the dead man, the prosecution had to depend upon circumstantial evidence, but the conduct of the Crown counsel was marked by the utmost fairness. All the evidence for the prosecution had been made known to the defending counsel before the trial.

Palmer was thirty-one. He was described in the calendar as of superior education. He was a short, rather stout person, with a round head and face, scanty hair of a sandy colour, and a ruddy complexion. There was nothing in his expression or carriage which indicated cunning or cruelty. Throughout the long trial he was composed and interested. He paid close attention to the evidence and passed notes to his counsel at frequent intervals.

The Attorney-General's speech occupies thirty-three pages of the Law Cases section of the Annual Register. He said that the accused had been trying to raise money on bills ever since 1853, and traced his gradual drift into racing and betting. He had been present at the post-mortem, and when it was announced that no trace of strychnine had been found, he turned to one of the examiners and said, "Doctor, they won't hang us yet!" One of the most important witnesses for the prosecution was the chambermaid. She had attended the dead man during his attacks, and he had asked her whether she had ever seen anyone in such agony as he had been through during the night and said that it had been due to Palmer's pills. She tasted the broth that she had brought up for Cook's last meal, and it had made her ill. After more than an hour's retirement the jury found Palmer guilty, and he was sentenced to be executed at Stafford. After his conviction he played the part of an innocent man admirably. On the morning of his execution the high sheriff asked him if he acknowledged the justice of his sentence. He replied with energy "No, sir, I do not. I go to the scaffold a murdered man."

At Stafford there was a barbarous custom of burying executed prisoners without a coffin. Casts were taken of Palmer's head, and phrenologists were allowed to make a study of it. Palmer seems to have been endowed with an extraordinary power of influencing others. Even during the inquest on Cook the coroner appeared to be under his control and accepted suggestions from him about the line he should pursue. This strange power was shown in a sequel to his trial, in the following March, when Samuel Cheshire, the postmaster at Rugeley, was charged with opening a letter in transit through the post. He described at his trial a visit he had paid to Palmer's house on December 5, when Palmer gave him a hint to report to him anything he might see in letters passing through his hands on the subject of the result of the post-mortem. So the postmaster opened a letter from Dr. Taylor to the attorney, Gardner, and the terms of this letter were circulated about the town almost in its very words. It was thus that the postmaster's offence came to light. Cheshire was sentenced to twelve months' imprisonment.

On March 28, 1856, the last gibbet in England was demolished by men working on the North-Eastern railway dock at Jarrow-on-Tyne. The last criminal to be gibbeted on it had been a young miner, named William Jobbing, in 1832, for the murder of a magistrate, Mr. Fairles, who was trying to uphold the law during a colliers' strike. A disused law had been revived in Jobbing's case, and the memory of the poor wretch swinging in chains by the side of a great public road was still fresh. There was therefore much satisfaction when the navvies took it down on a dark night and either sank it in Shields Bar or buried it under the walls of Jarrow Monastery.

On February 3 a horrible scene occurred at the execution of a man named Bousfield, who had murdered his wife and three children in Soho. He had then surrendered himself at the Bow Street police station. In removing him to the Marlborough Street police court, the crowd was so great that a strong body of police were employed to force their way through. It was pleaded in Bousfield's defence that he had been attacked by a frenzy of jealousy. He was sentenced to death. Probably he was insane, for it is recorded that he maintained a "sullen violence" to the last, and when he reached the scaffold he was so much prostrated that he had to be lifted on a chair. His sitting position broke the fall, and by an immense muscular effort he raised himself to the level of the scaffold and tried to lift his pinioned arms to the rope. There was a terrible scene when the prison officers attempted to control him; three times he succeeded in getting his feet on the scaffold; finally he was held until all was over.

All this time shrieks, yells, and hisses from the spectators added to the horror of the moment, and all this time the bells of the neighbouring churches were pouring forth merry peals on the announcement of the armistice after the Crimean War. There can be little doubt that this horrible scene prepared the way for the decision to conduct executions within the walls of the prisons.

In 1857 there was a growing public alarm about the prevalence of crimes of violence which were attributed to the ticket-of-leave system. The Home Secretary, Sir George Grey, disclosed the figures of outrages committed in various parts of the country and agreed that there was some foundation for the alarm, though the facts had been greatly exaggerated. He was able to show that, during the previous two years, committals for trial for felonies had actually decreased by 25 per cent, notwithstanding the disbandment of the militia. As a remedy he proposed to remove all obstacles to the transfer of convicts sentenced to penal servitude to Western Australia or other penal settlements. As to those in convict prisons at home, he proposed to maintain the power of granting tickets of leave.

In March 1857 the detectives were employed in unearthing the headquarters of a great gang of forgers, headed by "Jim, the Penman," who was caught and sentenced to transportation for life. After his conviction there was a short respite for the banks, but in May 1859 a new gang, under the leadership of men named Wagner and Bateman, both ticket-of-leave men, liberated in 1856, was at work. Ostensibly they were carrying on a law stationer's business in York Buildings, Adelphi, but this was a blind for their real activities. Detectives from Scotland Yard kept them under observation for more than a year and found that the place was frequented by eight or ten persons who were employed in the manufacture of base coin with remarkable skill.

At that stage they did not think it safe to raid the premises, but at last a forged cheque for £265 was presented at the Union Bank. One of the gang, an old German of eighty named Kerp, had spent his life in forging signatures and had acquired extraordinary skill. He could not be found, but two members of the gang, Chandler and Glendinning, were arrested, and while awaiting trial in prison they explained the whole system to a class of admiring detectives. Wagner and Bateman were sentenced to penal servitude for life; Humphreys to twenty years' and Bramwell and Foster to ten years' penal servitude. They had obtained from £8,000 to £10,000 from bankers, and would have obtained double that sum from cheques but for the fact that the cheques had been dishonoured. One of them offered to disclose to the detectives for £3,000 the system whereby the Exchequer was annually defrauded of huge sums by means of forged stamps—an offer that was not entertained.

In August 1859 the police had a new rôle thrust upon them—to keep order in church. The rector of St. George's-in-the-East seems to have been one of the first "Ritualists." With vestments, incense, and images he raised a storm among his Protestant congregation, who retaliated by interrupting the services by loud mimicry and mock responses. Thereupon the rector sought the help of the police to maintain order; but since brawling in church is an ecclesiastical and not a civil offence the police were powerless to intervene until some overt act of violence should take place. This the disturbers of the services were careful to avoid. A letter from the Bishop of London and an undertaking from the rector to abstain from illegalities brought some relief, but in July 1860 the storm broke out again in an aggravated form. Two thirds of the congregation consisted of rough boys and girls, and there were scenes of great disorder. The Bishop of London induced the rector to take a year's holiday and put in his place a man of more moderate opinions who removed the offending church furniture and conducted his first service to a congregation of three hundred policemen.

THE RICHMOND MURDER

Perhaps next in importance to the Rugeley poisoning case was that of the poisoning of Isabella Bankes at Richmond. The facts were simple enough. A doctor named Smethurst committed bigamy deliberately by marrying a woman of some private fortune, named Isabella Bankes, who had been staying at the same lodgings as himself and his wife. At the end of December 1858 he left his wife and went to live with Miss Bankes at Richmond. In March 1859 Miss Bankes was taken ill, and in April Dr. Smethurst called in a good firm of doctors in Richmond, but he would never allow these gentlemen to be alone with their patient, and Mrs. Bankes's sister was not allowed to prepare an invalid diet or to sit with the patient. Finally she was told that her visits were too much for her sister.

On April 30 Dr. Smethurst called in a solicitor to draw up Miss Bankes's will. In this document she described herself as a spinster and signed the will, leaving her property to Smethurst. Her medical men were far from satisfied; they made private analyses of her excreta and communicated with the police. On May 3, three days after executing the will, the woman died, and after the inquest Smethurst was arrested for murder.

The trial began in July, but it had to be postponed because a juryman had been taken ill. In August the prisoner was again placed at the bar before another jury. The medical witnesses all agreed that there had been continuous administrations of some irritant poison in small doses, and that these counteracted the medicines prescribed by the doctors.

The prisoner was found guilty, and Chief Baron Pollock sentenced him to death.

Thus far the trial had been quite normal, and there

seemed no reason why the sentence should not be carried out; but in cases where a possible doubt of a prisoner's guilt may be entertained and the public is profoundly interested in the case, one can never tell what eccentricity the public may exhibit. At the time of the trial everybody believed the prisoner to be guilty, but no sooner had he been found so by the proper tribunal than people began to discover his innocence. Controversy raged in the press, and a weak Home Secretary (Sir George Cornewall Lewis) announced to the lord chief justice his decision that there was sufficient doubt of the prisoner's guilt to make it his duty to advise the grant of a free pardon. He softened this outrageous decision by intimating that it was intended to prosecute the man for bigamy. The maximum sentence for this minor offence was imposed—twelve months with hard labour.

On his release Smethurst immediately claimed the money left him by Miss Bankes, and as she had made her will in her maiden name and no flaw in the will could be discovered, the property had to be made over. It was what the man in the street would call "getting away with it."

In April 1860 there occurred a remarkable instance of the inequality of sentences. A boy suffering from mental deficiency, with water on the brain, had been sent by his father, Mr. Cancellor, a master of the Court of Common Pleas, to a private school for boys at Eastbourne, without informing the schoolmaster, Mr. Hopley, that this boy, Reginald, who was aged fifteen, was mentally defective. Hopley, who is described as a person of "high attainments," treated his pupil with consistent cruelty because of his silence and stupidity. Finally he entirely lost his temper with him and, going into his bedroom one night, beat him so unmercifully that he died. The servant was awakened by cries, but fell asleep again. In the morning, before the doctor was fetched, long stockings and gloves were put on the boy's limbs to conceal their macerated condition.

Hopley was tried at Lewes Assizes for wilful murder, but, doubtless to the surprise of most people who read of the case, the judge awarded him only four years' penal servitude.

In November 1862 there was a fresh outbreak of garrotting in the London streets. The garrotters became bolder with impunity. They did not confine their assaults to darkness, but committed them in broad daylight with police constables quite close at hand, and in some cases, after half strangling their victims, they stunned them with blows. The dangerous spots were Lincoln's Inn Fields, Long Acre, Pall Mall, and Cockspur Street. Finally a member of Parliament for Blackburn, Mr. Pilkington, was attacked near the Crimean Memorial, and this caused Parliament to intervene. The commissioner of police was ordered to pay special attention to this class of crime. In several outstanding cases of savagery the perpetrators were caught and very severely punished. The public became so much alarmed that people were afraid to leave their houses in the evening. As the evenings grew longer, the evil increased. Police were concentrated on the more dangerous streets and were able to arrest and bring to trial a number of the worst ruffians. Certainly the sentences were exemplary. For a brutal attack on a medical student one man was given penal servitude for life; in another case, twenty years. To make the effect of these sentences more marked, the prisoners were taken to Newgate after conviction and brought up for sentence later in the day. Baron Bramwell, the judge, was much commended for his conduct of the trials. In each case he gave a short sketch of the criminal's career before sentencing him. The effect was twofold: on the one side, the garrotters thought the risk not worth taking, and on the other the life histories of the criminals stiffened the attitude of the public towards the administration of the criminal law. All these men had been convicted over and over again, and it was alleged that they had been allowed to live in too great comfort in prison.

In 1863 Sir George Grey introduced a bill for amalgamating the Metropolitan and the City police, on the ground that the City police had proved to be insufficient on the occasion of the entry of Princess Alexandra into London for her marriage to the Prince of Wales. The Duke of Cambridge favoured the bill and testified to the efficiency of the Metropolitan Police, but there was fierce opposition from the City of London, which was up in arms as usual about its chartered rights. The bill was abandoned.

On the night of the wedding, when the City was crowded to excess, six women were crushed to death. Besides these it was supposed that at least a hundred others had sustained injuries from the terrific pressure of the crowd. The Prince of Wales addressed a feeling letter to the lord mayor on the subject of the accidents.

The year 1864 was remarkable for its amendments to the criminal law. Sir George Grey reported as Home Secretary that, in spite of an increase in certain forms of crime towards the end of 1862 and an almost total discontinuance of transportation, there had been a decrease of crime during the past two years. He ascribed this to the vigilance of the police. The public impression that the penal system was not sufficiently deterrent was, he said, quite erroneous, and any augmentation of the punishment under penal servitude was undesirable. Some of his conclusions would startle the penal reformers of these days; for example, that no sentence of penal servitude should be less than seven years— short sentences were useless; that all convicts should suffer nine months' imprisonment in separate confinement at the beginning of their sentences; and, finally, that all sentences of transportation should end in Western Australia, whither it was proposed to send six hundred convicts a year.

Immediately there was an outcry from the colony in question, and before the end of the year the government announced the total cessation of transportation.

On February 22, 1864, five of the seven pirates convicted of the murder of the captain of the ship *Flowery Land* on the high seas on September 10, 1863, were hanged in front of Newgate prison in the presence of a huge concourse of people.

THE FIRST TRAIN MURDER

The first train murder took place in 1864. On the night of Saturday, July 9, a suburban train on the North London railway was boarded by two bank clerks, who entered an empty first-class carriage. They had scarcely sat down when one called the other's attention to bloodstains on his hand. They left the compartment and called the guard, who discovered bloodstains on the cushions, on the window, and on the handle of the door. He found a hat, stick, and bag which he removed. The carriage was locked up and taken to Bow Station.

Half an hour later the driver of a train of empty carriages noticed a dark object on the line. He stopped his train, got down, and found that the object was the body of a man lying between the rails. The man was still alive, but quite unconscious from wounds inflicted on his head. He was soon identified as Thomas Briggs, chief clerk in the bank of Robarts & Company, Lombard Street. He remained unconscious until his death twenty-four hours later; he was close on seventy.

The police took up the inquiry and found that Briggs had dined with some relations at Peckham and had left their house at 8:30. At Fenchurch Street he had been seen by the ticket collector. The bag and stick were recognized as his, but not the hat; his own had disappeared, and that left in the carriage was lower in the crown than the ordinary high hat, and inside it was the name of the maker, "J. H. Walker," and his address.

This hat seemed to be the only possible clue to the identity of the assailant. It was assumed that Mr. Briggs had been attacked while dozing; robbery had been the motive, for though £5 in money had been left in his pocket, his gold watch and chain and gold eyeglasses were missing. It seemed probable that after the crime the assailant had pushed his body out of the carriage.

Rewards were offered. The first clue came from a jeweller of the not inappropriate name of Death, who said that on Monday, July 11, a man of about thirty, apparently a German but speaking good English, had called at his shop at Cheapside and had exchanged for a gold chain and a ring, valued at £3.10.0, a gold Albert chain, which Death recognized as one worn by Mr. Briggs on the night of the murder.

For six days longer, rumour was busy, but on July 18 a cabman named Jonathan Matthews made a statement to the police which was of the highest value. He said that he had heard nothing of the murder—he did not appear to be a bright man—until a man on the cab rank spoke of the jeweller named Death. He then remembered that he had seen this name on a jeweller's cardboard box which had been given to his little girl by a young German named Franz Müller, who had at one time been engaged to one of Matthews's daughters. Müller, it appeared, was a native of Saxe-Weimar, twenty-five years old. He had been working as a tailor, but he was dissatisfied and had declared his intention of seeking his fortune in America. He had left England on Friday, July 15, by the sailing ship *Victoria*, bound for New York.

The hat found in the railway carriage was shown to Matthews, who immediately identified it as one he had himself bought for Müller at the shop of Mr. Walker, whose name was in the hat. He was also able to give the police a photograph of Müller. This was shown to Mr. Death, who at once identified it as that of the man who on Monday, July 11, had visited his shop to exchange Mr. Briggs's gold chain.

The case was entrusted to Inspector Tanner, who was described by one of his colleagues as the most brilliant detective officer in the Yard. At any rate no time was lost. Matthews made his statement late on July 18, and on the following evening Tanner, accompanied by Detective-Sergeant Clarke, the jeweller Death, and the cabman Matthews, were on their way to Liverpool with a warrant for Müller's arrest. On July 20 they embarked on the steamship *City of Manchester*, which was timed to arrive at

New York two or three weeks before the sailing ship *Victoria*.

In those days there was no wireless telegraphy to inform the police that their quarry was on board the *Victoria*. They arrived in New York on August 5 and had to wait twenty days before the *Victoria* came in. By that time New York had become as excited as London over the expected arrival of Müller.

The *Victoria* arrived, and the officers boarded her in the pilot boat. The steerage passengers were ordered off for medical examination. Müller was called into the cabin and charged with the murder. He turned very pale but said that he had never been on that railway line. His keys were taken from him, and in his box were found the watch and what was believed to be the hat of Mr. Briggs.

On August 26 extradition proceedings were begun before Commissioner Newton and concluded on the following day. Müller was represented by Mr. Chauncey Schaffer. He made no reference to the charge in his speech, but he appealed eloquently to prejudice. It was just a year since the claims arising out of the depredations of the privateer *Alabama* were submitted to arbitration, and he argued that the wickedness of the British had made any extradition treaty a dead letter. It was a fine effort of oratory, but extradition was granted, and on September 3 Müller and his captors sailed for England on the steamship *Etna*. Considering that the Civil War between the North and the South was then raging, it was quick work.

The *Etna* reached Queenstown on September 15. Müller's conduct on the voyage had been exemplary. He was taken to Bow Street to be charged and was then removed to Holloway Prison. One fresh piece of evidence was in the hands of the prosecution: the hatters who made Mr. Briggs's hats identified the hat found in Müller's box as one made by them, but it had been cut down one and a half inches and sewn together by an amateur, and not as a hatter would have done it; moreover, the part of the lining on which the maker's name was shown had been cut away.

Müller was tried at the Central Criminal Court on October 27. The court was crowded, and there was a big array of distinguished counsel. As the Solicitor-General remarked, a stronger case of circumstantial evidence had rarely, if ever, been submitted to a jury. Matthews, the cabman, was very severely cross-examined, but his evidence was not shaken. The son of the dead man identified both the watch and the hat found in Müller's box as the property of his father.

After an absence of fifteen minutes the jury returned with a verdict of guilty, and sentence of death was passed. As Müller left the dock his firmness gave way and he burst into tears. His public execution on November 14 furnished a scene more disgraceful than usual. A crowd composed of the dregs of the population spent the night shouting and singing doggerel verses alluding to the murderer. Just before the drop fell, Dr. Cappel, the German chaplain, besought the doomed man to admit his guilt.

"Müller," he said, "in a few moments you will stand before God. I ask you for the last time, are you guilty or not guilty?"

Müller replied, "I am not guilty. God knows what I have done."

"God knows what you have done. Does He also know that you have committed this crime?"

"Yes, I have done it." (*"Ja, ich habe es gethan."*)

THE ROAD MURDER

In June 1860 occurred the Road murder. The infant son of a Mr. Kent, aged three, was found in the morning to be missing from his cot; his body, with the throat cut, was found in a lavatory in the garden. It seemed evident to the police that the murder had been committed by someone in the house. The chief constable of Wiltshire asked for help from Scotland Yard, and Williamson, who afterwards became chief constable of the C.I.D., and John Whicher, whom a contemporary described as a "prince of detectives," were sent down to Road to investigate the case. The first to be suspected was the child's nurse, but she was soon cleared; she was very much attached to the little boy, and her replies to questions were quite straightforward.

Mr. Kent had been twice married. By his first wife he had three daughters and a son, and by his second three children, who were still quite young. The two detectives from the Yard submitted the entire family to a rigid examination, eliminating one after another from suspicion. Meanwhile the local people had quite made up their minds that the guilty persons were Constance Kent, a girl of sixteen, and her brother William, aged fourteen, and that their motive was petty jealousy. Whicher took the same view of Constance, and having obtained a warrant from the local Bench, brought her before the magistrates on the charge of murder. The chief ground for suspicion against her was that one of her nightdresses was missing. Whicher produced two of her schoolfellows, who deposed to her having shown jealousy of her little brother on account of the attention shown to him in the family. The nursemaid, when asked whether she had shown any animus against her little brother, said, "No, sir," and Constance herself said, "He was a merry, good-tempered little boy. I had played with him often. He appeared to be fond of me, and I was fond of him."

It was a weak case on the evidence; the girl was admitted to bail and was ultimately discharged for lack of evidence.

There was great indignation, not only in Wiltshire, but all over the country. The magistrates and the police were held up to obloquy for their incompetence. Whicher returned to London to find that the police authorities considered his theory incredible and that he had lost the confidence of the commissioner. Still convinced that he was right, Whicher lost heart and retired from the police. The magistrates of Bath sent a memorial to the Home Secretary praying for a special commission to investigate the crime, but he replied that such a course would be "unconstitutional."

But the public was not allowed to forget the case. Nearly

a year later it became known that Constance Kent had made an alleged confession to one of her relations, and another attempt to investigate the crime was made by the detectives who had incurred the censure of a large portion of the press. They found, however, that the new information was vague, and that Miss Kent herself had been sent to a convent in France. In all, four inquiries were conducted, but the case remained unsolved.

Four years passed, when suddenly it became known that on June 29, 1865, the Bow Street magistrate was informed that Constance Kent was on her way to London to surrender herself to justice. It appeared that on returning from France she had entered a sisterhood at Brighton. There she had come under the influence of a Mr. Wagner, perpetual curate of St. Paul's, Brighton. A fortnight before her appearance at Bow Street she had told him of her intention to confess publicly to the murder of her little brother, and Mr. Wagner himself brought her up to Bow Street. The chief magistrate was exceedingly anxious that she should not incriminate herself without realizing fully what she was doing, and he warned her several times, but she adhered firmly to the truth of her statement, which, as Mr. Wagner testified, was entirely voluntary and had been made without any suggestion from him.

Her confession created an immense sensation, vindicating, as it did, the soundness of Whicher's judgment. She was tried on her own confession, found guilty, and condemned to death. The government requested Dr. Bucknill, a mental expert, to inquire into the state of her mind. He reported that at the time of the murder she was probably abnormal, as she was arriving at puberty. She told him during their conversation that she had made up her mind to confess if the nursemaid were convicted, and to commit suicide if she herself were convicted. She described to him in detail how she prepared the crime, by secreting one of her father's razors; how she waited until the household was asleep before taking the sleeping child from his cot, and how she carried him out into the garden. She wished it to be known that she had received nothing but kindness in her home. In the doctor's opinion she was perfectly sane, but with her peculiar disposition prolonged solitary confinement might bring on insanity. He urged this point for consideration. On this report her sentence was commuted to penal servitude for life. She served the usual period in a female convict prison and was released in good health after serving the statutory minimum period.

But for the Scotland Yard detectives her confession had come too late. Whicher had long retired from the force, and there was no public vindication.

Every public service governed by regulations is destined to become hidebound and sterile unless it keeps pace with changes. This is specially true of the police, who are in constant touch with all classes of the population. Manners change, and unless the directors of a service are quick to change with them, the service becomes out of date. It was so with the Criminal Investigation Department at Scotland Yard. To the present generation it would seem incredible that for twenty-two years there were but eight men in plain clothes to investigate every case of crime committed in London and that when, in 1864, the number was increased, it was only raised to fifteen.

It is scarcely surprising that criticism of the police was growing. In the early years the commissioner had been overwhelmed with applications to join the force; in the sixties there was difficulty in obtaining good recruits. The pay had fallen below the pay of some other forces. There was, besides, discontent regarding pensions and the long hours of duty, and the status of a policeman was still considered lower than that of any other functionary. The public was becoming alarmed. Garrotters were making the streets unsafe at night, and crimes of violence were increasing. This, no doubt, was due to the new factor of the ex-prisoner, who was being liberated on ticket of leave in England without any proper system of supervision.

The old suspicion of the force as a blue army had died down, and in 1864 the top hat gave place to the helmet. At the same time people were beginning to contrast the police organization unfavourably with that of the army. Numerically the force amounted to a division of troops, but it had fewer officers than a battalion.

It was at this stage that the riot in Hyde Park in July 1866, in consequence of the prohibition of meetings in the Park, took on alarming proportions. Sir Richard Mayne, then a man of nearly seventy, who himself took charge of the police, was wounded in the face by stones. The Park railings were torn down, and the police were so hard pressed that troops had to be called in to help them. It was the first instance of military intervention in a riot in London since the establishment of the force. There was worse to come.

There was a rude awakening from the lethargy that had overtaken the detective branch. In the early sixties the Irish Republican Brotherhood was being secretly transplanted from the United States to England, where it spread rapidly among the Irish labourers.

In 1867 there were serious disturbances in Manchester, and two of the leading Fenians, T. J. Kelly and "Captain" Deary, were arrested. The local Fenians knew the hour when the prison van would pass through the city carrying these two leaders from the prison to the courthouse, and they lay in wait for it. The van was stopped in the street, and a demand was made upon Sergeant Brett, who was in charge of it, to deliver up his keys to the assailants. This he refused to do, and he was immediately shot dead. Four men were arrested for the crime and were subsequently convicted and hanged. With the usual lack of logic that is found in the Irish patriot, these men were dubbed "The Manchester Martyrs," on the ground, we may suppose, that the Fenians were at war with England and that an Englishman who dared to do his duty unarmed could not complain if he was killed.

Acting on information from Dublin, Thomson, one of the best detectives in Scotland Yard, succeeded in arresting two

Fenians named Burke and Casey, who for some time had been acting as agents for the importation of arms, and they were both committed to Clerkenwell prison. Sir Richard Mayne was so much impressed with Thomson's usefulness that he promoted him to the rank of superintendent.

Burke set to work immediately to plan his escape. His friends were to blow down the prison wall where it abutted on the exercise ground, and a white ball was to be thrown over the wall as a signal to Burke to run for safety. Particulars of the plot had reached Sir Richard Mayne in an anonymous letter from Dublin, on Thursday, December 12, and he had informed the governor of the prison that an attempt to undermine the prison wall was to be made. On this the governor had arranged to exercise his prisoners in another yard, and had asked the police to place a cordon round the prison to keep people away from the wall, adding that he would "take care of the kernel if the police would take care of the shell."

On Thursday, December 12, a policeman on duty in Corporation Row, a street of densely inhabited small houses, had seen several men depositing a parcel at the foot of the prison wall, and then, after an interval, taking it away. Though it was not known at the time, this had been an attempt to carry out the plot, but the fuse was damp and the powder did not explode.

Emboldened by their immunity, the conspirators resolved to make another attempt on the following day. On the Friday afternoon two men, Allen and Despond, and a woman named Ann Justice wheeled a barrel to the boundary wall of the prison. They borrowed a light from a boy who was smoking, set fire to a squib, and made off after throwing it into the barrel. At a quarter to four, the usual hour for exercise in the prison yard, the explosion took place; it was heard for miles. The houses in Corporation Row were shorn of their front walls "like so many dolls' houses, with the kettles still singing on the hobs." After the smoke had cleared away, a crowd of people rushed into the yard through the breach in the wall. Captain Codd, the prison governor, ordered them to disperse, and as they hesitated to obey, he ordered a volley to be fired with blank cartridge. The intruders scattered in every direction.

As in most of these Irish conspiracies the inevitable informer came forward. He said that the few conspirators who lived in the decayed streets near the prison were rather invertebrate until they were reinforced by Barrett and Murphy from Glasgow, where the plot was hatched. The conspirators received a letter containing a plan of the prison, with an arrow showing the place where the boundary wall was weakest because a sewer ran under it, and saying that a barrel of gunpowder must be obtained, and it would "blow the wall to hell"; that they must get money to buy the powder, a little at a time, and blow down the wall about four o'clock; if they did not do it, "they ought to be shot."

They held a council on the night of December 11 at which Barrett flourished a revolver which went off and wounded one of the conspirators named Ryan. It was decided to make the attempt next day, but in the meantime the governor had received warning, and the prisoners were exercised in the morning instead of the afternoon. It was remembered afterwards that the prisoners were much on the alert and that Burke in particular was much excited.

A policeman was patrolling the wall, but he had had no instructions about the intended outrage. He saw the barrow left near the wall and pursued the men who left it. As he was passing the barrow the explosion took place and he was hurled to the ground, but he got up and continued the pursuit. Another policeman stopped two of the fugitives and also the woman, Ann Justice. Barrett, the man who fired the powder, was run to earth in Glasgow on January 14. A constable heard a shot fired in the street and arrested two men, though they pretended that they had been letting off fireworks and offered him a drink. On the way to the police station one of them made a leap as if to stretch his limbs, and in the leap threw away a revolver. Inspector Williamson and four subordinates came from London and identified the man as Barrett.

This was Sir Richard Mayne's first bad slip in a service of nearly forty years. He went over to the Home Office and tendered his resignation, but the Home Secretary declined to accept it. Mr. Liddell, the Under-Secretary, was reported to have said to a friend, "We told him that he had made a damned fool of himself, but that we intended to pull him through. We weren't going to throw him over after his long public service." But for a man of Sir Richard Mayne's temperament the deaths of innocent people who might fairly have laid their misfortune at his door weighed heavily, and he was dead within the year at the age of seventy-two.

The fact was that he was getting past his work. He had served for seven years beyond the maximum retiring age for the Civil Service, and he had never really recovered from the rough handling he had from the mob in the Hyde Park riot of 1866.

He had been one of the judges of the Court of King's Bench in Ireland when Sir Robert Peel selected him as one of the commissioners of the new force in 1829. Cavanagh, who served under him, thus describes him:

He was sixty-three, but didn't look it. He had a very piercing glance. He was about five feet eight inches high, spare but well-built, with a thin face, a very hard compressed mouth, grey hair and whiskers, an eye like that of a hawk and a slightly limping gait due to rheumatism in the hip joint. He was respected but feared by all in the service. He was a very strict disciplinarian. Having given out one Christmas that any man reported for drunkenness would be dismissed, he kept his word with about sixty men . . . even some with twenty years' service. Another time he dismissed three inspectors, one of whom had a record of twenty-eight years. They brought an action against him and although he won it on a technical point he never got over the ordeal of going into the witness box. Latterly he became beyond his job, but would go on.

The fact was that Mayne had saddled himself with duties that were far beyond the power of one single man. He had the common fault of energetic administrators that he would seldom delegate his powers. The force had grown from 1,000 men in 1829 to nearly 8,000. He had kept the detective branch, such as it was, in his own hands, and this had been his undoing. It was hard that a man with so brilliant a record should have had to retire under a cloud.

The Clerkenwell explosion had far-reaching effects. The panic had spread to the House of Commons. Three days after the outrage the Home Secretary issued a circular calling for volunteers to act as special constables, and a body of over 50,000 men was enrolled within a month. Parliament also authorized an increase in the number of Metropolitan Police, but the increase was not made until after the retirement and death of Sir Richard Mayne.

Though the public did not know it, there had been no connection between the attack on the Manchester prison van and the Clerkenwell explosion. Five men and the woman Ann Justice were brought to trial at the Central Criminal Court on April 20, 1868, and the public was treated to the novel spectacle of a prison van guarded by policemen armed to the teeth going through the streets to the Old Bailey. The woman Justice tried to hang herself in her cell, but she was cut down in time. All the accused were acquitted save Michael Barrett, who also made use of lying alibis, but without effect. His execution, the last public execution in London, took place on May 26, 1868. A huge crowd greeted his appearance on the scaffold with yells of execration.

There was little short of a panic in the country. There would have been more if it had been known that the explosion might have been prevented if Sir Richard Mayne had taken notice of the warning that had reached him and had put the matter into the hands of his detective department.

Mayne's successor was Sir Edmund Henderson, who set to work immediately on the reorganization of the force. He used the authorization for an increase in its strength almost at once and appointed four district superintendents to assist him in controlling the force. These district superintendents clashed with the authority of the superintendents of divisions, and not unnaturally they took the line of least resistance and did as little as possible in return for their pay. Whenever vacancies occurred in the rank they were not filled up by officers from the divisions. The new appointments were all given to military officers, and they were placed under the orders of the assistant commissioner who controlled the uniformed force. Their duties were confined to inspection of the men, their equipment, and their quarters, but they had few executive functions and naturally had not enough to do.

While the public was demanding more and more from the police the latter became restive about their conditions of service. There was an epidemic of strikes in 1872, and in the autumn the infection spread to the police. A monster meeting of the constables, with a member of Parliament in the chair, was convened to discuss their grievances at the Cannon Street Hotel. Other meetings were convened, and a representative committee of delegates from all the divisions was set up to formulate demands for increased pay, higher pensions, and a reduction of hours from nine to eight per day. The demands for higher pay and reduced hours were conceded, but the pension question was hung up until 1890.

The men had not decided what they would do if their demands were not conceded, but the settlement arrived at did not satisfy all of them, and in November 1872 about 180 men belonging to three stations refused duty. It appeared that this "lightning strike," if it was worthy to be called a strike, took place in consequence of the news that the constable who had acted as secretary to the delegates had been dismissed for insubordination because he wished to make the delegation a permanency and refused to obey an order prohibiting further meetings. The 180 strikers were dismissed from the force, but most of them were afterwards reinstated.

The news of insubordination in the force greatly disturbed the public. Leaflets were distributed, announcing that the "Revolution of the Police" was to be followed by like movements in the navy and the army. In the following year there were evidences that the police had lost public confidence. The Home Secretary described the feeling as "a dead set against the police," who were accused of "high-handedness and illegalities," due to absence of educated control. Unfortunately there occurred at this time the arrest of a Mr. Belt, who was wrongfully charged with drunkenness, and a scuffle between constables and officers of the Life Guards, who were unsuccessfully charged with drunkenness and assault outside the Argyll Rooms, and this added fuel to the flames. There were demands that more officers of social standing and education should be introduced as superintendents and inspectors, but the agitation gradually died away, the only change made being the appointment of a legal adviser to the commissioner, an appointment which was allowed to lapse, but has lately been revived.

The most important of the new commissioner's reforms was the expansion of the C.I.D. The fifteen men who had been working under Sir Richard Mayne at headquarters had been little more than policemen in plain clothes; they had had no specialized training, nor any regular duties. There are no means of knowing on what principle they were selected. In one or two cases we do know that their powers of observation were superior to those of the ordinary policeman. In the divisions there were no detectives at all; consequently, the principal equipment of a detective—personal knowledge of thieves—was almost entirely wanting.

Sir Edmund Henderson took the step that should have been taken many years before by attaching detectives to each division. The original department at Scotland Yard was considerably enlarged, and it became the Central Office for the whole department. At that date there were 207 detectives of all ranks, of whom 180 were stationed in the twenty-one divisions and 27 at Scotland Yard. This new organization included one superintendent, three chief inspectors, three inspectors, forty sergeants, and 160 constables.

On paper the distribution was all that could be required. It was impossible to foresee at that date that friction was bound to arise between the detectives who had their own superintendent and the uniform superintendent of the division, who felt that the detectives attached to him were an *imperium in imperio.* The friction was lessened in 1878 by an arrangement which will be described later.

Unfortunately, at this critical stage in the history of the C.I.D. a grave scandal occurred which shook public confidence in the Department. The turf frauds which occupied the criminal courts for twenty days in 1877 led to the reorganization of the whole Department. The days were long past when journalists could raise the cry of domestic espionage against detectives, who were now regarded by the public as a necessary protection. The danger was recognized to be corruption of the detectives by the men they were set to watch.

A certain William Kurr, who had started life as clerk in a railway office and had passed into the service of a West-End moneylender, had gravitated towards speculations on the turf. None of his bogus betting offices prospered, and he began to look farther afield for victims, but he spoke no foreign language, and his education was not equal to the composition of grammatical English. He advertised for a journalist without allowing it to be supposed that the business was not orthodox. His advertisement specified that the journalist should write French. It was answered by Harry Benson, a young Jew born in Paris of a French mother. His father had been a prosperous merchant with offices in the Faubourg St. Honoré; the son was well educated, a linguist, a musician, the possessor of charming manners, but a man who could never run straight. If Kurr supposed that he was entering into partnership with an honest man he was quickly undeceived. Young Benson had already seen the inside of a prison. During the Franco-Prussian War he had taken refuge with other French in Brussels under the name and title of the Comte de Montagu, the son of a Bonapartist general. He entertained lavishly in Brussels and was accepted at his own valuation.

One day he called at the Mansion House in London to beg for charitable aid for the citizens of Chateaudun, which had been sacked by the Germans. He obtained from the lord mayor's fund a grant of £1,000 which he converted to his own needs. The imposture was discovered, and he paid a second visit to the Mansion House, this time in handcuffs. He was sentenced to a year's imprisonment, during which he set his cell on fire and burned himself. Afterwards he was obliged to use crutches, but once, when his party in the convict prison was overtaken by a sudden thunderstorm and the men ran for shelter and laughed as they watched the cripple limping painfully through the downpour, a sudden crash of thunder with a blinding electric flash caused the cripple to drop his crutches and "run like a hare."

Kurr, under the name of Gardner & Company of Edinburgh, had come under suspicion, and his case was in the hands of Detective Meiklejohn, who had been detached from Scotland Yard for temporary service with the Midland Railway Company. On Benson's advice, Kurr approached him and bought him over.

Benson, being intimately acquainted with French ways, saw a great opening for turf frauds in France. The firm moved over to French soil and issued a circular setting forth the advantages of their system of betting. This was distributed broadcast through the country, accompanied by a copy of a sporting paper numbered 1713, though it was the only copy of that paper that ever appeared. It contained everything—leading articles, foreign news, paragraphs, police news and advertisements, and several of the articles referred in the most complimentary manner to an imaginary Mr. Montgomery (Benson's alias) and the excellence of his system of betting investment.

It was stated that this Mr. Hugh Montgomery had already netted half a million by his system and it was open to readers to reap the same handsome profit. All they had to do was to remit money to the firm at any of its numerous offices. Many simple-minded French people swallowed the bait, and none more readily than the Comtesse de Goncourt, a well-to-do lady of means with an unfortunate thirst for speculation. The time-honoured trick was followed: she was first allowed to win; then her transactions grew larger until at last they reached the sum of £10,000. Bogus cheques were sent to her for her alleged winnings, but she was advised not to cash them before a certain date, in accordance with the English law. Yet these rapacious scoundrels were not content. They wrote to the poor woman demanding another £1,200 to complete certain formalities. She tried to raise the money in Paris through her notary, and this led to the discovery of the whole fraud.

Benson thought he was safe by extending his system of bribing detectives. He approached Detective Druscovitch, who was specially charged with the Continental business at Scotland Yard, a well-meaning but weak man. He was in very straitened circumstances and he fell before the tempting offers of the plausible Benson, who was living in a charming house at Shanklin in the Isle of Wight, with a good cook, a staff of servants, and a carriage. Learning that Inspector Clarke had been instructed to hunt down sham betting offices, Benson invited him down to the Isle of Wight and sounded him about accepting a bribe. Clarke rejected the proposals, whereupon Benson played upon his fears by seeming to incriminate him. Then he offered a substantial bribe which Clarke was wise enough or honest enough to refuse.

Meanwhile the French police were taking active steps. They requested Scotland Yard by telegraph to intercept letters from Paris which would contain large remittances. Benson had early notice of this from Druscovitch, and contrived to intercept the telegram, but Druscovitch was becoming uneasy. He had many secret interviews with his paymasters and told them plainly that he would have to arrest somebody. He warned Benson to look out for himself. It was time for the conspirators to examine their line of retreat. They held most of their booty in Bank of England notes which could always be traced through their numbers. Benson decided to convert these into Scottish notes because the numbers of the latter were not always taken on issue. Through Meiklejohn he thus disposed of £13,000 worth of Clydesdale notes. To cover this operation he had deposited £3,000 of good money in the Alloa Bank.

He was actually dining with its manager when a telegram was put into his hands, warning him to decamp because Druscovitch was on his way down with a warrant to arrest him. Benson did not stop to finish his dinner, but he forfeited his deposit of £3,000.

Druscovitch still lingered over his job, but England had become too hot to hold Benson. The authorities had the numbers of some of the Clydesdale notes, and the men holding them were being watched. Benson took passage to Holland, but there he and his friends were arrested. They had an associate, Froggatt, a low-class attorney, who forged a telegram from Scotland Yard to the Dutch police to the effect that they had arrested the wrong people. The fraud was discovered in time, and the prisoners were handed over for extradition to a party of London police headed by Druscovitch in person. His complicity was not yet suspected, and he was compelled to carry out his orders.

Benson and Kurr had no idea of suffering alone. One of their first acts in Millbank prison after their sentences to penal servitude was to implicate the detectives. When these were put upon their trial it was found that the swindlers had long secured the support of three policemen and Froggatt. Clarke was acquitted. A letter from Meiklejohn to Kurr was read:

DEAR BILL,
Rather important news from the North. Tell H. S. and the young one to keep themselves quiet. In the event of a smell stronger than now they must be ready to scamper out of the way.

It was alleged by the prosecution that Meiklejohn received £500 for this little service.

Benson enjoyed an exemplary character in prison and was released in 1887 after earning his full remission. He did not trouble to report himself to the police as required by law, nor did Kurr. Finding that his father had left nothing to him by his will, he sought out Kurr and they crossed the Atlantic together as company promoters. They seem to have done well out of this new fraud, for presently we find Benson in Brussels selling mining shares. The Belgian police arrested him, and he served two years in a Belgian prison.

Thence he went to Switzerland and set up as an American banker of large means. Here he met a retired surgeon-general of the Indian army and made furious love to his daughter. When the father consented to the marriage he entrusted all his savings, about £7,000, to the son-in-law, who received forthwith a telegram summoning him to New York. The unhappy daughter tried to follow him, but her father took a shorter cut. He applied for a warrant, and Benson was arrested when actually on the steamer. He was taken back to Geneva, but was liberated on refunding £5,000 out of the £7,000. It was then discovered that his presents to his fiancée were all in sham jewelry and that the scrip he had given to his father-in-law in exchange for the £7,000 was really worth nothing.

That was not the end of Benson. We find him next in Mexico, impersonating Mr. Abbey, Madame Patti's impresario, selling tickets on her behalf to the amount of $25,000. The fraud was discovered; he was arrested and taken to New York, where he was lodged in the Tombs. There, wearied by the law's delay, he threw himself over the railings from the top story, fracturing his spine.

All the detectives concerned in the De Goncourt case, except Inspector Clarke, were found guilty and sentenced to two years' hard labour—a very light sentence, considering what they had done. The immediate result of the scandal was the appointment of a committee of inquiry, consisting of Sir Henry Selwyn Ibbetson, Colonel Fielding, Mr. J. Maile, Q.C., and Mr. Overend, Q.C. They went very thoroughly, not only into the conduct of the detectives, but also into the general organization of the Department. A young and briefless barrister, Mr. Howard Vincent (afterwards Sir Howard Vincent), was clever enough to see his opportunity. Speaking French fluently, he went over to Paris and studied the French detective system. Probably the prefect of police and his officers helped him under the impression that their neighbours across the water would flatter the French by imitation, although anyone who knew what the French system was, as compared with Scotland Yard as it was even before the inquiry, can scarcely have been impressed by it. A brave show of efficiency was—and is—made at the Prefecture, but the real reason for its successes is the power given to police officers in Paris to interrogate prisoners, and even to wring confessions from them—a system that would not be tolerated in any British court.

At any rate Mr. Vincent took pains; he is said to have rewritten his report eighteen times before he sent it to the committee. They were impressed with it because it contained information which they could not otherwise obtain. Lest anyone should think that Mr. Vincent's object in taking all this trouble was altruistic, his biographer made it clear that he had foreseen that an important new post in the police would be created and he was determined to get it if he could. As soon as he learned what the recommendation of the committee would be he applied for the post, stating his legal qualifications and enclosing a recommendation from the Attorney-General.

His application was successful. He was appointed director of criminal investigation at a salary of £1100 a year. His status was to be equal to that of an assistant commissioner, his only superior being the commissioner himself, but his position was invidious. An assistant commissioner had statutory authority over his department, and he had not, and there could be no question of amending the Police Act only to regularize his position. Moreover, he had been told by the Home Secretary that he was to come to him when he wanted advice and not to go to the commissioner.

It may be well to say here that the director of criminal investigation is not and has never pretended to be an expert in detective work. His function begins and ends with controlling the Department, bestowing commendations, rewards, and censure whenever they are deserved, satisfying himself that the best possible use is being made of the existing staff, and promoting the most deserving officers, irrespective of their length of service. His most useful function lies in encouraging the men under him, and in fostering a good understanding between the detectives of the various divisions and of the various police forces, because the only really efficient methods of detection lie in teamwork.

Vincent increased the strength of the Department to nearly eight hundred men. He greatly improved the filing of criminal records and took care that the various sub-branches of his department worked smoothly together. For the first time a divisional detective-inspector was made responsible for the detective work in the division, with a staff of sergeants and constables or "patrols" as they are called. He laid it down that pecuniary transactions of any nature with the public, unless they were authorized by the director, would entail immediate dismissal.

The centralization of the work at Scotland Yard had its disadvantages. There was too much writing, too many reports to be filed, too many bulky files of papers to be gone through. All these consumed valuable time. There had been no co-operation between the divisions, or even with the Central Division of Scotland Yard. This was a great defect in cases where speed was an essential, and yet if any central control was to be maintained all this circumlocution was necessary.

This new departure did not run smoothly. The detectives enjoyed a slightly higher rate of pay than the constables in uniform, and these, not unnaturally, resented it. In one division handbills were circulated among the sergeants and constables, convening a monster meeting to voice their grievances. Howard Vincent succeeded in preventing this meeting, and the commissioner promised that a hearing would be given to all reasonable complaints. Sir Matthew White Ridley, the Home Secretary, appointed a committee of inquiry, and a solution of the main grievance was found that might well have been thought of before. This was that every report drawn up by the divisional detective-inspector should be submitted through the uniformed superintendents before they went to Scotland Yard. This gave the superintendent a feeling that the men were under him and that by affixing his initials he was in some measure taking the credit for the efficiency of the C.I.D. It worked like a charm, for thenceforward any help that the C.I.D. might need from the uniform branch was at once accorded.

It must be remembered that when Howard Vincent took office there was no training school for detectives; no finger-print identification; no crime index; no proper filing of photographs; no indexing of the methods practised by criminals. All these improvements came after his time. It is indeed surprising that when there was so little mechanical aid to detection the early detectives did so well.

Bॅ OTH THE BRITISH PUBLIC AND THE POLICE were destined to undergo a period of terror during the eighties. Fortunately there was an exceptionally strong team in the Criminal Investigation Department, during the period of alarm, in James Munro (who afterwards became commissioner), Adolphus Williamson, the most famous of the superintendents, and men like Chief Inspector Littlechild and Detective-Inspector Sweeney. The Fenian movement of the eighties differed widely from that of the late sixties, which had been regarded by Irishmen as a rising for independence. The movement of the eighties was intended to bring the British people to their knees and to force them to crave for mercy at the hands of Ireland.

Between March 1, 1883, and January 31, 1885, there were no less than thirteen dynamite outrages in London alone, all of a serious nature. The dynamiters were entirely indifferent to human life, but in the first outrage, at the *Times* office on March 15, the bomb was badly placed and little damage was done. During the evening of that day there was an explosion in the Local Government Office in Whitehall. Much damage was done to the stonework, but there was no loss of life. On October 30 there were two explosions on the underground railway, one between Charing Cross and Westminster, which injured no one but did much damage, and the other at Praed Street Station. More than sixty people were injured by that explosion, which was believed to have been caused by dynamite thrown from the window of a carriage.

Early in 1884 the dynamiters turned their attention to railway stations. On February 27, 1884, innocent-looking portmanteaux were left in the cloakroom at Victoria, where part of the station was wrecked by a clockwork detonator. It was found that two strangers with suspicious-looking black portmanteaux of American make had left a hotel in Great Portland Street the evening before and had deposited their baggage at Victoria in the cloakroom. In April a desperado named Daley was arrested at Birkenhead; on him were found two phials of high explosive and five clockwork detonators. He was sentenced to penal servitude for life. Detectives now visited the other London stations and examined the baggage deposited in the cloakrooms, with the result that portmanteaux containing explosives with clockwork detonators were found at Charing Cross, Paddington, and Ludgate Hill. This was dangerous work and it was very well done.

Meanwhile a discovery was made by a smart Birmingham police sergeant, who found a small factory conducted by a man named Whitehead. Making himself up as a painter, he called there to ask for work, and the demeanour of Whitehead was such that the police sergeant revisited the building at night with a skeleton key and there found enough evidence to convict Whitehead, who was arrested. Norman, alias Lynch, the agent of the gang, had returned to London with his "material" and was arrested at his hotel in Southampton Street.

On May 30 the dynamiters decided to attack authority nearer home. During the morning a police officer noticed unusual deposits at the foot of the Nelson Column in Trafalgar Square. Seeing what appeared to be a fuse attached to one of them, he summoned help. The fuse was cut, and sixteen cakes of dynamite were carried off by the Inspector of Explosives. That same evening Detective-Inspector Sweeney was writing out a report in the office in Old Scotland Yard; another inspector was with him; both had left the building about fifteen minutes when a terrific explosion blew down part of it, destroying, curiously enough, a mass of documents dealing with the dynamite conspiracy. The desk at which Inspector Sweeney had been working was blown to pieces. The Rising Sun public house was badly damaged, but its landlord more than recouped himself by making a charge for admission to sightseers.

The experts who examined the offices at Old Scotland Yard were satisfied that the explosive had been placed in a lavatory in the northwest corner of the building. The débris was searched minutely, but it was never discovered how the bomb had been ignited.

Six months later, on January 24, 1885, two men named Burton and Cunningham were arrested in connection with an explosion at the Tower of London, and these were strongly suspected of placing the bomb in Scotland Yard. They were sentenced to penal servitude for life.

There were also attempts to blow up the Junior Carlton Club and London Bridge. In the latter case a big hole was blown through one of the buttresses, but no one was hurt. There was a mystery about that case. The police reported that the perpetrators, whoever they might have been, had lost their lives in the attempt and that they were almost certainly men named Lomasney and Fleming. It was not until three or four years later that Sweeney discovered Fleming's effects at the house of his sister, who said with many tears that she would never see her brother again.

In January 1885 there was a bomb explosion in Gower Street, and a few days later Westminster Hall might have been wrecked but for the courage and promptitude of a constable named Cole. A lady visitor pointed out to him that one of the mats in the crypt was on fire; it was smoking. Cole picked up what proved to be a parcel of dynamite and carried it out into the yard before it exploded, but two police officers were seriously injured by the explosion.

Sweeney's own view about this recrudescence of outrages in the eighties was that it was due partly to the Phoenix

Park murder in 1882, and partly to an unfortunate remark of Mr. Gladstone, who, when referring to the Clerkenwell explosion, said that Ireland would never secure anything except by force and by disestablishment of the Church.

Sweeney believed that the body responsible for the renewal of hostilities was the Clan-na-gael, a secret society founded by the American Irish in 1870. It was the most violent secret society in America, and its methods were brought over to England.

Sweeney was rewarded and commended by the commissioner for his work on the dynamite plots. His knowledge of the Irish language was very useful to him.

The use of explosives to avenge public and private injuries proved to be infectious. In 1888 it was applied to Tussaud's Waxworks. Mr. John Tussaud had employed a man named White for forty years as an expert in fixing hair to wax. This man had taught the art to John Tussaud himself. When the old building was pulled down and the new one erected in Baker Street, White, who was considered past his work, was discharged, apparently without a pension. To revenge himself he sent John Tussaud a box filled with gunpowder and so arranged that when the lid was lifted ever so carefully a number of fuses embedded in the powder would catch fire. Tussaud received the box from the postman, but not liking the look of it he summoned the police, who opened it with infinite care. Sweeney noticed that the postmark was Fetter Lane, E. C., and there he found a clerk who remembered that the parcel had been handed in by an old man, with extreme caution. The old man was tracked to Shepherd's Bush, but when Sweeney arrived he was told that the old man had gone out. While there, a little girl went down into the area and removed a suspicious-looking parcel. Its contents came to light when she had been followed to a house where White was run to earth. It proved his guilt. Tussaud was not vindictive; indeed, he pleaded the great age of the prisoner—eighty-two. White was convicted of attempted murder and was sentenced to twelve months' imprisonment, which was considered an unduly light sentence.

I have spoken of Adolphus Williamson, who was regarded by his subordinates as a man of outstanding ability. He spoke French well and set himself to learn German when he was past forty. He "needed knowing." He struck strangers as heavy and unimpressionable, but he had an astonishing power of gripping the points of a case, however intricate, and needed ten words of explanation where others needed fifty. He was always pleasant and courteous, and he inspired confidence in the most timid. He was full of dry humour. There were conferences on Sunday mornings, and these were attended by Williamson, who drew out the men engaged in difficult cases. He used to tell stories against himself, as when he went to attend a funeral of one of his former officers at Brompton Cemetery, and stopped to speak to a fine-looking labourer, digging a grave, whom he thought he recognized as having been formerly in the police force.

"Hallo! Don't I know you?" he asked. "Weren't you in the police?"

"No," said the man. "Thank God! I've never sunk so low as that yet."

Williamson was active in the suppression of the dynamite outrages, but he held the majority of the conspirators in great contempt. It was too much for his gravity when he was told that Fenians were practising cavalry exercises in Jerry Flanagan's backyard in Theobald's Road.

With such a Christian name as Adolphus, it was inevitable that he should be called "Dolly" behind his back by his subordinates.

In 1886 there was a change in the commissionership—a change which was not due to the handling of the dynamite scare. It illustrated the fact that a commissioner of police is sitting continually on a volcano of intermittent eruptions.

On Monday, February 8, there were to be two meetings in Trafalgar Square; one, of the unemployed, and the other, of the Social Democrats. As always happens on these occasions, a mob of roughs from the East End hung about the fringe of the meetings. When the crowds were beginning to disperse, these men marched west instead of east, and finding themselves without police shepherds they stoned the club windows in Pall Mall and St. James's and attacked shops in Oxford Street. A few mounted police would have prevented this, but the mounted men were patrolling the roads and lanes in the outer divisions. A message was sent to call up police reserves but the words "Pall Mall" were mistaken for "The Mall"; consequently the reserves marched to protect the Palace and Marlborough House, which were in no danger, instead of following the mob, who were quite easily dealt with in Oxford Street by a handful of men under an inspector.

This Monday riot was followed by a panic on the following Wednesday, when on the advice of the police the West End shops were closed and barricaded during a dense fog against an imaginary enemy from the East End.

A new Home Secretary, Mr. Childers, was now in office and he threw the blame of what had happened on the commissioner, who had no alternative but to resign. The public confidence in the police seemed to be shattered, and there was a widespread demand for a better organization in the higher posts at Scotland Yard. It was felt at the time that discipline would be maintained only by men of military training. Public opinion had travelled far from the days when the one fear about the police was that it was a military force disguised in top hats. A second Royal Engineer officer, General Sir Charles Warren, was summoned from his command in Africa to succeed Henderson, the Home Secretary thinking that the appointment of a distinguished soldier would restore public confidence.

A committee appointed to inquire into the riot found that the chain of duties among the superior officers was defective and suggested that more officers of military experience should be appointed. A second committee, of which Sir Charles Warren was a member, confirmed this finding and blamed the system under which men were selected for the higher posts by superintendents who had been promoted from the ranks. The only result was to appoint seven men —four as chief constables and three as assistant chief constables—to take the place of the old district superintendents.

Warren's contribution to the Metropolitan Police was the introduction of five military officers and a large increase in the number of inspectors and sergeants. His term of office has been quoted as a proof of the failure of soldiers in the Metropolitan Police, but the real reason for his early retirement was his objection to the civilian control of the Home Office. It was characteristic of him that his annual reports omitted all reference to crime in London, though space was given to the question of boots and saddles. Unfortunately for him the winter of the first Jubilee year, 1887, was marked by unemployed riots. There were constant disturbances in Trafalgar Square, which were repressed with military vigour.

At that moment the public was greatly disturbed by the Cass case. A Miss Cass had been arrested on a charge of soliciting in Regent Street on Jubilee night, 1887. Her arrest caused the defeat of the government in the House of Commons. It is always difficult for the police to overtake "police scandals." All that is now remembered of the Cass case is that a respectable young woman, who had been engaged in business all day, took a late walk in Regent Street, when she was falsely charged with an act which affected her moral character; what the public did not know was that the constable who arrested her was, after a prolonged magisterial inquiry, acquitted of any wrongful act and reinstated in the force.

Warren's reports were most unfortunate in their military brevity. For example, his reference to the events of November 13, 1887, when, after a struggle between the police and demonstrators in Trafalgar Square, the Guards had to be called out and troops drawn up to protect the National Gallery, while a magistrate rode up Parliament Street under the escort of a troop of Life Guards, was that "during the Autumn, attempts were made by unruly mobs to riot in the streets of Trafalgar Square, which proceedings were successfully coped with by the Police."

This raised the whole question of the legality of political meetings in Trafalgar Square, which was afterwards settled by allowing such meetings to be held subject to notice being given by the conveners to the commissioner.

That was not all. Warren wrote an article in a magazine in which he disputed the right of the Home Secretary to apply the Official Secrets Act to the commissioner or any member of the police force. He disputed the powers of the Receiver, and began to interfere with the administration of the C.I.D.—so much so that Munro, the assistant commissioner in charge, resigned, because he found it impossible to work with his chief.

At length Warren took up the standpoint that the Home Secretary could not issue orders to the force, and consequently he was called upon to resign. He might have been successful as a commissioner if he had been more tactful and less quarrelsome.

At the moment of his resignation great importance was attached to the work of the C.I.D., and especially to that of the newly established branch, known as the Special Branch, for dealing with criminal political conspiracies and dynamite plots. Consequently, Mr. James Munro, who had lately resigned from the C.I.D., was recalled to succeed Sir Charles Warren. Munro had been for twenty-seven years in the Bengal Civil Service and for a time inspector-general of police. He had shown great ability in unearthing the perpetrators of the dynamite outrages, but the dynamite outrages had been suppressed.

The "Jack the Ripper" murders now filled the public mind to the exclusion of all other police questions. The name was taken from the signature of one of the writers of bogus letters published by the police. The victims in every case were prostitutes who were ripped up by what appeared to be surgical knives of extreme sharpness. After the second of these murders the public took alarm, and there was widespread criticism of the C.I.D. Altogether five (with a possible sixth) murders were ascribed to "Jack the Ripper," and no arrest was made. After the last of these murders the police had brought their investigations to the point of suspecting one or other of three homicidal lunatics. One was a Polish Jew reported by Police Constable Thompson, the one police officer who caught sight of the man in Mitre Court; the second was an insane Russian doctor who had been a convict both in England and in Siberia. This man was reported to be in the habit of carrying surgical knives in his pockets. At the time of the outrages he was in hiding; at any rate he could not be found. The third suspect was also a doctor on the borderland of insanity. His friends had grave doubts about him, but the evidence was insufficient for detaining him with any hope of obtaining a conviction. After the last of these crimes in Miller's Court on November 9, 1888, this man disappeared, and seven weeks later his body was found floating in the Thames, the medical evidence being that it had been in the water for a month. Whether this identification was accurate or not, there is a strong presumption that "Jack the Ripper" died or was put under restraint after the last of the murders.

In blaming the detective police at this time it must be remembered that as compared with forces in other countries they work under a great handicap in not being allowed to arrest on suspicion or question the man they suspect.

In one case only, as I have already said, did a policeman have sight of the criminal. A young officer named Thompson was patrolling Chambers Street when a man came running out of Swallow Gardens towards him. On seeing the police uniform the man turned tail and made off at top speed in the other direction. An experienced officer would have pursued him, but Thompson turned into Swallow Gardens and almost stumbled over the mutilated body of Frances Coles. This error of judgment preyed upon the constable's mind: he seemed to think that it presaged misfortune for himself. His forebodings came true. The first time he had gone on night duty he had discovered a murder; some years later he himself was murdered by a Jew named Abrahams who stabbed him in the street. The jury returned a verdict of manslaughter, and Abrahams died in prison.

Unfortunately for Munro as commissioner, there was a recrudescence of industrial trouble in London which culminated in the great dock strike of 1889. This was handled by the police with success and restraint, but Munro had taken up the cudgels for his men and chose to regard the Pensions Bill, about to be introduced by the Home Secretary, as inadequate, when as a fact it made liberal provision for them.

Munro was also an alarmist about the growth of crime and was pressing for a large augmentation of the C.I.D. at a moment when the criminal statistics showed a change for the better. He had further taken into his head that the Home Secretary intended to appoint his private secretary to a post as assistant commissioner, and his resignation was intended to·be a protest; actually, no such appointment was made; the post was given to his own nominee. He resigned in June 1890 and returned to India to organize a medical mission.

A soldier was nominated to succeed him. The new commissioner, Colonel Sir Edward Bradford, was a distinguished Indian army officer who had lost an arm in the service of his country. At the moment he had charge of the political and secret department at the India Office. In India he had acquired a reputation for firmness as well as tact, and these qualities were put to the test almost as soon as he took office. The police had been pressing for the recognition of a committee of delegates to represent their grievances, and of their politically minded secretary, against whom disciplinary action was taken; whereupon there was a police strike at Bow Street and a huge crowd collected outside the police station, partly out of curiosity and partly to show sympathy with the strikers. A detachment of Life Guards was called out to disperse the mob; the strikers were all dismissed, and the improvements in pay and pensions which had been the points on which Munro had resigned were embodied in the Police Act, 1890.

On the whole the period of the nineties proved to be unexpectedly free from the organized crime that had been so harassing to the police, and particularly to the C.I.D., during the previous decade, and there was time to look round. The teamwork of the men improved every day, and the control of habitual criminals was largely responsible for the exceptionally low figures of crime at the end of the century. The second Jubilee in 1897 passed off in an atmosphere of peace which had been quite unknown in the festival of ten years earlier.

On Sir Edward Bradford's retirement in 1903, Mr. Henry (later Sir Edward Henry, Bart.), succeeded him and served in that capacity throughout the Great War. It was a time of stress for the police, for strike followed strike, and Scotland Yard had to send large contingents of men to reinforce the police in South Wales, Lancashire, and elsewhere. It was during this period that occurred the anarchist troubles which culminated in the "siege" of Sidney Street, which may here be described.

THE SIEGE OF SIDNEY STREET

Ever since the "Jack the Ripper" murders in 1888 the east of London had become a city of refuge for aliens whose own countries had become too hot to hold them. They were a continual cause of anxiety to the C.I.D., but though many of them were known to be getting their living by nefarious means, they were too astute often to figure in the assize calendars. They were white-slave traffickers and drug sellers, receivers of stolen goods and instigators of burglaries, but the feeling in Parliament and the press was against persecuting the persecuted, and the government saw no reason for tightening up the restrictions on the entry of aliens who presumably were seeking asylum in England from political persecution in their countries of origin for political offences. Without a far more stringent supervision of aliens at the ports of entry, the police were powerless. If aliens broke the laws of England they could be deported at the end of their sentences, but that was all. The safeguard of requiring passports had fallen into disuse.

On December 16, 1910, a Mr. Isenstein, who kept a fancy-goods shop in Houndsditch, the Jewish business quarter on the City side of Whitechapel, reported to the police that he had heard mysterious noises at night in the rear of his premises, as if someone were engaged in breaking through the wall. Investigations were made, and it was found that burglars had been trying to break through the rear wall, not of Mr. Isenstein's shop but of that of a Mr. Harris, a jeweller who every night locked up £30,000 worth of valuables in his safe. The police took measures the next night to capture the gang, but the burglars were armed with Mauser pistols, and there was a running fight in the dark and narrow streets. Up till then there had been no need to equip the police with firearms, except in emergencies like those created by the Irish gunmen of the eighties, because the home-bred burglars in London well knew that the use of firearms would double or treble their sentences. And so, having only truncheons for their defence, the police came badly out of the unequal contest. Three sergeants were shot dead, and several constables were wounded. The affair created an immense sensation in London, for, apart from the outrages by Irishmen, the criminals had conducted their business with a prudent regard for human life. It was known to the detective force that the leader of the gang was a Latvian, a sign writer born at Riga, named Peter Straume, alias "Peter the Painter," who had for some years been a leading figure in the Lettish colony in Whitechapel. He called himself an anarchist, and the police had been keeping him under casual observation.

The three murdered sergeants belonged to the City of London force, and to meet the intense indignation aroused by the murders they were accorded a funeral in St. Paul's Cathedral. Both the City and the Metropolitan forces were determined not to relax their hunt for the criminals until all had been brought to justice. They proceeded to comb out

East London for foreigners of doubtful reputation and for concealed arms.

Some ten days after the murders they were engaged in raiding the premises of a Mr. Moroutzeff in Gold Street near Sidney Street, Stepney, which lies about a mile to the east of Houndsditch. There they discovered an automatic pistol, six hundred cartridges, 150 Mauser bullets, a dagger, bottles of nitric acid, a quantity of nitroglycerine and other dangerous chemicals, and a manual on the manufacture of explosives. The newspapers described the house as "an Anarchist arsenal."

On this both forces of police combined to pool their information. It was known to them that some of the men they were in search of had found a refuge in the rooms of a Russian seamstress in 100 Sidney Street. Very early in the morning of January 3, 1911, fifty police officers closed in upon the house, fifteen armed with revolvers and four with rifles fitted with Morris tubes of small calibre. It was a bitter winter night, with snow lying in the streets.

Having been cautioned against a discharge of firearms, the police knocked on the door of No. 100, but they failed to arouse the inmates. By 4 A.M. strong reinforcements had arrived—one hundred from the City and an equal number from the Metropolitan force. As they could get no answer to their knocking, the police threw stones at the windows of the second floor where the Russian woman lodged. The response was a salvo of shots from windows. A sergeant was hit in the chest but not badly hurt, and an inspector received a bullet through his cap. When daylight came the police were 750 strong, and seventeen men with two non-commissioned officers of the Scots Guards and a Maxim had been brought from the Tower of London. Some of the soldiers were sniping No. 100 from the brewery opposite; others were lying in the streets on boards to protect them from the frozen mud and were firing at the house as if they were engaged in a rifle competition at Bisley.

The author of this little history was at the time employed at the Home Office as secretary to the Prison Commission, while his brother, a retired artillery officer, was in the same office as an inspector of explosives. I confess that we were both astounded by the news that the newly appointed Home Secretary, Mr. Winston Churchill, had himself started in one of the police cars for the scene of the siege—it was erroneously believed to take command of the operations. He was a tempting mark for the anarchist offenders, for he was wearing a silk hat and a fur-lined overcoat with an astrakhan collar—articles of wearing apparel that are rarely seen in the East End of London. With him went the commissioner of the City police, Sir Melville Macnaghten, chief of the C.I.D., and Superintendent Quinn, head of the Special Branch at Scotland Yard.

Naturally, the newspapers made the most of this unusual excursion of a Cabinet minister. Perhaps a more retiring Home Secretary who wished to see for himself what was going on might have slipped down to Stepney and escaped notice, but Mr. Churchill—soldier, statesman, and journalist—was followed by the limelight which he did not seek. He exposed himself to fire quite as much as the Scots Guards who were present, and his counsel as a professional soldier may have been valuable to the superior police officials who were faced with this unprecedented task, but whatever gossip said about his adventure, it was not true that he interfered with the orders given to the soldiers and the police, or that he himself issued a single order. It is true, apparently, that he agreed with the suggestion to bring a couple of field guns from the Horse Artillery Depot at St. John's Wood and hold them in reserve, and that a party of Royal Engineers from Chatham might be useful if it were decided to undermine the building. Apparently he did suggest that casualties might be avoided if light steel plates were brought from Woolwich to serve as portable cover for the military sharpshooters. But he never overstepped official correctitude.

It must be remembered that the strength of the garrison of No. 100 Sidney Street was still unknown. There might have been thirty or forty instead of what proved to be the

.actual number. Soon after one o'clock smoke was seen oozing through the broken windows of the second floor. By half-past one it became clear that the attic from which most of the shots had been fired was well alight and that the flames were creeping down to the floor below. The fire brigade arrived and gallantly offered to go into action forthwith, but the police forbade them to do so, and the Home Secretary agreed—a point on which he had to meet strong criticism later. There would, however, have been a far stronger ground for criticism if he had countermanded the orders of the police.

In a very few minutes the firing from the house ceased. It was alight from top to bottom. After waiting ten minutes a police inspector, accompanied by Mr. Churchill and a Guardsman armed with a double-barrelled sporting gun, advanced to the front door and kicked it down. The inspector shouted an order to surrender, but there was no reply. The fire engines then got to work and extinguished the smouldering flames. In the ruins were found two charred bodies which were identified as those of Fritz Svoars and Jacob Vogel—the entire garrison. No trace was found of Peter the Painter.

On the side of the besiegers, one Guardsman was hit in the leg, a police sergeant in the chest, and three civilians were slightly wounded. Superintendent Quinn, the head of the Special Branch, was struck by a spent bullet but not badly hurt. The only person brought before the courts in respect of the Houndsditch murders was a cigarette maker, a young woman of twenty-three, named Nina Vassileve, who was charged with complicity in the murders. She was sentenced to two years' hard labour, but the sentence was quashed by the Appeal Court on the ground of misdirection by the judge. The episode of Sidney Street had useful results in spite of its theatrical setting. The Aliens Department at the Home Office was strengthened, and a new departure was made in excluding undesirable immigrants from the country, so that a department had not to be organized in haste on the outbreak of the Great War. The episode had one other result: the issue of modern automatic pistols to the police when engaged on dangerous duty.

At that time no one knew what had become of Peter the Painter, though later it was believed that he had escaped to Australia and that he died in America in 1914. It was certain that he was not in the Sidney Street house that night, and if he had remained in London the police would have tracked him down. Detective-Sergeant Leeson, however, claims that he met him by chance in a railway carriage while on a trip to the Blue Mountains in New South Wales. Leeson had been very badly wounded in the Sidney Street affray and had been invalided out of the police service. The meeting took place several months after the affray.

THE TRIAL OF Dr. Hawley Harvey Crippen for the murder of his wife on October 18, 1910, was the first case in which wireless telegraphy, then in its infancy for commercial purposes, was used for the arrest of a fugitive criminal. Psychologically it is of special interest.

Crippen was an American doctor, born in Coldwater, Michigan, in 1862. He had married a Polish Jewess who called herself Cora Turner, though her real name was Kunigunde Mackamotski. She aspired to be an operatic singer, though lacking any natural talent, but Crippen paid for her training and for her dresses and jewelry and brought her to London in 1900, where he obtained the post of manager for Munyon's patent medicines. Failing to get an engagement on the opera stage, Mrs. Crippen fell back upon the music-hall stage and failed in that; at her only engagement she was hissed off the stage. She was vain, thriftless, and ill-tempered; she amused herself with other men; but Crippen remained her patient household drudge and bore all her contemptuous reproaches meekly.

In order to keep in with the music-hall society that she loved, Mrs. Crippen accepted the treasurership of the Music-Hall Ladies' Guild—a fact that had for Crippen very disagreeable consequences.

This long-suffering and quiet little man had begun meanwhile to solace himself for his discomfort at home with the

198

society of his typist, Ethel le Neve (or, to use her real name, Neave). The liaison became known to his wife, who saw in it an excuse for leaving him for another man in the character of an injured wife. In January 1910 she threatened to do this, and worse, to take with her all the funds in their joint names in the bank, together with her jewelry and wardrobe. This would have left the little doctor penniless. A few days later Mrs. Crippen disappeared. To her music-hall friends Crippen explained that she had carried out her threat to leave him, and a little later he announced that she had died in California and circulated a death notice and mourning cards in support of his statement. But in March he took Ethel Neave to live with him in his house in Hilldrop Crescent in London and allowed her to wear some of his wife's jewelry in public. It was this that first aroused suspicion among Mrs. Crippen's friends, for they knew that such a woman would never have left her valuable trinkets behind her. On June 30 a Mr. Nash came to Scotland Yard to ask the police to investigate the story of her disappearance.

The case was entrusted to a very astute and pertinacious detective, Inspector Dew, who interviewed Crippen at his office. Crippen at once admitted that his story of his wife's death was untrue; that he had invented the story to avoid the scandal of admitting that she had gone off with another man. He took the detective to his house, helped him to examine everything, and satisfied him that there was nothing inconsistent in his story. Apparently the case was cleared up, and Mrs. Crippen's disappearance might well have been added to the long list of disappearances among the eight million people in London.

But at this point something went wrong. Miss Neave's nerves failed her. Whether she knew the truth or not, she was not equal to the strain of further police interviews. Crippen was sincerely in love with the girl and wished to spare her. At any rate he took the fatal step of running away with her, after disguising her as a young boy and describing her as his son. He had laid his plans well, but it chanced that on July 11 Inspector Dew called at his office to ask some supplementary questions before closing the case. There he learned that Dr. Crippen had left the country, and immediately the case took on a new complexion. Dew now justified the character he had acquired for thoroughness. He revisited the house in Hilldrop Crescent and, having dug over every inch of the garden, turned his attention to the bricked floor of the cellar. On the third day of his search he discovered that one of the bricks was loose; he removed the bricks and after digging a few inches down he unearthed a compact mass of animal remains which were pronounced by the experts to be human, though the head, limbs, bones, and organs which would have determined the sex were missing. A warrant of arrest was obtained, and a description of the fugitives was widely circulated. Here is the description of Crippen:

About 50. Height 5 ft 3. Hair scanty, inclined to be sandy; bald on top; sandy straggling moustache; grey eyes; wears gold-rimmed spectacles; may be wearing beard or not; slovenly; throws out feet when walking; slight American accent; very plausible and quiet-spoken; shows teeth a good deal when he smiles. False teeth.

Fortunately the description reached Antwerp just before the R.M.S. *Montrose* sailed for Quebec. The captain had read it; his attention was called to two of his passengers who had registered under the names of Mr. Robinson and his son. The boy quite evidently was a girl in disguise; the description fitted the fugitives exactly. Without arousing their suspicions, the captain sent a wireless message relating his discovery. The *Montrose* was a slow boat; there was time for Inspector Dew, by taking a boat from Liverpool, to arrive in Quebec before her.

The fugitives were arrested, extradited, and after a trial lasting five days, Crippen was sentenced to death and the girl was acquitted.

The case had excited immense interest on both sides of the Atlantic. At the trial the medical experts surpassed themselves, but it may be doubted whether the identity of the remains could have been established but for the fact that they had been wrapped in a torn pyjama jacket which was proved to have belonged to Crippen. A further fact determining the sex was the discovery, among the remains, of some Hinde's hair curlers. The man in court who was least moved was the prisoner himself. His one concern was for the young woman who sat beside him. During the three weeks that elapsed before his execution his one thought was for her, and it is not too much to say that he endeared himself to the prison officials by his gentle unselfishness.

Ethel le Neve was subsequently charged with having been an accessory to the murder after the fact and was defended by Mr. F. E. Smith (afterwards the Earl of Birkenhead). She was acquitted. Later she became a dressmaker in London.

Crippen was proved to have killed his wife with an overdose of hyoscin—a drug little known in 1910 as an anesthetic, but extensively used in these days. His counsel, the late Sir Edward Marshall Hall, wanted to put forward the plea that Crippen had administered the drug as a sedative to his exacting wife, but the prisoner, in his anxiety to clear his paramour of complicity, refused to allow this line of defence. He preferred to die with a lie on his lips.

THE TRIAL OF THE SEDDONS

The importance of the Seddon case lies in the fact that if Seddon had not given evidence himself the prosecution could not have obtained a verdict of wilful murder against him. It was, therefore, a classical example of the working of the Prisoner's Evidence Act in capital cases. Further, it was the only capital case on record in which two persons were indicted for the same offence and in which the same evidence was offered against both of them and yet the jury convicted the husband and acquitted the wife. Seddon was convicted, not because the prosecution succeeded in proving his guilt, but because he failed to prove his innocence. What had become of the old maxim that "an accused person is presumed innocent until he is proved guilty"? That had always been a solid tradition of English criminal justice.

Frederick Henry Seddon and his wife were charged with the wilful murder of Eliza Mary Barrow at their house 63 Tollington Park, in the north of London, on September 14, 1911, by administering arsenic to her. In 1901 Seddon was appointed district superintendent for Islington under the London & Manchester Industrial Assurance Company. In November 1909 he came to live at 63 Tollington Park in a house of his own, a house considerably larger than was required for his family. On June 20, 1910, he instructed house agents to find a tenant for his top floor. He, with his wife and family, consisting of five children, occupied the lower part of the house, and the tenants were to have the upper portion.

The tenant who was found for him was Eliza Mary Barrow, a spinster forty-nine years of age. With her came a small orphan boy ten years of age, whom she had adopted. She was a woman of eccentric habits and uncertain temper. In 1909 she had gone to live with relatives, a Mr. and Mrs. Vonderahe. She paid them for the board and lodging of herself and the little boy and lived with them until July 26, 1910, when she removed to 63 Tollington Park, in consequence of a quarrel. She possessed a small fortune, amounting to some £4,000. She loved to hoard gold and bank notes which she did not trust to a bank but kept in a cashbox. Besides this she had £200 in a savings bank, and she owned house property, cashing the cheques for rent every quarter and hoarding the proceeds in the cashbox. At the time of her death her entire fortune, except the paltry sum of £4.10.0, had passed into the hands of the Seddons, who alleged that they had given her an annuity in exchange for her hoardings and her leasehold property. She seems to have had no friends: at any rate no one called upon her. It was therefore evident that the Seddons had every interest in getting rid of this woman, who was costing them this annuity of £1 a week and was a disagreeable tenant.

What happened afterwards? On September 1, 1911, she

was taken ill. During her illness Mrs. Seddon attended her, and Seddon himself went into her room several times. On September 11 she made a will appointing him sole executor and trustee; his father, who was living in the house, was called in to witness it. The will left her slender belongings to two children—the adopted boy and his sister—when they should come of age, the property being held in the meantime by Seddon as trustee. The doctor who was called in diagnosed that she was suffering from epidemic diarrhœa. She had been getting better, but as soon as she had made the will she became rapidly worse. She sent the little boy to call the Seddons, who called in no doctor, and in the early morning of September 14 she died. Seddon saw the doctor and obtained from him a certificate that death was due to epidemic diarrhœa. Seddon then went to an undertaker and arranged for the removal of the body to the undertaker's mortuary and for the funeral to take place from the undertaker's two days later.

None of her relatives heard of the death until September 20, four days after the funeral, though the Vonderahes lived less than a quarter of a mile from the house. Seddon assured Mrs. Vonderahe when she saw him that he had posted on September 14 a letter to her husband telling him of the death and the time of the funeral. No such letter was received by them. There existed among Seddon's papers a document which showed that Miss Barrow was entitled to burial in a family vault at Highgate, yet he told the undertaker that she had only £4.10.0 in the world, out of which the doctor's fee must come. The undertaker replied that for that amount of money there could be only the cheapest funeral and she would have to be buried in a public grave.

The Vonderahes became suspicious and demanded an interview with Seddon, but on September 22 the Seddons went for a fortnight to the seaside, and it was not until October 9 that the interview took place. So far from reassuring them, the Vonderahes became still more suspicious. They communicated their suspicions to the police, and Miss Barrow's body was exhumed and examined by the Home

Office experts, doctors Willcox and Spilsbury, who found evidence of arsenical poisoning. The coroner's jury found that arsenic had been administered by some person or persons unknown. The excellent preservation of the body when it was exhumed was consistent with arsenical poisoning.

On December 4 Seddon was arrested. There was evidence to show that on August 26, 1911, Seddon's daughter, Maggie, had purchased flypapers which contained arsenic, and the case for the prosecution was that the arsenic had been obtained from a number of these flypapers sufficient to cause death. Mrs. Seddon was not arrested until January 15th.

The case was passed to the director of public prosecutions, who applied to Scotland Yard to obtain the necessary evidence. The C.I.D. officers selected were Chief Inspector Ward, who was killed by a Zeppelin bomb during the war, Detective-Sergeant Cooper, and Detective-Sergeant Hayman, all experienced officers, and it was due to their work that the case for the prosecution was prepared. It entailed a vast amount of work in interviewing witnesses, examining accounts, and tracing bank notes.

When Ward arrested Seddon the latter asked, "Are you going to arrest my wife as well?"—a curious question for an innocent man to put. He went on, "Have you found arsenic in the body?" At the police station when left in charge of a sergeant he said, "Poisoning by arsenic—what a charge. Of course I've had all her money affairs through my hands . . . but I think I can prove my innocence."

The prisoners appeared before the magistrates and were committed for trial on a charge of wilful murder.

Now it is to be noted that there was no direct evidence to show that poison had been administered; there was no direct evidence to show that arsenic had been in the possession of the deceased woman: all that the prosecution could adduce was that the two accused people had purchased flypapers; had opportunities for administering the arsenic distilled from them and had a motive for getting rid of the victim. It was, therefore, a case largely resting on presumption. It appeared afterwards that Dr. Willcox, who believed in Seddon's guilt, did not believe that he used any decoction of flypapers. It is possible that the idea of flypapers, introduced by Seddon himself, was a blind and that he used arsenic in the form of rat poison or weed killer. A day or two after his arrest Maggie Seddon, the daughter, was sent at her father's suggestion to buy some Mather's flypapers. He had made this suggestion to his solicitor, because he had remembered that there were flypapers in Miss Barrow's room during her illness and he wanted his solicitor to have them analyzed and the quantity of poison in them ascertained.

It was not until Seddon himself went into the witness stand that the real nature of the man, his cupidity, his hardness, and his meanness came to the knowledge of the jury. He was as cool and collected as if he were concerned only in one of his business transactions. He never seemed to realize the sinister effect which this cold demeanour was likely to have on the jury and, for the matter of that, on the public, who heard or read the evidence.

Mr. Justice Bucknill, who tried the case, the most humane of men, allowed himself to be mastered by emotion both in his summing up and in his sentence. The jury were absent from court for an hour. It was noticed that when the two prisoners entered the dock again there was a doctor with them and that an officer stood close behind Seddon. You could have heard a pin fall. When the deputy clerk asked the jury the fateful question as regards Seddon and the foreman pronounced the word "Guilty," Seddon did not move or change his expression. The question was again put as regards the wife and the answer came, "Not guilty," and while the clerk was entering the verdict in his book Seddon crossed the dock to his wife and gave her a kiss which resounded incongruously through the deathlike silence of the court. Mrs. Seddon was supported down the stairs, and then came the question to the condemned man whether he had anything to say why sentence should not be passed on him. Quite calm in his manner he went through an intricate array of facts and figures, finally lifting his hand to take the Mason's oath and swearing by the Great Architect of the Universe that he was innocent. The judge was all but sobbing, and he had to pause before uttering sentence of death. Seddon was the least moved of anyone in court. He hitched his overcoat about him, took a drink of water, and went down the stairs that took him away from the world of men forever.

The inevitable appeal occupied two days. It failed. There remained only the appeal to the Home Secretary, Mr. Reginald McKenna—an appeal supported by upwards of 300,000 signatures. This also was rejected. Seven thousand people—an unprecedented crowd—assembled outside the gate of Pentonville prison on the morning of his execution.

A few months after Seddon's execution, his wife married again and emigrated with all her family to California, but the *Weekly Dispatch* of November 17, 1912, published a declaration signed by Mrs. Seddon to the effect that she saw her husband give the poison to Miss Barrow on the night of her death, and that he terrorized her into silence with a revolver. The painful impression about her was heightened when, a fortnight later, *John Bull* published an affidavit, sworn before a commissioner for oaths, to the effect that the alleged confession was untrue; that she had made it for payment and to put an end to the gossip of neighbours who pointed her out as a murderess. Seddon himself had maintained his innocence until the end.

THE THEFT OF A PEARL NECKLACE

In May 1913 a well-known London jeweller opened a registered parcel from Paris, which purported to contain a pearl necklace valued at £110,000. To his dismay he found in it nothing but a few lumps of coal. The box had been delivered with all the seals apparently intact.

At first suspicion fell upon the French postal servants, but inquiries made on both sides of the Channel established beyond a doubt that the wrapper and the seals were exactly in the condition in which the parcel had been delivered for registration; but pearls do not change into lumps of coal of their own volition, and therefore there must exist a counterfeit seal of the firm, which consisted of the initials "M. M." within an oval border. At Scotland Yard an experiment was made with a plaster seal. It was found that one could be made and used on melted sealing wax within four minutes, and therefore that at some point in the parcel's journey it would have been possible to break the seals, undo the wrappings, remove the pearls, and seal the parcel up again, without the loss of a post.

Now the basis of police action at Scotland Yard and elsewhere is in most cases the subterranean telegraph—that is to say, whispers from informants; and the most successful detectives are those who have won the confidence of such men and know how to handle them. It was not long before the names of Grizzard and three others were whispered in connection with the robbery. There was no difficulty in finding the men; they were already known; the difficulty was to find them with the stolen pearls on their persons. It was probably the most difficult case of observation that had been known for years. The men had no reason to suspect that they were being followed, and yet never for a moment did they relax their precautions. If they took a taxi to any rendezvous, they gave a false destination, paid off the taxi, and took another, sometimes repeating this process of mystification two or three times. If they met in Oxford Street to lunch together at an A. B. C. shop they would change their minds on the doorstep and go off to another; and all the while they had an aged discharged convict in their pay to shadow them and call their attention to any suspicious follower.

A day came when the four thieves entered an underground station together; they were arrested and searched, but on that particular day they had left the necklace at home. They were detained in order that a search might be made of all their hiding places.

It did not take the police long to unravel the details of the crime. They found an engraver who had innocently cut the false seal. Learning from the Post Office the round of the postman who delivered the registered parcels, they went down to Pall Mall seeking an empty office which had been lately rented, and there, nearly opposite Marlborough House, the London residence of the Prince of Wales, they found what they were looking for—a little room on the fifth floor which had lately been let to some Jews who had not been there after the theft of the pearls. The police found the postman, who confessed that he had left the parcel in that office for three or four minutes before taking it on to deliver it; they found a coal scuttle filled with the same kind of coal that was in the parcel. The thieves had expected diamonds, which are far more easily disposed of than pearls so large that in the trade each pearl had almost a history; they knew they could not dispose of them and were at first for throwing them into the Thames. The wife of one of the gang, fearing a domiciliary visit, put the pearls into a Bryant & May matchbox and dropped it into the gutter of the mean street where she lived: there it was found by a street sweeper who thought at first that the pearls were beads and was going to take them to his children to play with, but fortunately he first took them to the police. On my office desk unstrung and ungraded, it seemed incredible that they were worth £110,000. I rang up Mr. Mayer, the owner, who fell upon them chortling with joy. "I thought they were false," I said. "They look so yellow." "Yellow?" he protested. "They're r-r-r-ose-colour."

The thieves were tried at the Central Criminal Court and received long sentences.

THE SUFFRAGETTES

Let me now turn to a class of "crime" that taxed the police severely—the extravagances of Mrs. Pankhurst's branch of the female suffragists commonly known as the "Suffragettes."

There was an uncanny ingenuity about their methods of annoyance which seemed unworthy of the cause they advocated. Many of them were perfectly rational ladies in private life, but they drew into their ranks a number of mentally unbalanced women who must have been extremely difficult to control by the leaders. They broke windows with hammers; they assaulted Cabinet ministers and others they mistook for Cabinet ministers; they threw marbles under the feet of police horses and brought them down; they assaulted policemen, and when they were committed to prison they went on hunger strike and carried it on until their lives were actually in danger. To meet this aspect of the agitation the government passed in haste an act which permitted the release of a prisoner and her rearrest to serve the remainder of her sentence at a later date. It was popularly known as the "Cat and Mouse" Act; but while it was a great relief to the prison authorities, it threw many difficulties in the way of the detectives who had to rearrest them. They were amply supplied with money, and they had a host of sympathizers all over the country. A high-powered car met them at the prison gate and spirited them out of London to an unknown destination. Actually three of them were arrested on the morning when war was declared, but they were released on a promise that they would devote their energies to war work for the future. This undertaking was interpreted by some of them as an invitation to combat German espionage. It ceased to be Cabinet ministers who had their windows broken; it was any tradesman who chanced to have a German-sounding name.

As the war went on, the extreme group of these ladies became affiliated in some way with Russian Bolshevism. In one instance after the war they broke in upon the Two Minutes' Silence on Armistice Day by singing and shouting at an open window in their office. The police went up the stairs to reason with them, but some resolute-looking ladies called them back and claimed to be allowed to deal with them themselves. It was reported later that this was very thoroughly done.

The war brought many changes to Scotland Yard. There was in England, as in all the belligerent countries, a spy scare. Denunciations of suspected spies—most of them quite innocent people—poured in by every mail, and it was not safe to ignore any of them. When the Zeppelin raids began, there was an outbreak of the signalling scare, and this too had to be investigated in every case. Fortunately there was not very much ordinary crime to take up the time of the C.I.D., since a large number of habitual criminals were satisfying their love of adventure by fighting at the front.

It soon became apparent that the Admiralty and War Office intelligence services had not the outdoor personnel necessary for dealing with these cases, especially with the real spies who were arrested in England or stopped at the ports when landing, and it became the custom to make the office of the head of the C.I.D. the common meeting ground for the two services in which the statements of suspected persons were taken down in shorthand to be used after-wards, if necessary, at their trials. There were many dramatic and moving scenes at some of these interviews. As the war went on, the quality of the arrested spies continued to decline until it touched the lowest grade of commercial traveller, who could not, even if he had been free, have reported intelligently on anything that he saw. The explanation was that in Holland, whence these people came, both the naval and the military German intelligence officers were in active competition and they had ceased to scrutinize too closely the competence of the men they were sending.

CHAPTER XIX

The Criminal Record Office

THE CASE OF ADOLF BECK

THROUGHOUT THE DECADE OF THE NINETIES England had been dependent for identification on the Bertillon system of body measurements taken in the different prisons, but, carefully as these were done, there was always the personal equation to be reckoned with. One prison warder would press the caliper closer home than another, and one mistake of this kind threw the system out of gear. The fingerprint identification devised by Mr. E. R. Henry, and tested by him not only in Bengal but at Johannesburg, was now becoming known, and in 1901 he was brought to Scotland Yard as assistant commissioner of the C.I.D. to inaugurate the system. He got together a strong team of detectives as enthusiastic as himself, and the system was successful from the first.

The Beck case is important in the annals of detective science as having been the motive force behind the adoption of fingerprint identification in England. Here is the case in broad outline:

In 1877 a man who called himself John Smith was convicted at the Central Criminal Court for frauds on women of loose character, whereby he had obtained from them jewelry or money. His methods had been to introduce himself as a nobleman of wealth with an establishment in St. John's Wood, and to offer the position of mistress to his victim. He would then suggest that she would require a new outfit

and he would write out an order to some well-known tradesman at whose shop she was to deal and give her a cheque on
a non-existent bank. He would then on some pretext borrow
money or some article of jewelry and decamp. The name
under which he perpetrated these frauds was "Lord
Willoughby." He was sentenced to five years' penal servitude and was released from prison on license in April 1891.

Towards the end of 1894 the police began to receive complaints from women, mostly of loose character, that they
had been defrauded by a man who called himself "Lord
Wilton" or "Lord Winton de Willoughby," with an establishment in St. John's Wood. The methods were identical
with those employed in the Smith case. The description of
the man by these women varied, but the cheques appeared
to be all in the same handwriting. The police failed to find
this offender, and their attention was first drawn to Mr.
Beck on December 16, 1895. On the afternoon of that day,
Ottilie Maissonier, who had been defrauded in November,
happened to meet Mr. Beck in Victoria Street. She charged
him with having robbed her; he protested that he had never
seen her before. She followed him along the street until
they met a policeman to whom they both appealed, and as
the woman persisted in her charge they were both taken to
the police station, where a charge was entered against Mr.
Beck. A large number of the women who had been defrauded were given opportunities of seeing Mr. Beck and
identifying him if they could. Several did so and gave evidence against him at the police court.

When reports of the proceedings appeared in the newspapers, a gentleman who had been interested in the Smith
case, and who was entirely unconnected with the police, came
forward to say that he had no doubt that Mr. Beck was
identical with the ex-convict Smith. Upon that information a retired police constable who had arrested Smith in
1877 was found. He swore positively that Mr. Beck was
Smith and was confirmed in his opinion by another officer
who had been concerned in the Smith case. Mr. Beck was
committed for trial on all the charges brought against him

and was sentenced to seven years' penal servitude. His defence was that the real culprit was the man who had
been convicted in 1877 and that he was not that man. In
prison he was classed and treated as a man who had been
previously convicted, and this was embroidered on his prison
dress.

Immediately after his conviction, Beck sent a petition to
the Home Office alleging that his case was one of mistaken
identity. This was followed by several other petitions, to all
of which came the stereotyped reply that the Home Secretary saw no grounds for interference with the sentence.
In May 1896 his solicitor wrote to the Home Office demanding that the case be reopened. Then for the first time
the Home Office instituted inquiries and elicited the fact
that in 1879 Smith had been examined by the prison doctor,
who had reported to the governor in writing that he had
undergone the rite of circumcision. Orders were given to
have Beck examined, and it was found that he had not
undergone this rite. On this new fact the Home Office consulted the judge, with the result that Beck was ordered to
have his previous conviction struck out, but to undergo the
sentence on the last conviction.

It was a strange fact that though this distinctive mark
was known to the prison authorities in 1879 and was communicated to the Home Office in 1898 it was not made
known either to the public prosecutor or to Scotland Yard
until July 1904, when Smith, the cause of all the trouble,
again fell into the custody of the law. Meanwhile in July
1901, Mr. Beck was released on licence after having served
his time.

Here comes the most astonishing episode in this tragedy
of errors. In April 1904—nearly three years after his release—Mr. Beck was again arrested on a charge similar
to those on which he had previously been convicted. He was
again convicted, and as he could not deny having been convicted in 1896, he was treated as having pleaded guilty to a
charge of a former conviction. Happily the judge felt misgivings and postponed sentence, and at last Fate stepped in

to aid this shuttlecock of ill-fortune. The ex-convict Smith was arrested for acts committed while Beck was in custody, and this led to further inquiries and the release and pardon of Beck in respect of both his convictions.

The fact that an innocent man could be not only once, but twice convicted, and that his petitions to the Home Office had led to no redress created grave misgivings in the public mind on the working of our system of criminal justice. The case had been dealt with throughout in good faith; the identifications made by a number of persons, among them men accustomed to checking identifications, had been positive; it was a case of mistaken identity, due to the fallibility of observation in the witnesses, but the strangest fact of all in this strange case is this: when it had been proved to the Home Office in 1898 that Beck was not Smith, he was, nevertheless, made to serve out his term, which was longer than it would have been if he had been a first offender. Moreover, if the Home Office had notified the police that they had been wrong, it must have affected their action on the second arrest and trial.

A strong committee of inquiry headed by the Master of Rolls himself went into the whole matter and entirely exonerated Scotland Yard. There was some slight resemblance between Beck and Smith, but after Smith's arrest in 1904, Mr. Beck owed his release to the intervention of an intelligent police officer, Inspector Waldock, who was in charge of the case. He happened to have had a previous acquaintance with Beck and did not believe in his guilt. While Beck was in custody, Inspector Waldock caused him to be stripped, for the purpose of comparing his bodily marks with those recorded in Smith's description, and he failed to find on Beck the corresponding marks. He communicated his views of Beck's innocence to the assistant director of public prosecutions, but the case was soon afterwards taken out of his hands.

To put the matter shortly, Beck was hampered in his defence by lack of funds, and the Home Office had got into a habit of treating petitions from convicts in a stereotyped manner. The view of Scotland Yard was not that of the press and the public, who wrote of the "martyrdom of Adolf Beck" as if he were the victim of crassly stupid officials, but that both Smith, *alias* Wyatt, and Beck were practising the same kind of fraud on unfortunate women, a fraud that was common at the time, and that their superficial resemblance led to charges against first one and then the other.

Even granting that Beck was entirely innocent in this respect, it was a remarkable fact that the two men should both have been staying at the Grand Hotel, Charing Cross. Beck was an adventurer; pawn tickets relating to women's jewelry, brooches and rings, were found in his possession; the clothing described by the women, the white vest slips, spats, and patent-leather boots described by them were found by the police in his rooms, and all he could prove as to character was that twenty years earlier he had mixed with respectable people in a foreign country. He and Wyatt both spoke English with a foreign accent, but whereas Beck could speak English with scarcely any accent at all if he liked, his broken English in court only strengthened the conviction that he was a humbug. Both he and Wyatt, *alias* Smith, apparently were Germans. One at least of the defrauded women was accosted within a few yards of where Beck lived.

Beck's behaviour, too, weighed heavily against him. When the woman Maissonier accosted him and accused him of defrauding her, all he had to do was to shut his front door in her face and go upstairs. Instead of that, he ran away across the street and was chased by her until they met the policeman, when he used bad language.

On the second, as on the first, trial Beck could not account for his movements. On the second trial he went into the witness box and said that he was with a "Mr. Gajardo," but Gajardo was not called as a witness for the defence.

The investigating committee laid its finger on the outstanding lesson of this case—that "evidence as to identity based upon personal impressions is, unless supported by other facts, an unsafe basis for the verdict of a jury." The second lesson is that women are especially to be mistrusted in cases where the evidence is of this character; and thirdly it must be clear that the so-called corroboration really is corroboration and not merely evidence to show that the crime has been committed without indicating the prisoner as the one man who could have committed it.

Let us glance for a moment at the afterlife of Adolf Beck. The government awarded him £5,000 as compensation for the miscarriage of justice. He did not use this considerable sum to procure for himself some reputable employment; on the contrary, he dissipated the money in more or less riotous living. He frequented the lowest stratum of society and was convicted once of obstructing the police. He died in Middlesex Hospital in 1909, utterly destitute. Nevertheless, his case was of inestimable benefit both to the Home Office and to Scotland Yard, for it hastened the adoption of fingerprint identification and led to the appointment of a legal under-secretary at the Home Office who had had extensive practice in the criminal courts. These two reforms have made it practically impossible that such a case as that of Adolf Beck can ever occur again.

The Criminal Record Office, known as the C.R.O., is in itself a means of detecting criminals. It dates from the adoption of fingerprints as an unerring method of identification. Until 1901 the identification of criminals depended upon the system initiated by the Paris enthusiast, Dr. Bertillon, who adopted five body measurements as the basis of his system. During the late eighties the system was adopted in England, and the prisons were all furnished with his apparatus. The measurements were the length and breadth of the skull, the length of the foot and the cubit, the length of the middle finger. He distributed them as belonging to one or other of three equally numerous classes—small, medium, and large. Each of these primary headings is successively subdivided according to height, span, length and breadth of the ear, height of the bust, and colour of the eyes, this last providing seven divisions.

The system was first practically worked in France in 1883, and though France has since adopted fingerprints she still maintains the Bertillon system as a check. Gradually the anthropometric system spread to other countries, and the French turned to account the habit of criminals of having their arms and bodies tattooed by instituting a tattoo index. In March 1892 the system was introduced into the province of Bengal in India, where certain improvements were made in it. It was then extended to the rest of India, and by the end of 1898 nearly 200,000 cards had been collected. Meanwhile, Francis Galton had been investigating the use of fingerprints among widely scattered nations. He found the significance attached to their use to have been partly superstitious and partly ceremonial, citing the practice of the executant of a document, who lays his finger on a seal and declares "this to be my act and deed." As early as 1823 Purkenje, a professor of physiology, read a Latin thesis on fingerprints before the University of Breslau. His labours failed to attract the attention they deserved.

The next person to advocate the official use of fingerprints was Sir William Herschel, of the Indian Civil Service, who used them as a means of checking false personation, which was prevalent in all the Indian courts; but his report was allowed to lie stillborn in the archives, and the check he had introduced was abandoned. Galton had already proved that the skin ridges on the fingers persist from infancy to old age, and that there is some evidence to show that the patterns are transmissible, but none that shows any relation between the patterns and the character or faculties, or that the patterns are distinctive in different races.

Meanwhile Mr. (later Sir) Edward Henry of the Indian Civil Service had been quietly working out a system of classification. He told the author that the solution came to him in a flash in the course of a long ride through the Indian jungle. It chanced that Henry had just retired from the office of inspector-general of police in Bengal at the moment when the defects in the Bertillon anthropometric system were becoming apparent, partly, no doubt, owing to the idiosyncrasies of the measurers in the prisons. Moreover, the system depends upon catching the subject before his measurements can be taken, whereas if he leaves his fingerprints on the scene of a crime he can be identified while he is still at large if his fingerprints are recorded in the registry.

Henry's system had been adopted throughout India. A Home Office committee, which was investigating the subject in 1900, invited him to give evidence on the system, and this was followed by appointing him to the vacant charge of head of the C.I.D., which was followed two years later by promotion to the commissionership. This was the starting point of a system of identification which, as I have said, has since been adopted by the police of every civilized country.

It was also the starting point of the Criminal Record Office, which absorbed various subsections, the Crime Index, the *Police Gazette,* the Prisoners' Property Store, the Crime Museum, the Photographic Laboratory, Extradition, etc.

It was of the greatest importance that, before the courts and the public who are summoned as jurymen should be convinced of the efficacy of the fingerprint system of identification, no mistake should be made. Happily during the early months there were some startling identifications, which found their way into the press. A marauder scaled a gate with a line of spikes on its top, and in jumping down he caught his ring on a spike, tearing off the finger. A print was taken from this, and the man was identified. A hue and cry resulted in his arrest with the torn finger half healed. He was convicted on that evidence alone. Not long after this episode a candle was found on the scene of a burglary. Candles are naturally susceptible to the preservation of prints of the fingers which held them; there were three such impressions which were found to belong to a well-known housebreaker. His fingerprints were already in the collection and, despite the efforts of his defending counsel, he was convicted.

Such cases are, of course, less common than is generally

supposed. Burglars took to wearing gloves, and besides, many of the prints found on the scene of a crime are blurred and useless for identification. When depredators help themselves to the contents of a cellar by knocking off the top of a wine bottle the case is more hopeful, since the finger impressions are nearly invisible to the naked eye and have to be developed by dusting powder over them with a camel's-hair brush and blowing off the superfluity of powder. They can then be photographed and used for searching in the registry. One source of error has to be guarded against. It is an office rule that whenever a police officer brings an isolated fingerprint to the C.R.O. for identification he should submit to having his own prints taken. The author remembers a case in which a museum in a provincial town had been broken into and a police inspector had discovered a well-defined thumbprint on a neolithic axe blade of polished stone. His thumbprints were taken, and it was found that the impression on the stone axe was identical with that of his right thumb. He went back to report the result to his chief constable, a little crestfallen.

The Fingerprint Registry established at Scotland Yard was made available for all police forces, and in the first year the identifications of old criminals were nearly four times as many as those made under the anthropometric system. By 1934 little less than 400,000 identifications had been made. In the early days of the system habitual criminals were indignant. "Let a man come forward like a man and say that he recognizes me. I've nothing to say against that, but this fingerprint business behind a fellow's back, it's mean and un-English, that's what I say," was the comment of an habitual criminal to the author when he was told that he would be charged with being an habitual criminal. Not only is the system sure, but it is swift. When a criminal is arrested in London at night, his fingerprints and his criminal history are often ready for the magistrate next morning.

In England and Wales it has been doubted whether the police have power to compel a person to submit to the taking of his fingerprints before he is committed to prison. In

June 1933, however, the Judiciary Appeal Court of Scotland decided that the police were vested with a common-law right to take the prints of a person in custody without his consent if it was in the interests of justice. This common-sense view may ultimately be adopted by the English courts.

The discovery of a fingerprint on the scene of a crime or on some object connected with it is not conclusive proof of guilt. In some cases there may be an innocent explanation, or the Court may give the prisoner the benefit of the doubt and acquit him, but that does not imply that fingerprint identification is fallible. In such cases ill-informed newspapers proclaim that, after all, fingerprints are not infallible. They are not—but only in the sense that the chances of two persons having identical fingerprints are about one in 64,000 millions. This was proved by the researches of Sir Francis Galton. Both the English and Scottish Courts of Criminal Appeal have accepted the evidence of a single fingerprint, unsupported by other evidence. The risk they have taken is not great.

The Fingerprint Registry now contains a little over half a million prints. The number is growing, although it is constantly being cleared of dead men's prints, and of those of still living men who are considered unlikely again to get into trouble. The number of prints in the registries of New York and of Pretoria, which are not confined to persons convicted of serious offences, is very much larger than the number in the registry at Scotland Yard. When such vast numbers have to be dealt with, the Henry system has to be modified, and searches cannot be made with the speed and accuracy of Scotland Yard.

In 1930 Mr. Battley, the head of the Criminal Record Office, made a remarkable extension of the fingerprint system by inventing a system of classifying and filing single fingerprints. All other systems of classification are based on formulæ drawn from the patterns of the ten digits in combination and are therefore of little help where the problem is to identify the print of a single finger. Battley's system is based on points which are found in all finger impressions, and it is claimed that any finger mark found on the scene of a crime can be identified with any recorded print of the same finger. Hundreds of single-print identifications are made at Scotland Yard every year. The work of identifying prints found on the scene of a crime and sent to Scotland Yard from all parts of the country is harassing, because accidental prints are very often blurred. They run into thousands in the course of a year.

Identification by description is common enough, and here we come to a subsidiary register, the Crime Index. It is based upon the well-known habit of criminals to repeat the method of a crime that has already been successful: for example, a burglar enters a house by climbing a water pipe and escapes detection; he will repeat that particular method of housebreaking. The names, crimes, methods, and descriptions of criminals are entered upon cards under hundreds of classified heads and subheads. A person who has been victimized or robbed can be taken to the Crime Index room, where he describes the methods employed to rob him. He is then invited to inspect vast photograph albums in which the photographs of criminals who have used this particular method are brought together. The photographs, of course, are fallible for identification purposes, but often they furnish a good starting point. The Crime Index has proved particularly useful in cases of fraud, for all such cases are classified according to the class of persons defrauded and the character assumed by the criminal. Each of these classifications has numerous subdivisions. It is not so easy to subdivide burglars and housebreakers, but here a distinction can be made by the method of entry, the way of forcing the lock of a door or the catch of a window or shutter, the kind of food and drink taken by the intruder, and the method used for silencing the dog. When investigating a burglary detectives are specially trained to look for the points that would be useful for tracing the burglar in the Crime Index.

This index, like the Fingerprint Registry, is national in its scope. It is constantly used by the provincial police and in international and overseas cases. It includes about half a million criminals, but the various systems of classification simplify the task of searching for a particular individual.

Subsidiary to the Crime Index is the Property Index of identifiable articles which have been stolen or lost. The Property Index not only makes it possible to restore the property to its owner, but also to secure the conviction of the thief.

Certain publications intended for the Metropolitan Police, or for all forces, are issued by the C.R.O. First come the "informations" containing particulars of crimes committed, persons wanted or arrested, property stolen. The informations are circulated twice a day to all the London police stations and are read to the police when they parade for duty. There is also a pawnbrokers' list, containing a description of articles lost or stolen which have some identifying mark. This is distributed daily to every pawnbroker and dealer throughout London.

The oldest and most important of the police publications is the *Police Gazette*. It became a weekly newspaper a year before the establishment of the Metropolitan Police, under the title of the *Police Gazette*. Ten years later it became the principal medium for the circulation of criminal information. Actually the chief clerk at Bow Street was its editor until 1883, when it was transferred to Scotland Yard. It continued to be issued weekly until 1914, when it developed into a daily newspaper with stop-press news, which makes it possible to circulate information within an hour or two of reaching Scotland Yard.

Formerly it was on sale to the public, but its circulation is now confined to the police of Great Britain, and certain imperial and foreign forces without charge. It contains particulars with photographs of persons who are wanted by the police and also of those who are awaiting trial, in case they may be wanted elsewhere for other offences. It contains also the results of cases tried in the courts, special warning notices about criminals, particulars of property stolen and recovered, and a daily list of stolen motorcars and motorcycles. This last list is sent to all licensing authorities. There are five special supplements to the *Gazette* which are to all intents separate publications. Of these the most important is the "Illustrated Circular," now called "Supplement A," which appears once a fortnight, giving the portraits, descriptions, methods, and particulars of expert and travelling criminals liberated from prison—in fact, all the details which would enable a provincial police force to compile a miniature Crime Index of its own.

A second fortnightly supplement contains the same kind of information about criminals of the second grade—e.g., petty thieves, persons guilty of minor assaults, etc. The remaining three supplements are issued weekly; they deal with convicts on licence or on police supervision who have failed to report and with aliens and deserters from the navy and army.

Convict supervision is less important than it used to be because of the progressive fall in the last few years in the number of persons sentenced to penal servitude or to supervision by the police, but there are still enough of these people to make the check upon them an important part of the prevention of crime. When a convict fails to make his monthly report or is found to be missing from his registered address, he becomes an object of suspicion, and in most cases it is found that he is wanted for a crime under investigation, or that the reason for his modesty in failing to report is that he has committed some other crime.

Arrangements are made in the C.R.O. for the monthly reports of discharged convicts and the enforcement of the other restrictions to which convicts on licence are subject, but it must not be supposed from this that there is hostility between the ex-convict and the officers of the C.R.O., who do their best to befriend and if possible to reclaim their charges. They work in co-operation with the discharged prisoners' aid associations and are very careful to avoid any act which may prevent a man from earning an honest living, and so, when a convict tries to excuse a relapse into crime by saying that a police officer divulged to an employer the fact that his employee had been in prison, he is lying.

Everything is done to avoid betraying the past of a criminal who has started a new life in a district where he is unknown, but if a man chooses to return to a neighbourhood where everyone knows his history, it is of course almost impossible to conceal the fact that he is reporting to the police. The police do not know the criminal as the warders of convict prisons know him, and probably his good points are less well known to the officers of the C.R.O. than his bad, but it is quite a mistake to think that they hound down discharged convicts and make no effort to rehabilitate them.

In his interesting book, *Ten Thousand Public Enemies,* Mr. Courtney Ryley Cooper draws a comparison between Scotland Yard and the Division of Investigation under Mr. J. Edgar Hoover at Washington, somewhat to the disadvantage of Scotland Yard. It seems a pity that in his advocacy of the American organization he should not have got his facts right. It is true that help from Scotland Yard is not called in more than on an average of five times a year, but that is not due to jealousy on the part of the British provincial forces, but to the fact that their own detective forces have been vastly improved during recent years, and that Scotland Yard is the guardian of the only general crime index in the country upon which the success of the provincial detectives largely depends. It is not true that "the area covered by Scotland Yard lies within the city limits of London." The Special Branch of about 150 men has always operated all over the country, though its activities do not extend to ordinary crime. Moreover, the Criminal Record Office with its various publications—the daily *Police Gazette,* with its various supplements which are circulated to all forces—is a national institution, almost daily consulted by provincial forces. So far from jealousy preventing co-operation between the provincial forces and Scotland Yard, there is a perfect understanding between them which enables them all to work for the common good. The provincial forces would be the first to cry out if the activities of Scotland Yard were confined to London as Mr. Cooper states.

It is, of course, perfectly true that the crime problem in America is twentyfold more difficult to solve than it is in England, where lawbreakers commit their depredations unarmed and where the prisons have been under the control of the central government since 1877, but no good object can be served by misrepresenting the facts in order to enhance the undoubted efficiency, within its limits, of Mr. Hoover's organization.

THE C.I.D. IN WARTIME

It was by accident that my room at Scotland Yard became the centre for investigating charges of spying and of enemy activity during the Great War. The Admiralty, the War Office, the Air Force, and the Ministry of Munitions had each their own anti-espionage sections, but they lacked machinery for dealing with suspects—men to arrest them, cells in which to keep them, and trained staffs to prepare the prosecutions for the High Court: for these they had to come to Scotland Yard, and as the Admiralty and the War Office were equally interested in bringing spies to justice, it was arranged that the preliminary investigations should be conducted in my room and that the task of conducting the inquiry should fall to me. So, day after day I sat with a naval officer on my right and a military officer on my left questioning suspects about papers discovered on his person or in his baggage, with a stenographer recording question and answer. The police officers present all belonged to the Special Branch.

The British Empire is far-flung, and the Germans were busy trying to foment rebellions in India, Ireland, Egypt, South Africa, Australia, and the West Indies. In April 1916 they did succeed in bringing about a rising in Dublin which was quickly suppressed, but that was all. As for the spies they sent to England, they could scarcely have been worse chosen. This was due to the fact that two separate German spy organizations were competing with one another —the one military and the other naval. Both were amply supplied with money, and both were singularly incompetent. They sent musicians, dancers, music-hall actors, and commercial travellers who at the best could report only gossip picked up from fellow travellers on the railways, but nothing of value either to the naval or the military authorities.

I was destined to learn a good deal about the German intellectual limitations during those four crowded years. About the middle of 1915 we found that an active band of Indian revolutionaries were working with the Germans in Berlin and were maturing a plot for the simultaneous assassination of the leading men in the Allied countries. The King of Italy, Lord Grey, Lord Kitchener, M. Poincaré, and Signor Viviani were some of the persons mentioned. The bombs that were to be thrown at them had been manufactured in Italy and tested at the military testing ground near Berlin. At the English end of the conspiracy were certain British Indians: an Englishwoman was privy to their plans, and a Swiss girl acted as messenger between Switzerland and the English group. The case was difficult because the real culprit, Chattopadhya, lived in Berlin and was careful never to set foot on the soil of any of the Allied countries. When the evidence was complete, every member of the conspiracy who was in British jurisdiction was interned and kept in internment until the Armistice.

In the middle of October 1915 fresh evidence of the German-Indian conspiracy reached us. An Indian committee had been established in Berlin early in the war. Har Dayal, who had been conducting the *Ghadr* (Mutiny) vernacular newspaper in California, came over to Switzerland and went on to Berlin. The Germans took little notice of him at first, but later the Indians persuaded them to concert measures for starting a revolution in India under a German president. They had a press bureau and a working scheme for corrupting the loyalty of Indian prisoners of war. Yet, though tons of paper and lakes of ink were consumed, no headway was being made until March 1915, when an Indian landowner, named Pertabr, conceived the plan of going over to the Germans in the character of an Indian prince.

He had some slight claim to this title, since he was the son of the deposed ruler of a small Indian state. He landed in Marseilles and arrived in Switzerland, where Har Dayal took him to see the German consul. It does not take much to deceive a German official about Oriental matters. Pertabr was clad in native robes and was aloof and condescending: in fact, his haughty demeanour was exactly what the German consul would have expected from an Indian rajah. When pressed to enter the Fatherland, Pertabr declined to move without a promise that the Kaiser would receive him in person. After several journeys to and from Berlin, the audience with the Kaiser was arranged. It was characteristic that the German consul begged Pertabr to say a good word for him to the All Highest when he should enter the Presence.

Pertabr had daydreams of himself mounted on a fiery white steed at the head of conquering bands as the new liberator of India; of receiving the homage of native princes at Delhi. He may have imbued the Kaiser with some of these ideas, though one cannot imagine the imperial mind dreaming of Oriental conquest in which any other man but himself should prance on a white horse. Nevertheless, a mission did start for Kabul headed by "Prince" Pertabr, three German officers, and several released Indian prisoners of war. They passed through Constantinople during the first week in September, and then they disappeared into space. Later it was learned that they got no farther than Afghanistan and that they were wandering as homeless outcasts in the wilds of central Asia.

The headquarters of the Indian conspirators who were being manipulated by the Germans in America were at Berkeley, California. It was there that the *Ghadr* was being printed in the vernacular and arrangements were being made for shipping arms to India at German expense. It chanced that Mr. Nathan, a very able police official, had come over from India to assist us in dealing with the Indian conspiracy. There seemed to be no better way of getting the California police to take action as neutrals than to send him over to explain matters. When at last the police did act, they acted to some purpose. The two Indian leaders were arrested and charged with a breach of the neutrality laws. At the trial one of the accused, convinced—from the intimate knowledge of his secret activities disclosed by the prosecution—that his companion had turned informer, slipped a pistol from his pocket and shot him dead in open court. The deputy sheriff whipped an automatic from his pocket, and from his elevated place at the back of the court, aiming above and between the intervening heads, shot the murderer dead. And so, in less than ten seconds the sentence which the judge was about to pronounce was more than executed.

In the dreary procession of spies who passed through my room—some of them on their way to execution, others to internment until the end of the war—I learned certain psychological facts that I did not know before, facts that probably were known instinctively by native races for many centuries. The first was that if you want to get the truth out of a man you must have his eyes at a lower level than your own. There was in my room a leather armchair which had seen much service and, having lost a castor, had suffered the partial amputation of the other three legs to bring them to the same length. Consequently the seat was a bare twelve inches from the floor. It was on this seat that every suspect was required to perch when submitting himself to be questioned. Very soon we noticed that whenever an embarrassing question was put to him the suspect would try to raise himself by his elbows resting on the arms of his chair. A legal colleague who had noted the same thing, said, "I believe that it's the chair, B. T. Go and sit in it while I question you." Under his cross-examination I felt the instinct to raise myself to his level. If this be true, as I believe that it is, we go to work the wrong way in our criminal courts when we require witnesses to mount an elevated stand whence they look down upon their questioner. In native communities the chief stands erect when he questions an inferior, and the man cowers on the ground at his feet.

I learned also how very easy it was to "pull the legs" of

German intelligence officers. Early in 1915 it was discovered that a foreigner who could write fluently in English was sending regular communications written in secret ink to one of the spy-receiving offices in Holland. These letters were posted from various London post offices, and though nothing of real importance was disclosed, the writter had sufficient education at any moment to stumble upon information which might be of real value to the enemy. He was true to the spy type, always demanding money, and it was hoped that a remittance from Holland would disclose his identity, but in the end he was unmasked in quite a different way. A letter was stopped by the postal censor which disclosed secret writing. It was not written in the usual hand: the secret writing said only that "C" had gone to Newcastle and that the writer was sending the communication "from 201" instead. The postmark was Deptford, in the East End of London; "201" might or might not be the number of a house. We rang up Deptford police station and asked for a list of the streets in their division that ran to "201" houses. There was only one—Deptford High Street—and the occupant of that house had a German name—"Peter Hahn, Baker and Confectioner." No one was more surprised than the stout little baker when a taxi deposited a number of police officers at his door. He proved to be a British subject who had been resident in Deptford for several years. While he was being put into the cab, a search of his premises was made, and in a back room the police found a complete outfit for secret writing neatly stowed away in a cardboard box.

When seated in the low armchair, Hahn refused to answer any questions, but patient inquiry among his neighbours produced a witness who remembered that a tall Russian gentleman had visited Hahn at frequent intervals; that his name was believed to be Müller and his address a boarding house in Bloomsbury. The register of every boarding house was searched, and within a few hours the name of Müller was found. The landlady described him as a Russian and said that he had lately gone to Newcastle to visit friends. Within a few hours he was found in that city, arrested, and brought to London. He proved to be a tall, spare, worried-looking person. He had never seen Hahn; had never been in Germany and could not even speak the German language. For some time he stuck to the story that he was a Russian, but an inquiry into his past showed that he was one of those cosmopolitan, roving Germans who are by turn hotel keepers, commercial travellers, and motorcar agents. He spoke English with scarcely any trace of a foreign accent. He had gone through the usual spy routine of making love to impressionable young women and of winning male acquaintances by a promise of partnership in profitable speculations. He was an accomplished linguist and spoke no less than six languages. As Hahn was a British subject, the two were tried together at the Old Bailey in May 1915. Both were found guilty. Müller was sentenced to death; Hahn to seven years' penal servitude on the ground that he had acted under Müller's influence.

On June 22 Müller was transferred to the Tower of London. He was highly strung, and he broke down on the night before his execution, but on the following morning he pulled himself together and insisted on passing gravely down the rank of the firing party and shaking hands with each man.

Now follows the sequel. The Germans had not heard of his death, for letters containing remittances continued to arrive from his employers in Holland.

One morning the very astute military officer who had been handling the Müller case came to see me, bringing a dispatch case containing the Müller letters together with another letter in the selfsame handwriting recounting in German absurd fables about the war.

"Surely Müller never wrote this?" I asked.

"No, he didn't, but we have in our branch a young officer with a genius for imitating handwriting. It would be a shame to draw pay from the Germans and give them nothing in return for their money, and we have this advantage over Müller—that we can supply them with news really worth reading. We have Müller's secret ink and a good supply of

Standing left to right: Elias Bower, Alfred Ward, Thomas Divall, Frederick Porter Wensley, Charles Collins.

Sitting: Albert Lawrence, John McCarthy, Frank Froest, Henry Collins, Frederick Thomas.

At the time this photograph was taken Froest was superintendent and the remaining nine were Chief Inspectors. Ward was killed during an air raid in 1916.

his notepaper and envelopes. All we have to do is to badger them for more money, and then they will swallow everything we tell them."

"We can try it," I said; "but I'm sure that they will detect the fraud."

But I was wrong. For three whole months the false Müller continued to feed the German intelligence service with incredible information about mythical engines of war, about troop movements and projected attacks on the western front which caused the Germans to move divisions to meet them, and for three whole months they continued to pay us handsomely for the bogus information, until we had accumulated twelve hundred pounds with which a car was purchased for the use of the section which was gratefully christened Müller. After three months there came a day when the remittances stopped. We learned afterwards that the German "intelligence" had seen Müller's sister, who told them that her brother had been dead for many weeks— she could not tell them how many. And so we drew a mental picture of half a dozen German naval and military officers poring over those admirable forgeries in the hope of establishing the precise date when the real Müller was supplanted by the false one and how much money had been wantonly thrown away. I suppose that some poor devil lost his job over the business, which was unfair, since those forgeries would have deceived even the elect.

With a single exception the women spies engaged by the Germans were a sorry crew. What military information of value the Germans could have expected to get from dancers or housekeepers (the kind of women they employed), it is difficult to understand. One of their spies, Madame Popovitch, the Serbian, had to be certified as insane and removed to an asylum—yet she was one of their paid spies! The exception was Margaret Gertrud Zeller, better known as Matahari (Eye of the Morning). So much journalistic nonsense has been written about this woman that a dispassionate account of her may not be without interest. Her father was a Dutchman who, while in the Dutch East Indies, married a Javanese woman whom he brought home with him to Holland together with her little daughter, "Matahari." The girl became known as an exponent of a form of voluptuous Oriental dancing which was new to Europe in the late eighties. At the age of twenty she married a Dutch naval officer of Scottish extraction named Macleod, who afterwards divorced her. She was well known in Paris, and until the outbreak of war she was earning considerable sums of money by her professional engagements.

In July 1915 she was fulfilling a dancing engagement in Madrid when information reached us that she was consorting with members of the German secret service and might be expected before long to be making her way to Germany via Holland. The forecast was correct. Early in 1916 the steamer taking her to Holland put into Falmouth in accordance with the rule prescribed for all ships on their way to Holland or one of the Scandinavian countries. She was brought ashore, together with her very large professional wardrobe, and escorted to London.

I confess that I was expecting to receive a lady who would bring the whole battery of her charms to bear upon the officers who were to question her, but there walked into the room a tall, slender woman of middle age, severely practical, ready to answer any question with a kind of reserved courtesy. She seemed to feel so sure of herself and of her innocence that all that remained in her was a desire to help us. She was ready with an answer to every question, and of all the people that I examined during the course of the war she was the "quickest on the uptake." If I quoted to her the name of some person in Spain with whom it was compromising to be seen in conversation, she seemed astounded. He a suspect? Surely we must be mistaken.

"I see how it is," she said at last, "you suspect me. Can I speak to you alone?" The room was cleared of all but one officer and myself. She looked at him interrogatively. "I said *alone.*"

"Yes," I replied, "but this officer and I may be regarded as one person."

"Very well," she said, "then I am going to make a confession to you. I am a spy—not, as you think, for the Germans, but for the French."

At the time we did not believe her, but we were to discover a little later that it was true. She talked fluently about her adventures in the course of her work: we treated her narrative as highly talented fiction. At any rate she convinced us that she had been working for the enemy, but that any messages that she might be carrying had been committed to memory. On the other hand she had had no intention of landing on British soil, and with no evidence to support our view we had no excuse for detaining her in England. And so, at the end of our second interview with her I said to her, "Madame,"—she spoke no English— "we are going to send you back to Spain, and if you will take the advice of a man much older than yourself, you will give up what you have been doing." She replied, "Monsieur, I thank you from my heart. I shall never forget your advice. What I have been doing I will do no more. You may trust me implicitly." And within a month of her return to Spain she was at it again. She was, in fact, what the French call an *agent double*—a spy working for both sides.

This time she was captured on the French side of the frontier and, I was told at the time, with compromising papers upon her. I should have thought that so astute a lady would have avoided documents at all hazards. They carried her to Paris, put her on her trial, and on July 25, 1916, condemned her to death, but there was as usual in France a long delay, and it was not until October 15 that she was taken from St. Lazare prison to Vincennes for execution. A French officer who was present described to me what happened. She was awakened at 5 A.M., and she dressed herself in a dark dress trimmed with fur, with a large felt hat and lavender kid gloves. With an escort of two French soldiers, her lawyer, and a priest, she was driven to the execution ground. When she came in sight of the soldiers she gently put aside the ministration of the priest and waved a salute to them. She refused to be blindfolded and was in the act of smiling on the firing party when the volley sent her pagan spirit on its journey.

To describe Matahari as a miracle of grace and beauty, as so many journalists have done, is an abuse of language. When I saw her she was past forty, and she had led a strenuous life. The one thing graceful about her was her walk and the carriage of her head, but she possessed a quality far more attractive than ephemeral beauty—a quick and lively intelligence, and in this she transcended all the other women who were brought into my room during the war.

PART IV

THE C.I.D. TODAY

CHAPTER XX

The Forged Treasury Notes

THREE MONTHS AFTER THE DECLARATION OF WAR Eng-land was threatened with a creeping paralysis which, in its possible effect upon morale, was more deadly than the air raids. Every Englishman had been reared upon a gold currency, and he was to have gold in his pockets no more. He had accepted the first Treasury note rather unwillingly, as one of the necessities of war, and was just becoming accustomed to it, when I learned from the Treasury that its notes were being forged. The Treasury note of those early days was a plain invitation to the forger. It was printed on paper little better than the best typewriting paper, with the facsimile signature of Sir John Bradbury (hence its early nickname, "Bradbury"), and there was nothing in the body of the paper to defeat the forger except the watermark: "ONE POUND." They brought me specimens to see and compare with genuine notes; the differences between them were so slight that most people would have accepted the counterfeit without question.

"It's a very serious matter," said the Treasury official. "The forgeries that have already come in exceed £10,000, and if public confidence in our notes becomes shaken, the country will be in the soup. Oh, yes; I admit that the note is easy to forge. We are now at work upon a new one, and we shall recall all these, but it takes time, and in the meantime the forger must be caught."

237

It did not take Scotland Yard long to find out who was issuing the spurious notes. The method was simple enough. At five o'clock every Friday, a certain ex-convict, who chose to call himself "Elliot," arrived at a rendezvous in Jermyn Street with bulging pockets. No one knew whence he came, but not a few were ready to deal with him on terms that covered the risk. They bought his pound notes at half their face value; each chose his own street—preferably a mean street of little shops—and worked it at dusk. He would go in and buy a box of matches or a cake of soap, take his change in silver, until the last note in his bundle was disposed of, and then he would await Elliot's reappearance on the following Friday. We could have arrested Elliot and the smaller fry at any moment, but our quarry was the skilled printer who could fake a watermark.

Why, it may be asked, did we not shadow Elliot and let him lead us to the printer? In the detective stories, shadowing is most ingeniously done, but in real life it will be found that to shadow a gentleman of Elliot's experience defeats its object at the outset. Elliot knew all the tricks of the trade of shadowing—the trick of doubling, of playing off taxis, of "shaking free" in buses, subways, and tubes. He took no chances and made no confidants. All that we knew was that on Friday evenings he arrived with his merchandise and afterwards disappeared into space; and that somewhere among the eight million people in London was an artist who worked hard at his calling every Thursday in the week.

There was nothing for it but to embark in the trade ourselves, not, of course, by circulating counterfeit notes, but by appearing to do so. One of our men presented himself as a purchaser, and since he was a foreigner, Elliot was content to deal with him, taking the precaution to watch his proceedings. That was how the expense came in. Our man had furtively to substitute genuine notes for the counterfeits before he "worked" the street. Knowing that Elliot was watching him, he loaded himself with cakes of cheap soap, and, having accomplished his mission at the expense of the Treasury, he had to adopt Elliot's own tactics and shake him off before he could come to report progress to his employers. These barren and costly manœuvres had to be conducted for weeks until Elliot's confidence had been gained.

Meanwhile the forgeries had risen to over £60,000; we had spent £1,500 in good money, and we seemed no nearer the printer.

There came a Friday evening when the little upper room in Jermyn Street was crowded with gamblers, most of them customers of Elliot, and among them was our man who had been far too wary ever to ask Elliot questions. His eyes and ears were open, but never his mouth. The roulette board was in full play; men were staking their money in an atmosphere of tobacco smoke thick enough to cut with a knife when a thin-faced young man entered the room, watched the play for a few minutes, and staked nineteen shillings and sixpence. My man observed that his fingers were stained with printer's ink. He staked a second and third sum and lost them all. The amounts suggested that he had been dealing in his own wares, and yet not a sign of recognition had passed between him and Elliot. After his last stake he left the room in disgust.

"I remember that young fellow," said our man, casually. "He used to be a clerk in that betting office of yours."

"Never!" said Elliot shortly.

"Oh, yes, he was. I never forget a face and I remember his name now. It was Dixon."

"Will you bet on it?"

Our man put up his money.

"He's a printer, and his name's Williams. So pay up."

Our man concealed his triumph and paid. There was chastened rejoicing at Scotland Yard that night. If we could but find out where Williams, a printer, got his livelihood, our labours might be crowned. The usual message over the wires went out to every station in the Metropolis, and presently there came a reply from north London that on a wooden stable gate in a quiet back street the half-obliterated words "Williams—Printer" could still be deciphered.

The very next day, a Sunday, the long vigil began. The widow who let lodgings opposite that stable door must have been puzzled by the habits of her new lodger—a grey-haired man who received quite a number of male visitors in the afternoons—visitors who spent their time with their eyes glued to the street through the lace curtains. On the next Friday afternoon he had more visitors than usual, but they made no noise; they just sat watching the street down which nothing ever seemed to pass. Darkness fell, and things began to happen. First, the footfall of a pedestrian who stopped at the stable gate and kicked it. The gate opened and shut behind him. Immediately the grey-haired man and all his visitors trooped noiselessly into the street and ranged themselves on either side of the stable gate. Suddenly the gate opened and a man came out.

There was noise enough then to bring out every householder. In the middle of the roadway the man was fighting with the quiet lodgers, howling like a wild beast and spouting Treasury notes from his pockets like a centrifugal machine, until the roadway was carpeted. At last, when his features had been so modified as to defy recognition, he declared himself satisfied and said that he would go quietly. The detectives—for that is what they were—vaulted the gate and ran for the stable door. This was opened by the young man who had tempted fortune at the gaming table. Seeing the police, he fell limp on the floor in a faint. The place was crammed with machinery. Notes still damp were lying on the press. You had only to turn the handle to forge notes until your arms tired. This expert printer and his father had been making a fine art of forgery for years. When the author took the Chancellor of the Exchequer and Sir John Bradbury to the stable next morning, while Sir John fed in the paper, Mr. McKenna turned the handle. It was the first instance in history, I believe, that the British Chancellor had forged the currency, but it is fair to add that he was careful to write "FORGED" across each of his productions before he put them in his pocket.

THE CASE OF MADAME GERARD

As has been said more than once in this little history, the secret of success in criminal investigation lies in teamwork —a matter so well understood in the C.I.D. of Scotland Yard that it seldom fails even in the most difficult cases. "Teamwork" means that no individual detective who has come across a clue in an important case thinks of keeping it to himself and winning credit for his acumen. He passes it on to his official superior to form perhaps a fresh starting point in the investigation. The detective who solves mysteries in the manner of Sherlock Holmes exists, fortunately, only in the pages of fiction, or in the mind of the brilliant young journalist who keeps the thickheaded detective from making mistakes.

I am indebted to former Chief Constable Frederick Wensley for the details of the murder of Emilienne Gerard, whose torso was found on November 2, 1917. I remember the circumstances very well. Mr. Wensley considers it not only one of his most successful cases, but a conspicuous instance of the value of teamwork.

The case opened by the discovery, by a road sweeper, on Friday, November 2, of a parcel wrapped in sacking, which appeared to have been dropped over the railings in Regent Square, Bloomsbury. When the parcel was opened, the body of a woman without head, hands, or legs, was found in it; she had been wearing expensive underclothing trimmed with lace and blue ribbon. A sheet was wrapped round the body, and on a piece of torn wrapping paper the words "Blodie Belgium" had been roughly scribbled. The Square was searched; the legs were found in a paper parcel a short distance away. A medical examination showed that the woman must have been killed not earlier than two days before and that the mutilation of the body showed some anatomical skill.

The case went automatically to Divisional Detective-Inspector John Ashley of the E Division, in which Regent Square lay. We felt from the beginning that it was going to be a case of extraordinary difficulty, since in wartime London was packed with foreign refugees.

Fortunately, there was one, but only one, clue—a laundry mark, "114," worked in red cotton on a corner of the sheet. Inquiries were at once instituted among the laundries of the locality. Within forty-eight hours it was known that the sheet came from a house in Munster Square, Regent's Park. There it was learned that a Frenchwoman named Gerard had been absent from her rooms since a destructive German air raid on the night of October 31. Her husband was a chef who had been in England but was then serving in the French army.

There was nothing to show where the murder had taken place. The woman might have been killed in London or in the country, and therefore it became necessary to put the case into the hands of the senior detective chief inspector who could relieve the hard-pressed divisional detective-inspector of the E Division. Mr. Wensley went to Bow Street, where he found that valuable work had been done. It was obvious that the news that he was to take a hand in the inquiry was welcome.

In tracing the friends and associates of Madame Gerard it was found that at one time she had acted as housekeeper to a butcher named Louis Voisin, who was then living with a woman named Berthe Roche. Officers were sent to find them, and they were invited to come to Bow Street to make statements. They could not complain of this, because a number of other foreigners had been sent for in connection with the case. Thus far there was nothing to indicate even that the headless body was that of Madame Gerard—nothing except the telltale sheet which had been traced as belonging to her. Even if the body was that of Madame Gerard, there was nothing to connect her with Voisin except some evidence to show that Voisin and she had been on intimate terms. Whether he had murdered her or not, it was probable that he knew something about her.

There had been gossip among Voisin's neighbours, who had said that high voices of women had been heard in his room during the night. This might have been induced by the excitement of the air raid, but in some degree it provided a reason for questioning Berthe Roche.

When the two arrived at Bow Street, some twenty to thirty people were waiting to be interviewed. Voisin was taken first. He was a short, thickset man with heavy jaws and powerful frame; he faced Mr. Wensley aggressively. The interview was conducted in broken English, but Mr. Wensley had with him Detective-Sergeant Read, who spoke French fluently.

Voisin's line was entire ignorance. He had known Madame Gerard for about eighteen months; she had acted for some time as his housekeeper. On October 3 he met her with a young French girl named Marguerite, with whom she was going to France on a visit to her husband. She had asked him (Voisin) to visit her room for letters and to feed the cat, and he had done so.

It was a plausible statement. Voisin knew that the police had not yet proved the body to be that of Madame Gerard and that it would not be a simple task to prove that she had not gone to the war area and disappeared. At a later date the girl "Marguerite" was traced; she was brought back from France and she was prepared to swear that she had crossed to France alone.

In the course of his statement Voisin referred, quite unnecessarily, as it seemed at the time, to having killed a calf and to bringing home the head. This was intended to account for bloodstains that were afterwards found in his kitchen.

It will surprise foreign readers to hear that Wensley had now to take a serious responsibility that might vitiate the entire case for the prosecution, under what are known as the "Judges' Rules," which preclude the questioning of prisoners whom the police are about to charge with a serious offence. During the war these rules were held to be in abeyance in spy cases, but this was not an espionage case, and the rules still held good.

It will be remembered that on a torn paper wrapping on

the parcel containing the woman's trunk were the words "Blodie Belgium." The question was whether Voisin could be asked to write these words. The object of the Judges' Rules had been to prevent anything in the nature of what is popularly known as "the third degree," but they are a handicap to the police in England which does not exist in the United States, France or any European country. But the risk had to be taken. Voisin and Roche were detained for the night, and on Sunday morning, November 4, after a desultory conversation, Voisin was asked through the interpreter whether he would have any objection to writing the words "Bloody Belgium." "Not at all," he said. A paper and pencil were handed to him, and laboriously, for he was an illiterate man, he traced the two words. He wrote the words in the same misspelling—"Blodie Belgium"—but in characters much smaller than in the original. Wensley invited him to try again. He wrote the words five times, and in the fifth writing the words bore a perfect resemblance to the words on the wrapping paper. Wensley was then sure of his man.

Among the things found on Voisin when he was searched was a key which fitted the door of a cellar at 101 Charlotte Street which he rented. This cellar was searched by Chief Inspector Collins (then a detective-sergeant). In a cask of sawdust he found the head and hands of the murdered woman. They were examined by Sir Bernard Spilsbury, who found that she had been struck several times on the head with a blunt instrument. Bruises on her right hand showed how she had tried to shield her head. There were blood-stains all over Voisin's kitchen, especially on the inside of the door, which was taken from its hinges and produced in court at the trial. The stains were all of human blood and could not be explained away. When they learned that they were both to be charged with murder, the woman Roche was thunderstruck. She thought that her lover had betrayed her, and she broke into a torrent of abusive French. The man shrugged his shoulders and muttered, "It is unfortunate" as he was taken away.

Sir Bernard Spilsbury testified that the dead woman had

struggled hard for her life. A bloodstained towel was found, with one of her earrings in it. It was a fair inference that it had been held over her head to stifle her screams. Gradually the final scene was reconstructed. Madame Gerard had been Voisin's mistress. Whether or not she knew that Berthe Roche had supplanted her, it was clear that she had never met her. Wensley was inclined to think that she did not know of her existence. Shortly after 11 P.M. on October 31 an air-raid warning was given; Mrs. Gerard, like hundreds of others, left her rooms and sought safety in one of the tube stations. It was the worst air raid London had experienced, and when the refugees were turned out of the station after the "All Clear" signal had been given, the panic-stricken woman sought refuge in her lover's room in the basement of 101 Charlotte Street. There she found Berthe Roche sitting in a lighted room with her nerves all on edge. Probably the heavy-witted Voisin was snoring in his bed, and the two hysterical women had to face one another and demand explanations. A violent quarrel was inevitable. Berthe Roche, half mad with excitement, sprang upon her rival like a wild cat with the first weapon that came to hand, and Voisin, roused by the noise of the quarrel, seized Madame Gerard and stifled her screams with the towel, while the woman Roche continued to strike at her face and head. Then the butcher's instinct seized Voisin, and he finished the job.

This was Wensley's reconstruction of the crime, based upon the fact that a number of the earlier blows had been struck by a person of far less physical strength than Voisin's. During the remainder of that tragic night the pair must have sat up discussing what was to be done with the body. Voisin, with his professional skill as a butcher, must have been the first to suggest dismemberment, and he must also have charged himself with the disposal of the body. Wensley was inclined to think that they were perplexed about the disposal of the head and hands, and that they had come to no decision about this when they were summoned to face the police at Bow Street. They had, however, agreed upon taking the initial steps of a clumsy expedient to make it appear that Madame Gerard had been murdered in her own room, of which Voisin had a key. He called on her landlord and told him that she would be away for a fortnight or so; that she was expecting to receive a sack of potatoes, and would he see that it was put into her room when it arrived? It may have been on the occasion of this visit that Voisin purposely made the bloodstains that were found there, and that he took away the sheet in which the headless body was to be wrapped. It was a very clumsy story even for the thick-witted Voisin to have thought of, because when the contents of the supposed sack of potatoes came to be examined, the landlord must inevitably have remembered his conversation with Voisin and have communicated it to the police. The words "Blodie Belgium" also, as a device to lead the police off on a false scent, were futile.

A day or two later Voisin tried to adapt this story to fit in with some of the discoveries that he felt sure the police must have made. He said, "I went to Madame Gerard's place last Thursday at eleven in the morning. When I arrived the door was shut but not locked. The floor and carpet were full of blood. The head and hands were wrapped up in a flannel jacket which is at my place now. They were on the kitchen table. That is all I can say. The rest of the body was not there. I was so astonished at such an affair that I did not know what to do. I go to Madame Gerard's every day. I remained five minutes stupefied. I thought that a trap had been laid for me. I commenced to clean up the blood, and my clothes became stained with it. . . . I then went back to my house, had lunch, and later returned to Madame Gerard's rooms and took the packet to my place. I kept thinking this was a trap. I had no intention to do any harm to Madame Gerard. Why should I kill her? I didn't want any money. Madame Gerard owes me nothing, and I owe her nothing" (actually he owed her £50). "I cannot see why I should do such a thing as that to Madame Gerard. I wanted to see Monsieur Gerard because I knew Madame Gerard was being mixed up with bad associates and had taken people to her flat. I knew that she had taken somebody there that night, and there are letters to show that she had been meeting men."

We must give this ruffian one mark to his credit. At the same interview he tried to exonerate his paramour. "She is not concerned in this crime at all," he said; and when both were committed for trial, he said, "Madame Roche is entirely innocent. All that was found was taken from Madame Gerard's to my home."

There was some legal argument as to whether the circumstances under which Voisin had consented to write the words "Blodie Belgium" invalidated that part of the evidence for the prosecution. The judge, Mr. Justice Darling, held that it was admissible. "It was quite proper," he said, "for the police to ascertain who was the person who wrote 'Blodie Belgium.' It would be greatly in favour of Voisin if his handwriting did not resemble the writing on the paper. What was done was not setting a trap for a man; it was a legitimate attempt to assist the police." Nevertheless, it was made the principal ground for Voisin's appeal on the point that Voisin had not been specially cautioned before he wrote the words. The Court of Criminal Appeal upheld Wensley. The mere fact, said Mr. Justice Lawrence, that there were police officers present, or that the words were written at their request, or that Voisin was being charged at Bow Street police station did not make the writing inadmissible. There was nothing in the nature of a "trap," or the "manufacture" of evidence. The identity of the dead woman had not been established, and the police had not decided to charge the prisoner with the crime. It was desirable in the interests of the community that investigations into crimes should not be cramped, and the Court was of opinion that they would be most unduly cramped if it were held that a writing voluntarily made in the circumstances proved in this case was inadmissible in evidence.

The evidence against Berthe Roche was less conclusive than that against Voisin, and on the second day of the trial she was, by direction of the judge, acquitted of the charge of murder. On an indictment as accessory after the fact she was found guilty and sentenced to seven years' penal servitude. She became insane in prison, and a year later, after her removal to an asylum, she died. Voisin received his sentence of death with the same composure that had marked his attitude throughout the trial. He was executed on March 2, 1918.

This case was remarkable, not only for its example of successful team work, but for its celerity. If the police investigation had been allowed to drag—and for that there would have been ample excuse when the country was in the throes of a great war—Voisin would have found some way of disposing of the head and hands, as well as the incriminating bloodstains in his rooms, and without that evidence the case might well have joined the long list of unsolved crimes. The body was discovered on a Friday. Thanks to Divisional Detective-Inspector Ashley's energy its probable identity had been established on Saturday. On that day Voisin and Roche were detained, and on Monday the case against them was practically established. That Chief Constable Wensley regards it as his best case is not surprising.

THE BRIDES IN THE BATH CASE, 1915

Probably the worst man in the criminal annals of England was George Joseph Smith. After a few weeks spent in attending British courts, an American lawyer said, "British justice? It's dear, but it's prime!" and considering that Smith was tried during the war, when the flower of manhood was falling on the fields of Flanders and the country was spending fifteen million dollars a day, it was remarkable that the country should have spent many thousands of dollars in bringing the most worthless man in England to justice. It took the evidence of 150 witnesses to do it.

Smith had begun his criminal career at the age of nine. Even now it is not known how many murders he committed. He was indicted for three. His method was always the same —under an assumed name to make love to women and, having ascertained that they had savings or property, either to abscond with their savings and leave them destitute, or to induce them to make a will in his favour and then insist upon their taking a bath. While they were in it he would take them by the feet and hold them head under water until they were drowned. He contrived always to avert suspicion by playing an organ or carrying on some noisy occupation except at the moment of the crime, and then he ran for help and wept copious tears before going to the office for the insurance money. Tears were his strong suit: he had complete command over his lachrymal glands.

It was one of those cases that are brought accidentally to light by the newspapers. If the inquests on three of his brides had not been reported, Smith might still be carrying on his system, because he changed his name and his address with every fresh venture and never worked the same town twice. Nevertheless, it took a long time before anyone noticed the coincidence between the newspaper reports of the inquests. The first person who did so was the father of Alice Burnham, whom he had married in Portsmouth and, after insuring her life, had drowned in her bath at Blackpool. He had not even troubled to bury her decently; a deal coffin and a common grave was good enough for her; he had drawn the insurance money and absconded. Reading an account of the inquest on a later bride, the father had sent it to the Aylesbury police. About the same time a Mr. Joseph Crossley called the attention of Scotland Yard to the coincidence between the cases. Margaret Lofty, the daughter of a clergyman, had married Smith under the name of "Lloyd" and was drowned within a few days at lodgings in London. Scotland Yard then began investigations in over forty towns and took statements from 150 witnesses before they had enough evidence to justify them in charging him, and even then it was necessary to arrest him on the minor charge of giving false information to the registrar of marriages. The difficulty was to find a man who seldom passed for three months under the same name. Fortunately, they felt sure that "Mr. Lloyd" would call upon a lawyer named Davis in order to get from him the money of his murdered wife, and they were sure that the bait would attract the fish if nothing were done to alarm him. Day after day the police stood keeping observation upon Davis's office with a witness who knew Smith by sight. Then the witness became restive and refused to waste any more of his time. At the very moment when further persuasion had failed, the witness saw Smith approaching the office, and the police arrested him. He tried hard to elicit from them whether any further charges were pending, but received no satisfaction.

Not until after his arrest did they learn of the murder of Beatrice Mundy, the daughter of a bank manager with a fortune of £2,500, which was tied up in the hands of trustees. He took lawyer's opinion as to how he could get possession of the capital and was advised that each must make a will in favour of the other. That was Beatrice Mundy's death warrant, for he went straight to an ironmonger, in Herne Bay, bought a bath tub, and five days later she was dead. He had not even taken the trouble to warm the water for her. Then he obtained probate of her will, and not a word was said to the police, because the coroner's verdict had exonerated him from suspicion. The judicial scandal of this case was that the woman's brother had written to the coroner demanding a post-mortem. The murder took place on a Saturday, the inquest on the following Monday, the funeral on Tuesday, and no post-mortem was held, nor was time given for the brother to attend the inquest. In three cases, therefore, a coroner's inquest proved to be no protection at all against murder. The murderer's tears at the inquest had quite disarmed suspicion.

Never in his whole life had Smith succeeded in making a friend of his own sex. Physically he was repulsive, sordidly mean in money matters, illiterate, common in his speech, and a bully; only once in many years had he been known to take a bath; and yet, for some obscure reason, he succeeded in winning the affections of a little army of women who acted blindly under his direction and, having suffered every indignity and humiliation at his hands, were always ready to welcome him back. It is easy, of course, to say that he had hypnotic power over them. One or two women spoke of the magnetic quality in his eyes. It was noticed at the police court and at his trial that the public was largely composed of women, who appeared to be following the proceedings with an unhealthy interest. There let me leave this part of the case for others to explain; Smith, no doubt, was himself conscious of his power and exercised it to the full.

The trial lasted eight days; the inevitable verdict was delivered in a very few minutes. Like other bullies, the prisoner collapsed, and a doctor had to stand near him while sentence was being pronounced. He appealed, and the appeal was rejected. Then he abandoned himself to self-pity and made a contemptible exhibition on the scaffold at Maidstone. He had, in fact, almost to be carried to the execution shed and to be held up there by warders during those last few seconds. But while he had abundant pity for himself, he had had none for his wretched victims, whom he stripped and robbed and then did to death in cold blood, in order to possess himself of the insurance money, and these were women who had loved and trusted him.

CHAPTER XXI

The Police Strike

O N AUGUST 30, 1918, eleven weeks before the Armistice, London learned with consternation that more than six thousand of the Metropolitan Police and practically all the City of London force were on strike. Their demands were:

The official recognition of the National Union of Police and Prison Officers; an increase of pay and a war bonus; and the reinstatement of Police Constable Thiel, who had been discharged from the force by a discipline board for his action in connection with the police union.

General Smuts was deputed by the Prime Minister to see the men and endeavour to persuade them to return to duty, but he found the task beyond him. The fact was that the nerves of many people in London had succumbed to a kind of war hysteria from the strain of four years' fighting. The author had evidence of this when he had to make his way through the strikers on the first morning. They filled the approaches to Scotland Yard in plain clothes, shouting and booing, and among those who were shouting the loudest were men that he knew almost intimately as calm, energetic, and conscientious officers. Mass influence had entirely changed them. There was a strange, hysterical light in their eyes, but he saw them recover their balance as he passed, and one of them made a shamefaced gesture of salute.

At about 4 P.M. several thousands who had changed into mufti marched from Scotland Yard to Smith Square, where they were joined by other contingents from an area covering Greater London within a radius of fifteen miles from Charing Cross. As they crossed Old Palace Yard on their way, they hooted and jeered at a few officers of the Special Constabulary, calling them "scabs" and "blacklegs." From Smith Square they marched in column of fours to Tower Hill behind a solitary piper, a policeman who had brought his pipes with him from Scotland. At the Blackfriars end of Queen Victoria Street a City constable on duty held up the traffic for this unfamiliar procession. At Tower Hill they listened to harangues from officials of their union and of the London Trades Council before marching to Whitehall again to await the result of the negotiations of their leaders with one of the ministers.

The absence of the police from their usual stations seemed to make little difference to the public safety; the traffic managed itself. They were more missed as guides and advisers of the public, for the special constables could not fill that gap. Prisoners on remand could not be escorted to the courts, but the strikers had notified the authorities that in the event of an air raid they would resume duty.

The tragic part of this strike when the armies at the front were at death grips with the enemy was that the demand for higher pay—the real cause of the strike—was on the point of being granted. It was waiting only for actuarial calculations to be worked out, and the commissioner, Sir Edward Henry, declined to be hurried over this essential. The pay of a constable at that time was thirty-eight shillings a week, with a rise of one shilling after fifteen years, and a further shilling after twenty-one years. The war bonus was twelve shillings, with further allowances for married men.

On September 1 and 2 the Prime Minister, Mr. Lloyd George, intervened by receiving a deputation, not from the police union, but as simple constables, introduced by a member of Parliament, and offered them improved terms (virtually not much more than had been under consideration before the strike), of an addition of thirteen shillings a week of pensionable pay and a noncontributory pension to widows of ten shillings a week, on condition that they returned to duty the same evening. On one point Mr. Lloyd George stood firm: he refused to give official recognition to the police and prison officers' union, on the obvious ground that a disciplined force could not serve two masters. The clause granting a pension for widows was very well received by the men. Whitehall was packed with Metropolitan and City constables in civilian clothing who were waiting to know the result of the conference. Most of them were wearing the red-and-white ribbon of the union, but even without that they were easily to be distinguished from the rest of the crowd. One man, when asked the cause of the strike, jerked his thumb towards the august buildings and said "Dilly-Dally. You'll find him in all these buildings."

Unfortunately, he was right. If, at the outset of the agitation, a scheme had been drawn up embodying the government concessions, and this had been communicated to the men, no strike would have taken place. As it was, the strike was unpopular with the majority, but, as always happens, a noisy minority forced the quiet men to join them. It is worth noting that only a minority of the C.I.D. men joined the strikers.

The retirement of Sir Edward Henry was inevitable, though the fault of the delay did not entirely lie with him. As the *Times* said: "He may have been the victim of circumstances, but it is the main business of a man in his position not to allow circumstances to make a victim of him." He was succeeded by General Sir Nevil Macready, who took office on September 9 and met delegates from each of the Metropolitan Police divisions to settle minor points that had not been disposed of. He proposed to the men that they should elect representatives to meet him and set up machinery for the formation of committees to report grievances to him. At once the National Union was up on its hind legs declaring that the Prime Minister had promised that the executive committee of the union should meet the Home Secretary to set up these committees. On this Mr. Lloyd

George appeared to give way to the extent of saying that he and the Home Secretary would receive a deputation from the men's representatives. The meeting took place at the Home Office on September 13. In reply to a question at the House of Commons, the Home Secretary, Sir George Cave, declared that there could be no recognition of the union by the police authorities, but that no objection would be made to members belonging to it as long as it did not interfere with the regulations and discipline of the service.

Sir Edward Ward, chief staff officer of the Metropolitan Special Constabulary, issued an order saying that he would gladly accept the regret expressed by the whole force of regular police for the conduct of some of their members in the recent strike. This referred to acts of violence towards middle-aged volunteers by young hotheads among the strikers, who persisted in treating these unfortunate men as blacklegs.

In March 1919 there was still an aggressive attitude on the part of the leaders of the police union. A clash had taken place between the representative board and Sir Nevil Macready on the interpretation to be put upon a reply he had made to a resolution. The board members were defiant, and the commissioner declined to deal with them, but suggested the formation of another committee. A week later, the negotiations had come to a deadlock. Sir Nevil Macready had refused to treat with members who had been responsible for a letter written on February 21 regarding pay for overtime. The committee resolved to appeal to Parliament and to the public. On March 8 the Home Secretary received a deputation of six constables from the representative board on the minor point of the constitution of the board, but this they declined to discuss, bringing up a number of irrelevant subjects which Sir George Cave would not listen to until they had been submitted through the proper channel. On their side the men refused to discuss the question of the new constitution of the board of representatives.

The National Union now appealed to the press, with the gentle flattery that its attitude disproved the Commissioner's statement that the union had lost the confidence of the public. It was the union's fight for existence. On March 14 the Cabinet decided against recognizing the union. The Labour correspondent of the *Times* pointed out that Mr. Lloyd George's statement during the strike—that the government could not recognize the police union during the war—did not commit the government to recognizing it when the war had ended. A stronger argument for recognition, he said, was that the men were allowed to join the union as members of the force. "The present position," he added, "could not continue indefinitely."

On June 2 the union announced that there was to be another police strike, this time for recognition of the union. According to Mr. Hayes, the secretary, nearly 45,000 votes had been given for a strike, and only 4,324 against, and yet the strike was not called. Mr. Hayes said that this was because the authorities wanted a strike and were making a last bid for autocracy. The union was going to wait till more men came home from France.

What had really happened was this: The government had announced that policemen would receive a definite minimum wage of nearly seventy shillings a week and that other improvements were in contemplation. Government was determined not to recognize the union or the right to strike, and public opinion was behind it. Moreover, the opinion in the force itself had hardened against a strike.

On July 17 the Home Secretary introduced the Police Charter Bill, amending the law relating to police and exacting penalties for disaffection. The police union had been losing ground. On August 2 the *Times* published a remarkable letter from Charles Green, a Metropolitan police constable, saying that the arbitrary conduct of the committee of the police union had caused many members to resign; that the leaders "to their eternal shame" had chosen a time "when the country was on the edge of a volcano," but the good sense of the majority would not allow them to be carried away by the frenzy of a few fanatical leaders of the so-called National Union of Police and Prison Officers. On the same day the union was unwise enough to call a strike. Only 854 out of 20,000 of the force responded, and they were dismissed. On that day the Police Charter Bill passed its third reading.

Under the police charter, branch boards were instituted for inspectors, sergeants and constables, with representatives from each rank—one inspector from each division, one from the commissioner's office, one from the Public Carriage Department, one from the C.I.D. The sergeants were to elect representatives from each subdivision, and the constables, one from each station, to be known as subdivisional and station representatives respectively. They were to bring up matters affecting the general welfare of the force and the conditions of service in their respective ranks. Matters that affected more than one rank would be discussed by a combined board of equal numbers of representatives concerned. But the most important condition of all was that under the police charter no one who was not serving as a police officer could meddle with matters that concerned the force.

Sir Edward Henry had been succeeded by a soldier. General Sir Nevil Macready had had, before the war, actual experience of police administration, when he commanded soldiers and police during the prewar industrial troubles. He accepted the post of commissioner with the reservation that it would be for three years only. His task at the outset was a difficult one, in consequence of the demand for a representative body in place of the police union, which the men were not allowed to join, but his task was made easier by the grant of large increases in pay and improvements in the conditions of service. Macready successfully repressed the strike of July 1919 and established the police federation with branch boards for each of the ranks.

In April 1920 Sir Nevil Macready took over the command in Ireland and was succeeded by Brigadier General Horwood, who had been chief officer of railway police and provost marshal of the army in France during the war.

In November 1928 Lord Byng of Vimy was brought in to

replace Sir William Horwood. Ill-health compelled him to resign the post in October 1931. During his three years' tenure of office he inaugurated many of the reforms afterwards carried on by his successor, Marshal of the Royal Air Force Lord Trenchard, appointed in November 1931. Lord Byng also purged the force of many evils which had come to light in the case of Sergeant Goddard, who was convicted in 1928 of having accepted bribes from night clubs to a large amount.

THE PLOT TO ASSASSINATE
MR. LLOYD GEORGE

One morning, a few days before the Armistice, a military colonel who had been appointed intelligence officer to the Ministry of Munitions with the duty of keeping the Ministry informed of impending strikes and sabotage walked into my room at Scotland Yard and proceeded to unfold a fantastic story. He told me that he had an informant in his pay who had become intimate with a family in one of the Midland towns and had been taken into the secret of a plot to assassinate the Prime Minister (Lloyd George) in such a way that the murder would never be detected. He said that the family consisted of a Mrs. Wheeldon, a widow, and her two daughters, of whom the elder was married to a druggist in Southampton and the younger was a school teacher and lived with her. The three women were militant suffragettes and were constitutionally opposed to any government; the married daughter had brought her druggist husband to her way of thinking, but the mother was the archinstigator, and it was she who had confided details of their plot to my friend's agent.

They had read in the newspapers that it was Lloyd George's habit to play golf on the Walton Heath course on Saturday afternoons. They understood that at various points on the course there were bushes large enough to conceal a stooping man. The druggist son-in-law knew of a rare South American poison, curare, in which the natives were wont to steep their arrows to poison them. All that was required was a bottle of this poison. Mrs. Wheeldon and her school-teacher daughter would do the rest at home. A little dart soaked in the poison would be discharged from a blowpipe at Lloyd George as he passed the assassin's lurking place; the dart would pass through his clothing, and he would be conscious only of a slight prick, less painful than a sting from a bee. He would suffer no pain and would be able to continue his game, but gradually he would be overcome with lassitude and would decide to be driven home to rest. Once safely at home, he would wish to go to bed and would quickly fall into a sleep from which there would be no waking. The doctor would be called in to examine the body and would certify that the cause of death was an apoplectic seizure in the night; no one would think of looking for a wound.

I asked the colonel to give me the name of his informant, or, if he preferred, to bring him to see me. He replied that he had already suggested this to the man, but that when he heard my name he showed great unwillingness to come and made a condition that his name should not be disclosed.

That set me thinking; either the agent was a person with a criminal history or he had invented the whole story to get money and credit from his employer. But I did not confide my misgivings to the colonel; on the contrary I proceeded to take down the names and addresses of the persons con-cerned as if I believed in this fantastic plot. There was a very simple way of putting the story to the test. According to this self-effacing agent, letters were constantly passing between the druggist and his mother-in-law, who was expect-ing to receive a registered parcel from Southampton con-taining a bottle of curare. In those war days there were facilities for stopping and examining suspected letters in the General Post Office and of photographing any of them before they reached the addressees. All that was required to legalize the proceeding was a warrant signed by a Secretary of State. This warrant I obtained, leaving the colonel to obtain from his agent any further information about the proposed date for the outrage at Walton Heath.

I confess that I was astonished next day to receive from the Post Office a photograph of a letter from Mrs. Wheeldon to her son-in-law, couched in violent language, in which the Prime Minister was referred to in opprobrious terms such as do not usually fall from the pen of a self-respecting woman, and there was a veiled reference to an expected parcel. There was therefore some truth in the agent's story, but I had an uneasy feeling that he himself might have acted as what the French call an *agent provocateur* by putting the idea into the woman's head, or, if the idea was already there, by offering to act as the dart thrower. Still, we had now documentary evidence of the plot, and it was no longer possible to treat it with contempt, since, if the curare could not be obtained, a pistol might be used instead. In those days Mr. Lloyd George was considered the keystone of the arch in the coming Peace Conference, and, quite apart from the question of a plot to murder, his life was at that moment of inestimable value to the Allies.

I saw the colonel again and told him that, whether his agent liked it or not, he would have to come to London to be at hand if required. He shook his head; told me that among his other gifts his agent was no mean poet, with all the nervous shrinking from publicity that is supposed to go with poetic inspiration. I said that I was sorry to have to outrage his poetic feelings, but in a case of such gravity I must insist. He promised to bring the overmodest poet up to London.

A day or two later the Post Office stopped a registered packet addressed from Southampton to Mrs. Wheeldon. It contained a bottle of liquid together with a very incriminating letter from her son-in-law. The bottle, he said, contained curare, and there were instructions to handle it with the greatest care, since if any of the liquid came into contact with a sore finger, death would result. Mrs. Wheeldon's fingers were spared any risk, because the packet was detained to be used in evidence against the sender.

Next morning a conference was arranged with the director of public prosecutions. My friend the colonel was present, with his agent waiting downstairs. I had taken with me as a precaution the superintendent of the Criminal Investigation Department and the superintendent of the Fingerprint Department, who had instructions to wait outside the conference room and cast a searching eye over the agent when he passed them on his way upstairs. After listening to my statement of the case the director demanded, as I had expected he would, that the agent, on whose evidence the case rested, should be brought into the room to be questioned. The colonel agreed to go and fetch him, and we waited expectantly. Then there walked into the room a thin, cunning-looking man of about thirty, with long, greasy black hair. My superintendent sat up and stiffened like a setter at the scent of game. He called in the fingerprint expert and whispered to him; the expert hurried off. The agent showed extreme nervousness when he saw the manœuvre, but he replied to all our questions readily enough. There was a knock at the door; the superintendent opened it a few inches and received from an unseen hand two cards, each bearing a photograph. He passed them to me. Both photographs were speaking portraits of the long-haired poet, but the names on each differed, and neither of them was "Gordon" —that given by the agent to the colonel.

We had to use the man; there was no alternative. We could only observe whether he would come with credit through his cross-examination.

There was no evidence against the married daughter, but Mrs. Wheeldon, her son-in-law, and her unmarried daughter were arrested simultaneously and charged with a conspiracy to murder. Their astonishment was unbounded. Mrs. Wheeldon had no words to express what she thought of the serpent that she had nursed in her bosom. The three were committed for trial at the assizes. The mother was sentenced to three years' penal servitude; her son-in-law and daughter to exemplary sentences. The bottle of curare, the mysterious South American poison, now reposes in the crime museum at Scotland Yard.

THE WAR GAVE RISE to several new offences. One of these was the melting down of gold and silver coin, at a time when the metal was worth far more than the face value of the coins. This offence continued after the war. In one case a raid made on the East End resulted in the discovery of a smelting works run by amateurs. The detectives found a furnace in full blast, crucibles full of coins, thirteen silver ingots, and an ingot of gold weighing fifty-nine pounds and worth about £5,600. Soon afterwards the C.I.D. unmasked a big conspiracy for dealing with gold coin. The men involved in it were not professional criminals. Among them were a barrister, a jeweller, and a moneylender. The first intimation that irregularities were going on came to the police when it was reported that a certain man of substance was exchanging large numbers of banknotes for gold. In this there was nothing illegal; it might have been the eccentricity of a wealthy man who preferred to hoard his money in gold, and at the outset this theory was probably right; but it was thought wise to consult a well-known inquiry agency conducted by a former chief inspector of Scotland Yard, who reported that gold was being dealt with illegally on an extensive scale.

The wealthy "crank" already mentioned had received a visit from a gentleman of doubtful antecedents who had dazzled him with a scheme that appeared fairly safe as well as profitable, and as time went on, other persons were drawn into it. Before they could be dealt with judicially it was necessary to prove that they were dealing improperly in gold coin, and positive proof was not at all easy to obtain, for the band were very clever in covering their tracks. At last one of the suspects was followed from a hotel in Southampton Row to a side street in Holborn. There a woman passed to him a heavy handbag, which he carried back to his hotel. The detective who was following him photographed the handbag on his brain, and it was well that he did so, for when it appeared again it was in the possession of another man who was accompanied by a woman. They took a taxi and drove to a narrow alley leading into Lincoln's Inn Fields. They carried the bag to the chambers occupied by the barrister. The detectives waited; they wanted to capture the entire gang. Presently another man was admitted to the chambers, and all this time observation had been kept without arousing any suspicion in the quarry. This was the moment for the detectives to follow and raid the chambers. They knocked and were admitted in time to surprise the barrister in the act of counting out banknotes in exchange for the bag. This was found to contain gold coins to the amount of £1,700. On another man caught in the place were found 1500 sovereigns. These considerable sums pointed to the fact that they were trafficking in gold coins, and they were arrested. A little later other people in the conspiracy were traced and ultimately seven were charged and convicted.

FRAUD IN CONNECTION WITH THE LATE LORD KITCHENER

A curious incident in connection with the drowning of Lord Kitchener was the story that his body had been found. This was given wide publicity, and a coffin was brought to London and placed in a room at the back of an undertaker's shop fitted up as a mortuary chapel. Of course no criminal offence had been committed, but Scotland Yard was appealed to, to put a stop to the proceedings if it could. The question was, what right had the police to intervene? It was Mr. Wensley who found the solution. The undertaker asserted that the coffin contained a body. Very well. Then where was the doctor's certificate showing the cause of death? There was none. Then, said the police, the body must be removed to a mortuary, pending a coroner's inquest. This at once put an end to the story, for the coffin could be opened and examined. It was empty.

The story reminds me of another incident with an undertaker which was not devoid of humour. He was reputed to be a receiver of stolen goods, and detectives were sent to his place of business to make inquiries. Though they were not armed with a search warrant, he received them politely and invited them to inspect his premises. They noticed a coffin that had been screwed down, with a newly inscribed name plate fastened to the lid. It did not occur to them to suggest opening it; in any case they would have hesitated to take such a step. It was not until later, when the undertaker was dealt with by the courts, that they learned that the coffin had been full of stolen property.

It was at this period that an important change was made in the organization of the Criminal Investigation Department. It had been under consideration just before the war, but the pressure of war work had postponed it. It was brought to the front again by a new development, the ease with which criminals can steal a motorcar and do their depredations far from their homes. It was no longer possible to deal with them in their own divisions; all London had become their hunting ground.

To meet this new portent the first step was taken in 1919 by dividing London into four detective districts, each controlled by a detective-superintendent who was invested with authority to take all the necessary steps for dealing quickly with a crime without referring to higher authority at Scotland Yard. Out of this grew the "Flying Squad," which began by using two police tenders, each of them working two out of the four districts, and both equipped with wireless receivers. This seemed to strike the imagination of the public from the first, when a squad under Detective-Inspector Crosse chased a gang of shopbreakers and arrested them after a fierce fight in the Buckingham Palace Road, but though the squad has been greatly improved since that time there does not appear to have been any diminution in our criminal population.

The fact is that the motorcar has served the criminal far more than it has served the police. A great deal of nonsense has been written about the Flying Squad. It has performed a great public service, but it is a mistaken notion that fast cars, wireless, police boxes, or any other mechanical device can ever supersede a single detective. It is true that quick information and instant action are invaluable, as for example when a policeman on his beat is able to tell Scotland Yard that he has seen five suspects in a car, which he is able to describe, heading in a certain direction, and thus Flying Squads can be warned by wireless to look out for it. In fact the only point in favour of the Flying Squad is its mobility, and perhaps also its salutary menace to the professional criminal now that its cars are undistinguishable from other private cars. It cannot take the place of a trained detective who knows every criminal in his division by sight.

The Flying Squad, like the individual detective, can act only upon information. It can get to any part of London quickly, especially at night, but to be effective it must have some definite objective. True, its cars patrol the streets night and day, but the number of criminals caught red-handed without previous information is absurdly small. It arrests thieves occasionally, because it knows thieves by sight and the thieves do not always know a Flying Squad car when they see it. In rare cases the men in the car catch sight of, say, a Hoxton criminal taking the air in a well-to-do residential district like Belgravia. "Hallo!" remarks one of the men. "That's John Jackson from Hoxton. What's he doing down here?" The car is pulled up out of sight of John Jackson, and its crew keep an unobtrusive eye upon him. As soon as he does something which a Hoxton man would not be doing in Belgravia unless his intentions were sinister, he is arrested as a suspected criminal, but such cases are necessarily rare.

A detective is as God made him. He cannot divine the intentions of a person whom he has never seen before, and to make police inquiries about a person whose face does not please him would take up more time than he can spare. To send a number of men from the Flying Squad into a district where there is an epidemic of crime would be worse than useless if they went without any knowledge of the men they were to look for, for the thieves would get to know the detectives before the detectives got to know them and would betake themselves to another district.

The Flying Squad methods were not entirely new. There was an occasion in the East End of London when a gang of suspected shoplifters were seen loitering together. They could not be followed, because they knew every detective by sight. Consequently the police borrowed a tradesman's van to track them in. In the van they had an assortment of hats and coats for changing their appearance in quick time. They would hide the van in a side street until the propitious moment arrived for arrest. The culprits were astonished to find that the detectives could describe the smallest detail of their proceedings over many hours. The defending counsel at their trial spoke of the meanness of the detectives in changing their clothes; which provoked the judge to retort with the question, "What is disguise?" and to tell the story of an Irish priest who was described as being in disguise because he was wearing a clean collar.

Shadowing a fast car in the congested London streets by another fast car is quite impossible, except when the streets are empty in the small hours of the night. The Flying Squad has never pretended to perform miracles. However modern its appliances may be, it can never take the place of personal contact, nor can it rely upon chance.

Take, for instance, the crime of safebreaking, an offence carefully planned beforehand and carried out in a place left unattended after business hours. By cultivating the society of some talkative employee or by personal observation the thieves have learned everything they wanted to know. A timetable is drawn up, and at the moment selected a signal is given, a car is driven up, and the safe is carried out to it and driven away. Unless a member of the gang is clumsy enough to rouse the suspicion of a neighbour, or unless a police officer happens to be on the spot at the moment, it is most unlikely that a detective should hear anything of the robbery until after it has happened.

Or take a "smash and grab" raid. There are said to be more than eighty thousand miles of streets in London. Unless the police received advance information of the raid, the chances of a Flying Squad car being on the spot at the time may easily be calculated. The criminals have made their plans, and the offence is committed in a few seconds. The chances against catching them in the act are too small to be considered. The police have a better way than that. Sooner or later the men who take part in these raids become known to the Squad. Then it is possible to take effective steps. Armed with knowledge of the gangs, the Flying Squad becomes valuable or rather indispensable if the gangs are to be broken up.

Modern preventive measures such as police boxes and the like are useful as far as they go, but no professional thief with a stolen motorcar at his command is likely to be caught by policemen on patrol. The professional usually avoids police officers on patrol, and it is generally the amateur or accidental criminal who is taken by them. It is true that in England and Scotland an habitual criminal seldom gets away in the long run, but the task of capturing him is far less easy than may be supposed. At present a Flying Squad patrol may see a well-known criminal driving a car. They may suspect him, but they have no power to interfere with him until an offence has been committed.

Former Chief Constable Frederick Wensley was the first to propose a simple expedient for stopping the use of cars by criminals, namely, by giving all judges and magistrates power, when sentencing those who have used motorcars for their crimes, to prohibit them from holding a driver's licence after their release except by permission of the police. The breaking of this condition would in itself become a punishable offence. This would mean that an unlicensed driver could be arrested at sight, as a convict licence holder is arrested when he leaves his registered address. If the men knew that they were running a risk in using a car, whether stolen or otherwise, this form of lawbreaking would be very much reduced. The arrangement would work quite smoothly except for the criminals. A police officer would see four or five criminals known to him by sight driving in a motorcar. He would either stop the car or send a notification that would result in their capture sooner or later. It might be objected that a man would take out a licence in a false name, but he could not use it for long without being recognized. But what, it may be argued, would prevent a gang from using an unconvicted friend as a driver? That would not last for long, for the supply of rogues who could be trusted and who had not yet been to prison would grow rapidly smaller.

The proposal would, of course, be restricted to persons likely to use a car for committing a crime. It would impose no hardship on an ex-criminal who really meant to turn over a new leaf and whose livelihood might depend upon driving a car. He would merely have to persuade the police of his sincerity, and a dispensation would then be granted to him without any publicity.

CHAPTER XXIII

The Work of Scotland Yard in Cases of Fraud

LEST IT BE SUPPOSED that the work of the Scotland Yard detective is limited to the detection of murderers, housebreakers, and thieves and to the patient and ingenious investigation of clues, let us consider it in relation to famous cases of financial fraud, and show the detectives in the guise of financial experts, versed in all the intricacies of company law and accountancy. How, it may be asked, can they acquire this? Surely it cannot be taught in any detective class? The answer is that it is acquired while working under senior officers to whom the inquiries have been entrusted, and who in their turn have gained their knowledge in the same hard school. These senior officers know how to select the younger men who have a natural aptitude for dealing with complicated accounts; their team for the investigation of a big case may number four, five, or even six officers taken from the central staff at Scotland Yard, and the senior himself has gained his knowledge by years of experience and hard work.

Whenever a big fraud is brought to the office of the director of public prosecutions, he requests the assistance of Scotland Yard to make the necessary investigations. Upon this the best officer who is free from other work is sent over to the director's office, and he then becomes the servant of the director of public prosecutions until the case is brought to trial and finished by the conviction of the accused. As far as possible, the chief inspector is allowed to select his own men to form his team.

The cases that will now be cited have been supplied to me by former Chief Inspector Alfred Collins, who was until his retirement probably the ablest officer in this difficult class of work. It is work that could never be taught in the widely advertised police college. It is acquired only by years of experience.

THE MANDEVILLE CASE

A few months after the war the British Isles were plunged into an orgy of speculation. It was the golden moment for the "bucketshop" operators, as the outside brokers and share pushers were called. Among these were three brothers, Alexis, Henry, and Walter Mandeville, who had cheated the investing public out of half a million pounds. The details of the case are too complicated to be given in full in these pages; the method was familiar enough. Probably no one who listened to the evidence guessed how many months of assiduous work were consumed by the police investigations; it is enough to say that the official receiver worked for more than two years on the case and had special rooms set apart to accommodate the vast pile of books and papers dealing with the numerous concerns which had been seized at the offices of the Mandevilles.

The three brothers were partners in a share-dealing enterprise called "The Financial Mail and Exchange." They were also the owners of the *Financial Mail*, which was edited by the eldest brother, Alexis. The paper was used to "boost" worthless stocks and shares and invite the public to buy them through the Financial Mail and Exchange. Another company, called Mandeville's, Limited, bought the stocks and shares. From time to time they declared profits and induced people to invest large sums, though no profits had been made at all.

On March 31, 1919, the position of the Financial Mail and Exchange showed a trading loss, during the previous

Former Chief Inspector
Alfred Collins

Sir Basil Thomson

Former Chief Constable Frederick Porter Wensley

THREE FAMOUS MEMBERS OF SCOTLAND YARD

three years, of £19,000, and there was an adverse balance, from the loan account, of £30,900, making a total adverse balance of approximately £50,000. Thereupon a "Financial Mail Operating Trust" was formed, and circulars were sent out showing that a profit of 30 per cent had been paid.

Subscribers were formed into groups, and alleged profits made by the early groups were paid out of money subscribed by later groups. In March 1920 the account showed that £494,000 had been subscribed and that £312,000 had been paid to the Operating Trust, leaving a balance in hand of £182,000; yet two months later all the money in hand was £55. The three brothers had misappropriated in all more than £500,000.

The eldest brother, Alexis, stood as a Liberal candidate for Parliament in 1904, but was not elected. He lived in Hill Street, Mayfair, and spent money lavishly. In 1915 he served as an officer of the Sportsman Battalion in France, and in 1918 he obtained an appointment in the Audit Department of the Ministry of Munitions which he held until February 1920. He was actually in the Ministry of Munitions at the time of these frauds. The other two brothers had also been in good positions; the younger of the two kept several hunters, and the three brothers had been principals in the London, Paris Exchange, Limited, which in 1909 failed, with liabilities of £424,437 and assets of £3. The failure of that company had brought ruin to thousands of people.

The money was used by the brothers in hazardous speculations. They had very expensive offices, with a huge and well-paid staff; all three were undischarged bankrupts. The case was an epitome of the old saying that the population of Great Britain was fifty millions, mostly fools.

All three brothers had the grace to plead guilty, and they were sentenced to six years' penal servitude, the judge uttering the pious wish that the investing public would take warning from the disclosures at the trial. The men came from a respectable family. Their father had held a post in the Colonial Office, and Alexis had shown aptitude for finance. He had always been a gambler with his own and other people's money; a figure at Monte Carlo and a squire at Cookham on the Thames. His friends for the most part were the smaller fry of the City, actors, and young sportsmen. To them he was quiet and unostentatious, and he was careful not to succumb to the easy fashion of dress in these postwar days. His silk hat was always fresh from the iron; his long-tailed black morning coat newly pressed; and the crease in his trousers was irreproachable. Watching him strolling across Berkeley Square gave the impression of some aloof person of distinction; that was his stock in trade. He was difficult to talk to; his Semitic hawklike beak seemed to muffle his speech, but the average man probably thought that his mind was wandering about the mountain peaks and that he was scheming, scheming. His facility with figures was amazing. There may have been no harm in him at the outset of his career; juggling with figures was the breath of his nostrils. He was no petty thief, whatever suffering he may have caused; his mania was to house his schemes in palaces. From the ashes of that first half-million crash he emerged like a phœnix in vulture's feathers. Apart from the years of his war service he never rested until he had housed an imposing staff again in palatial quarters, where an army of secretaries filed stacks of documents dealing with his frauds, while he sat for an hour with a gold pencil case between his fingers, covering sheet after sheet with figures. No crisis disturbed him; nothing ever ruffled his dignity; to the last his friends believed that "Mandy," as they called him, was more sinned against than sinning.

THE CASE OF E. T. HOOLEY AND OTHERS

When Ernest Terah Hooley was sentenced to twelve months' hard labour in 1912 for fraud, it was hoped that the last had been heard of him, and perhaps it would have been the last if there had been no war and no war profiteers to tempt him with their easily acquired wealth. Ten years later Hooley was at the game again. Hooley, as will presently be related, had been associated with the notorious Horatio Bottomley, and fraud was his livelihood. Shipowners in Cardiff and elsewhere had been making fortunes out of the war, and among them was Tom Lewis, whose father, also a shipowner, had done likewise. The son, it should be said, knew little about ships or indeed about anything except boxing. He had come up to London to witness the fight between Carpentier and Beckett, in which Carpentier won a lightning victory, and was staying at the Waldorf Hotel. There he met a Mr. Demery, who was also staying at the hotel. Demery brought the conversation round to cotton, in which at that time there was a boom. He asked his new acquaintance whether he would be interested in buying a cotton mill, for he knew of one that was going cheap. It belonged to a man named Fletcher, who owned two mills in England and others in Russia. The Russian Bolsheviks had seized his money and property, and consequently he was driven to sell one of his English mills cheap in order to raise funds.

It may be gathered from Tom Lewis's account of the conversation that he was an artless gentleman who was ready to take a stranger at his own valuation. He said at once that he knew nothing about cotton, but since Mr. Demery was out of a job and would give his whole time to the working of the cotton mill, he would buy the property on Demery's recommendation. What amount would he have to pay for it? Demery was quite ready with an answer. The owner, he said, would want £40,000 in cash and £55,000 in shares for the mill, and he, Demery, would expect £20,000 in shares as payment for his services in floating a company.

Then two new characters appeared upon the scene, named Wallis and Newton, who, according to Demery, were acting for Mr. Fletcher, the owner of the mill. After some conversation Mr. Tom Lewis sat down and wrote a cheque for £15,000, saying that he knew nothing about the value of the mill, but that he would leave himself in the hands of Mr. Demery to carry through the contract and protect his interests. Demery was clearly a man of business. He wrote out the following document for Mr. Tom Lewis's signature:

I authorise you to pay £15,000 on my behalf to purchase the Jubilee Mills, Walston, and to arrange the flotation of a company for £30,000 debentures and £150,000 shares, the balance of the purchase money in cash, if required, to be paid and 55,000 shares to be provided by me when called upon.

Mr. Tom Lewis signed this document with such alacrity that Demery tried him further and induced him to purchase the Isherwood Mills for £75,000. He agreed to advance £30,000 for the scheme, for which he was to receive half the profits on the promotion of a company with a capital of £1,250,000. Lewis got nothing for his £30,000, except a judgment in the High Court for £2,000 when the deal for buying Isherwood Mills fell through.

In another deal, this time with E. T. Hooley, Tom Lewis sold 68,000 shares at ten shillings a share, receiving £10,175 in cash and the balance in worthless shares in other companies. His total losses in dealing with Hooley, Demery and others amounted to £60,000. It will not be surprising to learn that a man so ill-endowed with prudence and knowledge of his fellow men eventually lost all his money through the slump in 1930 and became a bankrupt; or that his losses affected his mind.

To the reader the case may seem simple enough, but in fact it was highly complicated and took many months of tedious work in many parts of the country before there was sufficient evidence for the prosecution. It had created great public interest, owing to the notoriety of the principal defendant and the fame of the counsel engaged in it. The year 1922 was a profitable year for barristers and a record year for the Scotland Yard officers who were set to unravel the complicated series of fraudulent transactions which were brought to light by the victims. Six defendants appeared in the dock of the Central Criminal Court on April 8, 1922, charged with fraud—Hooley, Fletcher, the lessee of the mill, Macdonald, Demery, Wallis, the solicitor, and Breakspear,·Hooley's clerk. Fletcher and Breakspear were acquitted, but Hooley was sentenced to three years' penal servitude (after a previous conviction for fraud); Macdonald was bound over[1] for two years; Demery received twelve months in the second division (the intermediate grade of prison treatment), and Wallis, the solicitor, ten months. After the sentence Hooley approached Chief Inspector Collins with his usual smile and said, "Well Collins, this is the last day" (the trial had occupied five days). "I want to thank you for the kind manner in which you have treated us; throughout the case you've done your job well, without hitting below the belt." Then he turned to Demery and the others and said, "Now, look here, you fellows. I have had experience and I want to give you all a tip. When you get to Wormwood Scrubs you ought to get a job in the laundry if you can, because then you will have a chance of selecting nice clean clothes; otherwise you will have to look carefully through them."

From this it may be seen that E. T. Hooley had a resilient nature and was in no wise cast down by his sentence. He was aware that one of his associates in crime, Horatio Bottomley, was also coming up for trial for fraud within a few days, and he knew enough about Bottomley's case to feel sure that he would be sent to penal servitude. He was counting upon meeting him in prison and comparing notes with him. This was not destined to be, for two reasons—the first, that the prison commissioners were aware of the connection between the two men and ordered the transfer of Hooley to another prison for his separate confinement; the other, because on Horatio Bottomley's arrival at Wormwood Scrubs it was found that there was no prison clothing large enough to contain his vast body, and while the prison tailor was doing his best to fit the new arrival, Bottomley had to be kept unclothed in a hospital bed.

---

[1]Being bound over is somewhat comparable in English practice to the American system of being on parole. It is, however, more severe, for in addition to having to report regularly to his local police authorities the individual, on committing any subsequent offence, is automatically subject to sentence for the original as well as for the new offence.

THE BOTTOMLEY CASE

Probably no name was better known in England during the war than that of Horatio Bottomley. Lying rumour asserted that he was a natural son of Bradlaugh who had been the *enfant terrible* of the House of Commons in an earlier generation, but in fact his origin was less romantic. His father was William Bottomley, who, according to the son, died in a lunatic asylum. Horatio was born in Hackney, London, in March 1860. His father was a journeyman tailor. He was educated in an orphanage school in Birmingham. When he left school, he became for eighteen months office boy to a builder named Smith in Ryland Road, Birmingham. He then obtained a job with a haberdashery firm in London. This part of his biography is a little vague, but we know that at the age of nineteen he was employed in the office of a solicitor in Essex Street, Strand. It was a humble beginning for a man who was destined to loom so large in the public eye a few years later.

A year afterwards we find him with a firm of shorthand writers who still have a card bearing his name. It was there that he conceived the project of entering the House of Commons. He became a member of the Hackney "Parliament," and being a shorthand writer he founded the Hackney "Hansard." For some unrecorded reason he transferred himself to Battersea, where he founded a Battersea "Hansard." This concern became financially embarrassed, and Bottomley undertook his first venture in reconstructing failing businesses by amalgamating the unremunerative "Hansard" with the *Debater,* which printed reports of all the local "parliaments" in London.

At this period Bottomley was a devotee of the billiard saloon, where he was known as the "green-coated stranger." He was the mystery man among billiard players in the eighties; heavy bets were made upon his play, but he seldom spoke to anyone. He would enter the saloon, back his play, receive his winnings, and depart. Sometimes he was unfortunate, and then the settlement of his losses was postponed.

One of the principals of the solicitor's office in Essex Street had a relation, a young medical student, named Alfred Locke Cox. From 1879 onwards the two, Bottomley and Cox, were so closely associated that Cox was termed "Bottomley's Rubber Stamp." He was attracted at first by Bottomley's extraordinary oratorical powers. These had an attraction for others, as, for example, an old gentleman, long since dead, who was blamed by his family for entrusting Bottomley with nearly £40,000; he said, "I like this man. I have heard him speak. I won't have you say a word against him. I am not sorry I lent him the money, and I would do it again."

At this time Bottomley and Hooley used to sell the goodwill of their victims to each other; a document was found among Hooley's papers, signed by Bottomley: "In consideration of £125 I hereby declare that I am without any interest in any transactions you [Hooley] have with Mr. X." The victim in question had many transactions with Hooley. "You may think me foolish," he said, "but the reason is that I am eighty-three years of age . . . life is a complex system; anticipation is its greatest joy. Mr. Hooley can give me plenty of that, so I am prepared to pay for it." This poor old gentleman had, between Hooley and Bottomley, lost a sum of £92,000.

At the age of twenty-three or twenty-four Bottomley first began company promoting. His first venture was the Austrian printing company which failed. "The company has acquired no business in Vienna or elsewhere, has no property whatever, and its whole capital appears to be lost," was the summary of a committee of shareholders. There followed a number of companies in which Bottomley's name did not appear; it was only to be detected by the names of his nominees, but before long bankruptcy proceedings became inevitable. It was here that Bottomley shone. He had an extraordinary flair for dragging red herrings across the scent and making quite convincing excuses for himself, but on August 9, 1893, his first bankruptcy was concluded.

It would be wearisome to follow in detail all the enterprises that followed; all ended in the same way: the companies went into voluntary or forced liquidation: the shareholders lost all their money, and in 1911 he was again adjudged bankrupt. He had now become a member of the House of Commons, the editor of *John Bull,* and an associate of ex-convicts who conducted their business under assumed names. He was one of the first to realize the possibilities in sweepstakes. One of his ex-convict friends, Bargham, went to Lucerne under the name of Patrick O'Brien, and there started in 1913 a sweepstake under the high-sounding title of "The John Bull Derby 1913 Sweepstake." Under the Lottery Act this was an illegal enterprise, but it catered to a very general desire for an occasional "flutter." The sweepstake was widely advertised in *John Bull.* The result was a summons to the Bow Street magistrate's court, where Bottomley had to pay ten guineas costs. The drawing was supposed to be fair, but an examination of the winners' names was at least suggestive. Two were ex-convicts, one, a personal acquaintance of Bottomley, and the other, of Hooley; the third winner was a gentleman who led the cheers in Bow Street in favour of Bottomley.

In December 1913, Patrick O'Brien started two sweepstakes, one for the Grand National and the other for the Derby of 1914. Bottomley stated that he had been present at the draw—"it was fair and in order." The winner was stated to be a Madame Gluckad of Toulouse. *John Bull* published a moving article about her; she was blind. It transpired that she was the sister of a Jewish furrier, Saul Cooper, a close friend of Bottomley. This was shown in the books of Bottomley's bank. After a long search this lady was traced to Paris. She said that she had visited London at the request of her brother, and she remembered going to a bank to endorse a cheque for £25,000 which was handed to her by a representative of *John Bull,* who waited outside and took from her the whole amount, handing back only £280. Among the other winners of sweepstakes were the names of two other relations or friends of Mr. Saul Cooper, the furrier. One of these winners was interviewed; he admitted having endorsed the cheque and having given it to Mr. Cooper, whose servant he was.

Bottomley again found himself before the magistrate in Bow Street and was fined £25. He appealed, and the fine was remitted.

Then came the war, and Bottomley awoke to the fact that there was money in patriotism. He formed the "John Bull League," and having borrowed the London Opera House for recruiting purposes, he let himself go. He embarked on a lecture tour in the interest of his country, but he netted for himself the substantial sum of £27,000. He found time, nevertheless, to sue his traducers of the anti-gambling league for libel. The league had investigated the winners of his sweepstakes and had pronounced "the whole thing to be a swindle." He was awarded one farthing damages. Another of his ventures was the patriotic "War Skill Competition." The prizes were to be awarded to the competitor who most nearly forecasted the indemnity to be paid by Germany, and the country and the date where and when peace would be signed. The prizes ranged from £10,000 to £3,000; the entry fee was one shilling; the manager was Mr. Patrick O'Brien, formerly of Portland convict prison, and the judge was Mr. Bottomley. No one knows what happened to the money subscribed.

It is impossible to deny that Bottomley had won for himself a unique position during the war. He had been the most successful of recruiting agents; the soldiers at the front believed in him; when there was unrest in the trenches in 1917 he was invited to go out to talk to the men, and the result was a great improvement in morale among the troops. On the other hand his "League of the Man in the Street," which took up arms against the restriction of the liquor traffic, which he fought as a restriction on personal liberty, was an embarrassment to the government. In December 1915 he had formed a small party which he called "The

Business Government Party." He was now preparing for a return to the House of Commons.

John Bull had now a circulation of nearly 1,500,000, and Bottomley thought the moment ripe for launching a new scheme—the issue of "Victory Bonds." He received on his own admission subscriptions to the amount of £77,500, but it is believed that the sum was considerably larger. Being an undischarged bankrupt, he could not keep a banking account in his own name, so the money was banked under the name of "The Northern Territory Syndicate, Limited." There was grave reason for suspecting that the draw for prizes under the scheme was not conducted fairly, but the result was that Bottomley was now possessed of considerable funds, and by the summer of 1919 he was again a member of Parliament. He now promoted the "Victory Bond Club," which drew fresh money into his coffers, and there was a talk in *John Bull* of another sweepstake. Owing to the social position which he had now acquired through his influence with highly placed personages, he imagined no doubt that he would be immune from interference. There was supposed to have been three draws, but the names of the "winners" were suppressed, it was said, at their own desire. The method of the draws was extraordinary. According to Bottomley, he and six of his clerks put the discs into sacks and turned them out onto the floor. The lights were then turned out, and Bottomley went in with a candle to draw the highest prizes. Afterwards his clerks in order of seniority went in to draw the lower ones!

The sands were running out. On June 21, 1921, a well-dressed man of middle age appeared before the Bow Street magistrate on a charge of having in his possession a 5 per cent National War Bond numbered D 53438, believed to have been stolen. He refused to give his name or any account of himself and was remanded in custody. A week later he was brought up again; he admitted then that his name was Reuben Bigland and demanded that Bottomley should be called as a witness. There being no evidence that the bond had been stolen—on the contrary, the police had ascertained that it had been issued to the prisoner's own niece, who would make no charge against her uncle—the charge was withdrawn and the prisoner was discharged. "I do not want to be discharged," exclaimed Bigland. "I want Mr. Bottomley to be called. I represent 250,000 people."

"You are discharged," said the magistrate.

Having failed in his object in one way, Bigland adopted another. He wrote a pamphlet, "The Downfall of Horatio Bottomley, M. P. His Latest and Greatest Swindle. How He Gulled Poor Subscribers to Invest £1 Notes in His Great Victory War Bond Club," and employed masked men to distribute it all over the country. On September 17, 1921, Bottomley happened to be dining at the Eccentric Club when the cries of these masked hawkers of the pamphlet were wafted through the club windows. Very unwisely Bottomley lost his temper; he left the club and wrote a paragraph in his paper, the *Sunday Illustrated,* declaring that he intended to prosecute Bigland for criminal libel.

He could not now draw back. Nobody was more pleased than Bigland when the police came to arrest him. Among Bottomley's charges was one of blackmail. This was dismissed, the magistrate remarking, "I am unable to believe Mr. Bottomley on oath." On the libel charge Bigland was committed for trial. He read a statement in which he said that an offer had been made to his son by E. T. Hooley of £20,000 if his father would withdraw his statements. The bribe was indignantly refused.

A number of cross-actions intervened, and it was not until January 23, 1922, that Bigland faced a jury at the Central Criminal Court on a charge of criminal libel. To the surprise of the uninitiated in court, Bottomley's counsel rose and said that he proposed to offer no evidence. This meant that the jury must return a verdict of not guilty and that Bigland's plea of justification could not be read or find its way through the press to the general public. But Bottomley had to pay the costs—£1600—and this led to his third bankruptcy. Bigland now stood committed to the assizes in Shrewsbury on February 18, 1922.

Meanwhile the case against Bottomley was being very ably prepared by a team of Scotland Yard officers working under Chief Inspector Mercer of the Central Division. It entailed an immense amount of work and great intelligence. On the application of the director of public prosecutions a summons was issued from Bow Street, in answer to which Bottomley appeared in person, charging him with fraudulently converting £5,000—part of the proceeds of the Victory Bond Club subscriptions—to his own use. The jury, after retiring for thirty minutes, returned a verdict of guilty, and the judge in sentencing him said, "The crime is aggravated by your high position, the number and poverty of your victims, the trust they imposed in you and which you abused. It is aggravated by the magnitude of your frauds, and by the callous effrontery with which they were committed and sought to be defended. I can see no mitiga. tion. The sentence of the Court upon you is that you be kept in penal servitude for seven years."

Bottomley appealed against his sentence, but the appeal was rejected. Bigland, of course, was acquitted on the charge of criminal libel.

Among the army of cheats who have battened on the credulity of their fellow men Bottomley stands almost alone. His blustering eloquence, whether as a speaker or a writer, was due to his quick apprehension of the temper of his audience. He had a protean gift of instinctive knowledge of what people were thinking of him. Nothing pleased him more than pitting himself against the cleverest advocates at the Bar and scoring off them. He was armed at all points with vanity, but there was one weak spot in his armour: he could not stand ridicule. It is difficult to explain how he contrived to captivate so many lawyers and others in high places except by the suggestion that the whole country had lost its judgment and its balance in those early postwar years when people were dissipating the fortunes made so easily during the war.

Before the war Bottomley had accumulated money by company promotion, and in this enterprise he had hunted in couples with Hooley. They exploited the old men of substance and the young men by clever insight into character. Old men who had been hardheaded and hardfisted in trade were induced to speculate through the cupidity which is the characteristic of a man who has "hammered out his fortune." Hooley was the first to suggest speculaton. He would then take the victim to see Bottomley, who would point out how advantageously part of the fortune could be turned to account richly if invested in one of the companies controlled jointly by the two swindlers. They knew that he would never dare to admit failure, and so he could always be counted upon for further contributions in the hope of retrieving his losses.

The young were easier game. One of them was induced to part with £327,000 in the hope of making a million.

When the gullibility of the rich seemed to be nearing its end, Bottomley turned to the poor and, remembering the gambling instinct of the Englishman, he promoted sweepstakes on the Continent, where sweepstakes were not illegal. Years of self-indulgence did not seem to have impaired his self-confidence and alertness. His liquor bill in the House of Commons dining room amounted to £200 a year; he spent large sums in entertaining, and for years he had been spending as much as and more than he made by his frauds. Among the soldiers and munition workers he was regarded as the champion of the poor. There were several moments in his career when he might have pulled up and turned to honesty, but the parvenu's instinct to glitter before the world was too strong for him. His sentence of penal servitude was the end at last. He had lost everything, and there was nothing left but to quit the scene. For a few years after his discharge from prison he lingered in poverty, supported by the charity of friends, and at the last his mental powers were failing him. He died on May 27, 1933.

CHAPTER XXIV

The Thompson and Bywaters Case

Before the armistice, Scotland Yard was expecting a great wave of postwar crime. Certainly there was a rise in sensational crime, and this is not to be wondered at when we remember that a large number of criminals who had been absorbed by the army were relegated again to civil life without much prospect of finding jobs; that a considerable number of demobilized men were suffering from shell shock, and that the war which we were told was fought to make the world safe for democracy had not made it safe for men who were looking forward to a life of ease and comparative affluence. The savage slaughter of the Great War had affected even the civilian population in the low value it placed on human life, even among those who had taken no part in it. The crime that has now to be described is a case in point.

Among the sensational crimes of the postwar period which were solved by the C.I.D. of Scotland Yard was the case of Bywaters and Mrs. Thompson. On Wednesday, October 4, 1922, the divisional detective-inspector of K Division rang up Scotland Yard to report that he had what looked like "a nasty case of murder." A young married couple, Mr. and Mrs. Thompson, had been returning from a theatre a little after midnight when, while they were passing through an ill-lighted side street, the husband had staggered, callapsed, and died. The wife, who was sobbing hysterically, appealed to some passers-by for help. They ran for a doctor, who pronounced the man to be dead. Blood was coming from his mouth; it was assumed that he had had some kind of seizure. The body was removed to the mortuary, and a uniformed constable took the distracted woman home. A little later another policeman, when removing the clothes of the dead man, found that he had been stabbed several times and that a terrible knife wound at the back of the neck might have been sufficient to kill him. On this the detectives were sent to see Mrs. Thompson, whom they found in a very agitated state and quite incapable of giving any coherent explanation.

All she could say was that while they were walking home her husband had seemed to be suddenly overcome and that she had supported him until he collapsed against a wall. She could not account for his wounds, but it was noticed that both her face and her clothes were stained with blood. This, of course, was quite consistent with her story that she had supported him. The inspector added that he had seen her and that she was with him at the Elephant police station at that moment. A close search had been made for the knife that had caused the wounds, but nothing had been found.

Chief Inspector (as he then was) Frederick Wensley happened to be in temporary charge of the group of divisions which included K. He started at once for Ilford in his car; the rain was coming down in torrents. As soon as he arrived at the police station he saw Mrs. Thompson, the widow, who was in a state of genuine distress. She was still wearing the evening gown in which she had gone to the theatre. She was a woman rather above the average in culture and intelligence. She had come to the police station with one of her relations because it was convenient to have her there while inquiries were being made. There was also the hope that when she recovered herself she might be able to give a less disjointed account of the tragedy. There were no grounds for regarding her with any suspicion.

Wensley succeeded in getting from her in fair detail

what had happened up to the moment when her husband collapsed, but there she stuck. She was either unable or unwilling to go further.

Her husband, Percy Thompson, was a shipping clerk, thirty-two years old; she herself was twenty-eight. They had been married seven years; they lived in a little house in Kensington Gardens, Ilford. When he went to his shipping office, she went to her place of business as manageress and bookkeeper to a firm of wholesale milliners; between them they were making a very comfortable living. On the previous evening she and her husband had accompanied her uncle and aunt to the Criterion Theatre. They had separated at the theatre, and the Thompsons had caught a train to Ilford. It was while they were walking home from the station that the murder was committed. After several hours' questioning, that was as far as the detectives could get. They were led to suppose that the crime had been committed by a total stranger without any motive at all. Of course it was only four years since the war, and during that time there had been a few cases of crimes committed by ex-soldiers without any apparent motive. Again and again Mrs. Thompson had been urged to mention any person who might have had some fancied reason for killing her husband, but she shook her head. Those of her relations whom Wensley questioned were equally unhelpful.

One piece of information Wensley did get: the murdered man had a brother. This brother was sent for, and immediately the case took on a dramatic turn.

"What sort of a fellow was your brother?" asked Wensley.

The young man was perfectly frank in his reply, but in referring to his brother's domestic life he mentioned a young fellow named Bywaters, who, he said, had lodged for some time with the Thompsons and had become very friendly with his sister-in-law. Speaking of his brother, he said, "I never could understand how he tolerated the situation." At the same time he pointed out that Bywaters could

TWO VIEWS OF NEW SCOTLAND YARD

THROUGH the gates at the bottom pass the police cars and the vans
of the famous Flying Squad.

have had nothing to do with the crime, for he was then absent on a sea voyage.

From this Wensley inferred that the domestic life of the couple had not been running smoothly, a fact of which not the slightest hint had as yet been gathered. To their neighbours and the outside world there had been nothing to show that they were not leading a happy and contented life. If it had not been for that hint from the brother, the murder might have remained a mystery for all time.

Wensley lost no time in returning to Mrs. Thompson and the relation who was with her. "Who," he asked, "was Bywaters?" Mrs. Thompson replied that he was a youth who had known her since childhood, a ship's writer, who was often away on voyages but was then on leave and due to rejoin his ship on the following day. When had she seen him last? She began to fence with the question, but Wensley pressed it and at last elicited the fact that on the night of the murder Bywaters had visited Mrs. Thompson's sister at her parents' house at Manor Park and had left at about eleven o'clock.

Now Manor Park is only a mile or two distant from Ilford; on the other hand it would have been practically impossible at midnight for Bywaters to get to his mother's house at Upper Norwood by any rail or bus route. This set Wensley thinking. Why had Mrs. Thompson so carefully avoided any reference to this man? Why would she not speak about him in reply to a direct question? At last a hint of a motive began to loom in the distance.

One thing was obvious: by hook or by crook, Bywaters had to be found before they were twelve hours older. He might know nothing about the murder; he might know a great deal. As a matter of precaution it was decided to keep Mrs. Thompson at the police station until the police had probed the matter further.

It was here that a valuable reform in C.I.D. organization which Mr. Wensley had always advocated came into play. Instead of having to report progress to Scotland Yard and seek authority for every step he took, he was in a position to take instant action over a wide area. He used the Flying Squad and the local C.I.D. freely; every place where Bywaters was likely to go was covered. Had he eluded the detectives for another twenty-four hours, he might have got away to sea, and the evidence which the police were able to secure would have been destroyed. He might even have married Mrs. Thompson, and the two might have settled down respectably in a neat little suburban villa.

At six o'clock that evening the detectives who were keeping observation on the house of Mrs. Thompson's parents at Manor Park saw a young man who proved to be Bywaters. They accosted him and invited him to accompany them to Ilford police station.

Wensley was waiting with Inspector Hall in the C.I.D. office when Bywaters came in and hung up his overcoat. Wensley was quick to notice that there were small spots on the sleeves. He sent a message to the divisional surgeon to come down and say whether the spots were bloodstains or not, and saw him apply a rough-and-ready test that was new to him. The surgeon tore a strip from an evening newspaper, dipped it in water, and applied it to the smallest of the spots. The blood was drawn up by capillary attraction till it tinged the paper.

Bywaters was a tall, handsome young fellow of twenty, but both in appearance and in manner he seemed several years older. "What do you want with me?" he asked almost truculently.

Truculence was not the line to take with a man like Wensley, who knew from long experience that the ordinary person would have been anxious to help the police when they were inquiring into a cowardly murder, but Wensley showed no resentment; he told Bywaters civilly that his only object in seeing him was to ask his help in getting at the truth. However, when the doctor reported that the spots on the coat were bloodstains, though without further examination he could not say whether the blood was human or not, Wensley told Bywaters that the police would keep his coat and that he would be detained. He was indignant. "Why?" he exclaimed; "I know nothing about it."

He was going on to say more, but Inspector Hall intervened, warning him that he was not obliged to say anything, but that if he wished to make any statement, it should be taken down in writing. To this he assented.

It was not Wensley's practice to let a prisoner blunder into a statement without first giving him an opportunity of reflecting on what he intended to say. He told the young man that he wanted his version of his association with Mrs. Thompson, and his own movements on the fatal evening. Once or twice a question was put to him to clear up some ambiguity. At some of these questions there was a return to his old defiant manner, but Wensley calmed him down by telling him that if he wished to assist justice, he should tell all he knew. In the end he was clever enough to tell only what he knew that the police would find out for themselves. His statement amounted to this: Mrs. Thompson and he had always been good friends, and during the summer of the previous year he had stayed with her and her husband for about six weeks, at first as a guest and then as a paying boarder. One day he intervened in a quarrel between the couple, and the husband asked him to leave. He stayed with his mother for a time, and then signed on as a ship's writer. On his return he called on the Thompsons. The husband received him rather coldly, but they parted on good terms. Since then he had not visited them, but had met them once or twice at the house of Mrs. Thompson's parents. He had not seen Thompson since the previous June, but had met Mrs. Thompson without her husband's knowledge several times and had lunched with her on the day before the murder. He had known for a long time that she was not happy with her husband. He had written twice to her, and she had written to him in affectionate terms, but he had destroyed her letters.

On the day of the murder he had left home before midday and had spent the afternoon alone in the West End. About seven in the evening he had visited Mrs. Thompson's parents and had stayed at the house till after eleven o'clock. He caught a train to Victoria, but missed the last train to Gipsy Hill, and had had to walk home, reaching the house about three in the morning.

He was asked why he had not hastened to communicate with Mrs. Thompson as soon as he heard of the murder. He replied that he had had to take his mother to the City and that it was not until about five o'clock that he bought an evening paper and learned for the first time about the tragedy. He went straight to the house of her parents, and from there he had been brought to the police station. He denied that he had ever had a knife of the kind that had been used for the murder.

A party of Flying Squad men had been sent to keep observation on the house in Norwood where Bywaters's mother lived. No one was at home; it was not until 11 P.M. that the inspector in charge telephoned that Mrs. Bywaters had just arrived. The case was now sufficiently advanced to justify searching the house and bringing away anything that seemed to have a bearing on the case. In Bywaters's bedroom they found in a suitcase letters from Mrs. Thompson containing more than the usual endearments between lovers: ". . . Don't forget what we talked of in the tearoom. I'll still risk and try if you will . . ."

This was the stage reached at midnight, only twenty-four hours after the murder had been committed, but so far there was nothing more than suspicion to go upon, and it was unsafe to make a charge. Nevertheless the two were detained for the night at the police station. Bywaters was to sleep in the library; Mrs. Thompson in the matron's room. The only solid ground that had been gained during the day was that the two had been clandestine lovers; that Bywaters had quarrelled with the murdered husband; that there were passages in the wife's letters into which a sinister meaning might be read; that Bywaters's account of his movements on the fatal evening rested only on his own word. But there was not a tittle of evidence that he had been on the spot at the time of the crime.

On the following day inquiries were pushed on. It was not until the afternoon that Mrs. Thompson was asked whether she could give any further information about her husband's assailant. The letters found at Mrs. Bywaters's house were shown to her, and she admitted that she had been on affectionate terms with the young man. She said not a word about having seen him on the day of the murder, though the police knew that she had had tea with him at a confectioner's at five o'clock that day.

At the close of this interview there was a dramatic development. Neither of the suspects knew that the other was detained. In leaving the C.I.D. office to return to the matron's room, Mrs. Thompson had to pass through a yard from which the library drew its light, and she caught a glimpse of her lover through the window. Her nerve entirely deserted her.

"Oh, God!" she cried. "What can I do? Why did he do it? I did not want him to do it. . . . I must tell the truth." The divisional detective-inspector, who was escorting her, tried to warn her. "Do you realize what you are saying, Mrs. Thompson? It may be used in evidence." He brought her back to the office, made her sit down, and repeated what she had said in her hearing. Then she began to talk:

"When we got near Endsleigh Gardens a man rushed out and knocked me away and pushed me away from my husband. I was dazed for the moment. When I recovered I saw my husband scuffling with a man. The man whom I knew as Freddie Bywaters was running away. He was wearing a blue overcoat and a grey hat. I knew it was him, though I did not see his face."

When she had left the office Bywaters was brought in. He was told that they would both be charged with murder.

"Why her?" he exclaimed angrily. "Mrs. Thompson was not aware of my movements."

He went on to say that he had waited for the two to return from the theatre, had pushed Mrs. Thompson out of the way, and had told Thompson that he must separate from his wife. Thompson refused, and there was a fight in which Bywaters had used a knife and Thompson "got the worst of it." Mrs. Thompson stood by, "spellbound." "The reason I fought with Thompson," he went on, "was because he never acted like a man to his wife. He seemed several degrees lower than a snake. I loved her, and I could not go on seeing her lead that life. I did not intend to kill him. I only meant to injure him. I gave him the opportunity of standing up to me like a man, but he wouldn't."

Both prisoners were charged and remanded at the police court. The police inquiries were continued; they resulted in the recovery of a large number of letters from Mrs. Thompson to Bywaters, most of which were found in his ditty box on board his ship. They showed that the project of murdering the husband had long been in the minds of the pair, and that Mrs. Thompson had made several attempts to poison her husband. They were extraordinary letters, filled with vivacious gossip and endearments, and at the same time enclosing newspaper cuttings of poisoning cases and asking for instructions. The body of the murdered man was exhumed and examined by Sir Bernard Spilsbury, but no trace of poison was found in it.

The trial excited enormous public interest; people were offering large sums for seats in the public gallery. There was no real defence for Bywaters; for Mrs. Thompson it was urged that the incriminating passages in her letters showed only that she was living in a romantic world of her own, hoping to retain her lover by a pretence that she was trying to kill her husband for his sake. The woman elected to give evidence in her own behalf, but her admissions under cross-examination were deadly to her.

It struck Wensley that throughout the trial Bywaters was posing as a melodramatic hero, though his attitude was shaken when the judge spoke of "the unreal and unnatural atmosphere that had been created around an ordinary charge of a wife and an adulterer murdering a husband."

The trial lasted five days, and the jury was out of court for two hours before it returned a verdict of guilty against both prisoners. Bywaters squared his shoulders and addressed the judge. "I say that the jury is wrong. Edith Thompson is not guilty."

The woman was on the verge of collapse. "I am not guilty. Oh, God, I am not guilty," she cried.

The appeal of both prisoners was heard and dismissed; a huge petition for the reprieve of the woman was rejected by the Home Secretary, and the two were hanged on the same morning—January 9, 1923—the man at Pentonville, the woman at Holloway.

There was instantly an outbreak of the hysteria that from time to time warps the judgment of the British people, especially when the criminals are young and good-looking and illicit love is the motive for the crime. At such moments you hear no word of sympathy for the victim, in this case a young man who is enticed by a traitorous wife into an ill-lighted back street to give her lover an opportunity of doing him to death while she stands by without a cry for help until the deed is done. Bywaters's mother said afterwards that her son had always been ready when "dared" to do anything, and it was this quality on which the infatuated woman, eight years older than he, had consistently played. If the police had been less prompt, Bywaters would have got back to his ship and destroyed the letters which incriminated the woman. The pair might, as suggested above, have settled down in a suburban cottage to a life that would soon have become a hell for both of them. The man, head-strong and hot-tempered as he was, would soon have tired of his ageing wife; there would have been quarrels and re-criminations none the less bitter because each was in the power of the other. The scaffold was a more fitting end. Moreover, I think that the inexorable logic of the criminal law brought some measure of sanity to the unbalanced people who were living in a false world of their own making.

THE FAHMY CASE

At midnight on July 10, 1923, London was visited by a terrific thunderstorm. For more than two hours the sky

was illuminated by continuous flashes, and at least once
what appeared to be a gigantic fireball broke into a million
fragments of dazzling sparks. It was a weird and awful
night.

At 2 A.M., when the storm was at its height, a porter
wheeling baggage along one of the corridors of the Savoy
Hotel heard through the thunder three pistol shots fired
in quick succession. He ran to investigate and found a young
Egyptian prince, Prince Fahmy, lying dressed in his pyjamas
on the floor, with blood trickling out of his mouth. His
French wife was standing over him; she threw down a
Browning automatic pistol, and three empty cartridges lay
at her feet. The night manager was summoned; she cried
out to him in French, "What have I done? What will they
do to me? Oh, sir, I have been married six months and I
have suffered terribly." To Dr. Gordon, who was called in,
she said, also in French, "I pulled the trigger three times."
It was known that she had a pistol always near her to protect her jewels, which were of immense value.

The story of the couple who were staying at the Savoy
Hotel was remarkable. The prince was the son of a famous
Egyptian engineer and had inherited his father's colossal
fortune. He was then only twenty-two. He had bought his
title of prince by the most lavish generosity to charities.
While attached to the Egyptian legation in Paris he had
met a fascinating lady—Madame Marguerite Laurent—
whose maiden name had been Marguerite Alibert. The
prince had returned to Egypt, and thither she had followed
him to be married. Before leaving she wrote to a friend that
she was going out to live a "dream life" with the most
charming man she knew. She was destined to be quickly dis-
illusioned. For six months she had endured intense misery
and humiliation.

They arrived at the great London hotel in company with
the prince's Egyptian secretary, Said Enani. On the day before the tragedy, while the three were sitting at luncheon
together, the conductor of the orchestra, wishing to do

honour to the princess, came to their table and asked what piece of music she would like his orchestra to play. She said, "Thank you very much, but my husband is going to kill me in the next twenty-four hours, and I am not very anxious for music." The polite musician bowed gravely and said, "I hope that you will be here tomorrow, madame."

The case was put into the hands of Inspector Crosse of Scotland Yard. The part played by Scotland Yard detectives did not loom large in the published accounts of the trial, but in fact it was considerable. It was necessary to obtain from the Egyptian police a detailed account of the past life of the dead man and to arrange for the necessary witnesses to come over for the trial. Inquiries had also to be made in Paris. Terrible facts were revealed. It was shown that whereas Prince Fahmy had struck out the clause in the marriage contract which permitted the wife to sue for divorce, he was free on his side to divorce her by mere "repudiation" without any legal process; that whereas before marriage he had written to her, "Torch of my life, you appear to me surrounded by a halo. I see your head encircled by a crown which I reserve for you here in this beautiful country of my ancestors," he had written to his wife's sister, immediately after the marriage, "Just now I am engaged in training her. Yesterday, to begin, I did not come in to lunch or dinner, and I also left her at the theatre. This will teach her, I hope, to respect my wishes. With women one must act with energy and be severe." He had forced her to ride in a public tram as part of this "training."

On February 21 there had been a very serious scene. He had sworn on the Koran in her presence that he would kill her; she went from that day onward in constant fear of her life. From being a cheerful, fascinating woman she had become a broken and miserable wreck.

On February 23 the prince took her in his yacht to Luxor, ten days' journey from Cairo. There were six black servants on board—one of them a giant whose life the prince had saved; he became her gaoler. Dr. Gordon's evidence was likely to be very material. He said that Madame Fahmy had to undergo a very painful operation; that she wished to have it performed in Paris, but she had no money, and the husband refused to let her go there. Further, he knocked her about. She was in great physical pain, and on the fatal evening he had pestered her with his abnormal advances. Mortally afraid of him, she had picked up the pistol and had tried to empty the cartridges from it by firing one shot out of the window. Her physical condition was consistent with what she said. He had advanced upon her crouching, and she, meaning only to keep him away, had held the pistol to his face; somehow it had gone off.

There were three women on the jury; they began to understand the suffering this woman had had to go through, married to a sexual pervert and treated like a slave in an Oriental harem. While staying at the Savoy Hotel she had received an anonymous letter:

> Do not agree to return to Egypt. A journey means a possible accident, poison in a flower, a subtle weapon which is neither seen nor heard. Remain in Paris with those who love you and will protect you.

On the night of his death Fahmy had held before her eyes the money that would have taken her to Paris for her operation, but had refused to give it to her unless she submitted herself to his abnormal desires. He had then seized her by the throat and threatened to strangle her. There were marks on her arms of his violence. There were also witnesses brought from abroad to prove that the dead man had been a pervert.

But there it was. The woman had fired the shot; the British law does not admit the excuse of passion for a homicide; on the face of it, all that could be hoped by the defence was a verdict of manslaughter instead of murder. But Madame Fahmy was brilliantly defended by Sir Edward Marshall Hall—himself an expert on ballistics. He convinced the jury that the shooting was an accident; that the accused woman, intending only to scare her husband into leaving her alone—with her nerves all upset by physical pain and by the raging thunderstorm—had taken up what she thought was an empty pistol and held it to his face. The jury returned a verdict of not guilty, and the court had to be cleared of the cheering crowd before the judge's voice could be heard.

CHAPTER XXV

The Raid on the Premises of
the Russian Trading Delegation

Soon after the russians were allowed to open trade relations with England in 1926 they established a central agency in London called "Arcos Ltd.," with offices in Moorgate Street in a building specially constructed at a cost of over £300,000. It became known to the Special Branch that this office was not used exclusively to conduct trade, but was in fact the centre for political business that could not safely be transacted at the Russian legation. In fact, Arcos Ltd. was conducting in London an international campaign for the overthrow of existing institutions in all the so-called capitalist countries. It was significant that the building itself contained massive strong rooms with thick concrete walls and steel doors with elaborate bolts and locks. Within these strong rooms were heavy steel safes, and in other parts of the building steel safes were built into the walls behind the wood panelling.

All this had been known from early in 1926 onwards. It was known, moreover, that a number of subversive societies were drawing their funds from Russia through the medium of Arcos. British labour and British trade unionism were restless and indignant at the failure of the general strike, and though there was no evidence that the strike itself had been financed from Russia it was certain that one or two of the unions affiliated with the Trade Union Congress were receiving the greater part of their funds through Arcos.

The position was delicate. The Russian Soviet minister enjoyed the usual diplomatic privileges. Arcos, on the contrary, was ostensibly only a trading concern with no privileges other than those which could be claimed by any foreign trading concern, and yet the police had very strong reasons for getting to know what secret business was being conducted behind the walls of the imposing edifice in Moorgate.

It chanced that in May 1927 a British subject employed in the Air Force had been convicted of stealing two documents containing details of aeroplane construction, and the Special Branch received confidential information that one of these documents had been taken to the Arcos building and reproduced in the photostat room in the basement. On this, application was made to a magistrate of the City of London for a warrant under the Official Secrets Act, and a police raid upon the building was organized on May 12.

On their arrival in the building the police made straight for the photostat room, of which a Russian named Koling was in charge. Others entered the room occupied by the cipher clerk, Anton Miller. Upstairs the entire clerical staff was mustered in the corridors, and all were refused leave to quit the building. The door of one room was locked. It had no handle and could only be opened from outside by a key. The police demanded the key, but it was refused. Orders were then given to break into the room. There they found a member of the staff busy burning documents in the grate. He was taking them from a box full of papers, and there was a scuffle before he would give it up. The papers in the grate were burnt past recovery. The documents in the box and in some of the strong rooms in the building furnished abundant evidence that Arcos was carrying on a violently anti-British campaign. There was proof of a close association between Soviet organizers and Communists, both in England and in other European capitals, and that Arcos Ltd. was habitually used as a clearing house for subversive correspondence.

It was not surprising that the Russian press should have foamed with indignation at what they called the outrage, or that they should have printed mendacious reports of what had actually happened during the raid, but it was surprising to find a sober body like the Trade Union Congress General Council writing to the Prime Minister to protest strongly against what it considered the "unjustifiable proceedings of the Home Office."

The *Times* inquired in a leading article why a British Labour party should be stirred to a frenzy of passion because a house of business was searched by the properly constituted officers of the law. What was the bond of sympathy? There was no foundation for the theory that the date of the raid was carefully chosen to coincide with the committee stage of the Trade Union Bill.[1]

Although, probably, the raid might have been better managed, it had important results. The Prime Minister announced in the House of Commons that the government found itself compelled in these circumstances to terminate the trade agreement, to withdraw the British mission from Russia, and to demand the recall of the Soviet minister from London.

THE MURDER OF VIVIAN MESSITER (1928)

Mention has been made of occasions when detective officers of Scotland Yard have been called in to assist provincial police forces in investigating difficult cases of crime. For many years these occasions were rare, because the expenses of such detectives had to be paid out of county or borough police funds; but in recent years a concession was made by the Home Office and it was agreed that the cost should be borne by the Metropolitan Police Fund. Thereafter, such applications became more common. A good example of the value of such co-operation is to be found

---

[1]In the British parliament there are four stages in every bill—first reading; second reading; committee stage and third reading, after which the bill goes to the House of Lords before becoming law. The debates take place in the committee stage.

in the murder of Vivian Messiter at Southampton on October 1928.

In September Messiter was appointed manager of the Wolf's Head Oil Company in Southampton. He took lodgings in Carlton Road with some people named Parrot. On October 30 he left the house earlier than usual to keep an appointment with a man at 8:45 A.M. He did not return to his lodgings that day, and next morning it was found that his bed had not been slept in.

He was never again seen alive, but it was not until November 8 that Mr. Parrot, his landlord, reported to the police that his lodger was missing. A police officer was sent with him to 42 Grove Street, where the oil company had its local depot. This was a small warehouse for storing oil, but as a car was also kept there it was known as the garage.

Finding the outer gates shut, the two men climbed over the wall into the yard in front of the garage and tried the doors, but these were fastened on the outside by a bolt and padlock. This disposed in their opinion of any suspicion that Messiter might have committed suicide in the garage, but to make sure that there had been no foul play they broke a pane of glass in the window, thrust in a lighted candle, and satisfied themselves that nothing seemed to have been disturbed.

Meanwhile a new representative was appointed by the oil company in Messiter's place, and on January 9, 1929, this man called upon Mr. Parrot for the key of the garage. A search was made for it in Messiter's room, but it could not be found.

Next morning the new representative broke into the garage in order to begin his duties, and he came upon the body of a man lying in a narrow passage between packing cases of oil. He lost no time in informing the Southampton police, who found pools of coagulated blood on the floor and splashes of blood on the cases and walls. The state of the body showed that it had been lying there for some weeks. It was decomposed, and rats had gnawed away the flesh of the face. It was removed to a mortuary, where at first it was believed that the dead man had been shot through the head. A search of the clothing showed that nothing of value remained in it except a ring which was covered by a glove. In one of the pockets was found a letter from a man signing himself H. F. Galton, written from 163 Oakley Road, Shirley, Southampton.

The chief constable of Southampton immediately applied to Scotland Yard for help, and the case was assigned to Chief Inspector Prothero and Detective-Sergeant Young of the Central Office. On their arrival they received from the chief constable two books which had been found on the seat of the little Morris-Oxford car. The first step was to make a thorough examination of the body, to move the packing cases and drums of oil, and to search the garage thoroughly. The medical examination showed that the cause of death was not a bullet wound, but blows on the head from a blunt instrument. The splashes of blood on the packing case nearest the head seemed to show that the body was recumbent when the blows were struck; that the head was struck from behind, but that the body had been turned over—probably by the murderer, to make it easier to rifle the pockets. Near the door of the garage, twenty-eight feet from the body, was found a hammer with a few hairs and blood adhering to it. The medical officer was able to say that the hair closely resembled the hair of the murdered man, for there was no doubt at this point that the decomposed body was that of Vivian Messiter. The Home Office medical expert, Sir Bernard Spilsbury, was called in; he confirmed the view of the police surgeon that the hairs adhering to the hammer head had come from the eyebrow of the murdered man, who had received a crushing blow in the face. No fingerprint was found on the hammer.

The next step was to settle the date of the murder and to find out something about Messiter's past life and his associates. H. F. Galton, whose letter had been found in the pocket, proved to be an employee of the Southern Railway. He said that he had given Messiter an order for oil, writing to him through the newspaper in which he had read an advertisement, and that Messiter had delivered the oil on October 30 and had paid him two shillings and sixpence commission; that he did not know where Messiter lived, or where his place of business was; that the whole transaction had been personal. Messiter, therefore, was alive on October 30. A search was made of his lodging. In the bed-sitting-room were found two letters—one from his sister; the other from a man who signed himself "William F. Thomas," dated October 23. It ran:

5 Cranbery Avenue.

SIR,

Re your advert. of the present instant. Being in the motor trade and having a good connection among farmers and garage proprietors, I am sure that I can do you good service in oil lines. I am constantly asked my opinion of such and I am sure that I can build up a good connection of same.

Trusting I shall have a reply to the favour of such,

I am, Sir,

Yours truly,

WILLIAM F. THOMAS.

The letter from the dead man's sister made it possible to learn something of his history. He had spent several years in Mexico in touch with oil companies and had come home to try his luck as an oil salesman. The police learned one other fact of importance—that he had possessed a gold watch engraved with the initials V. M.

The mystery that enshrouded the case led to the widest newspaper publicity. The police were inundated with letters from all parts of the country, indicating persons whom the writers suspected. Ninety-nine per cent of such well-meaning communications lead to nothing, but all have to be investigated before they can be dismissed. In all such cases Scotland Yard believes that success depends upon hard work and luck in almost equal proportions. Thus far Chief Inspector Prothero and his assistant had put in an immense amount of hard work, and they had a right to hope that luck would still favour them. On the floor of the garage they found a tiny gold ring which had been bent as if detached by force from a gold watch, and in the sawdust covering the floor they found a torn scrap of paper with writing on it. It seemed to be part of a receipt.

On the back of the paper was some writing in indelible pencil, but it was so covered with oil and dirt that it was undecipherable.

This undecipherable receipt was taken to Mr. Ainsworth Mitchell, an analytical chemist, who cleaned off the grease and dirt and disclosed the words:

> 5 Cranbery Ave. . . .
> October 20th
> With thanks,
> Horne

Chief Inspector Prothero's heart beat fast when he read the mutilated address, "5 Cranbery Ave.," remembering that he had found this very address in the letter, to which he had attached little importance at the time, from William F. Thomas. The search was continued. In a little room at the end of the building was found a crumpled sheet of paper bearing the heading "Wolf's Head Oil Company," and written in pencil below were the words:

MR. W. F. THOMAS,
  I shall be at 42 Grove Street at ten, but not at noon.
                                    VIVIAN MESSITER.

No. 42 Grove Street was the address of the garage.

And then came a telephone message—the turning point in the case. A Mr. Mitchell of Downton, a village sixteen miles from Southampton, rang up the police to say that he had read in the press details about the murder, and thought that there might be some connection between the man W. F. Thomas and a man named Thomas who had entered his service just after the murder and had absconded with £143 belonging to him.

The next step was to trace Thomas's movements both before and after the fatal October 30. It was found that on the 20th a man who called himself Thomas had taken a room for himself and his wife at 5 Cranbery Avenue,

Southampton; that he had paid ten shillings in advance, for which his landlady, Mrs. Horne, had given him a receipt. It was half of that receipt which had been found in the garage. On October 22 it was found that Thomas had replied to two advertisements in the *Southern Daily Echo;* the first, that of Vivian Messiter for an agent to work on commission, and the other that of Mr. Mitchell, who wanted a motor mechanic. On the following day Messiter had called at 5 Cranbery Avenue to see Thomas and had driven off with him in his little car. On October 26 Mitchell had met Thomas by appointment in Southampton. As a result of both these interviews Thomas was engaged by both advertisers. Messiter was to pay him on commission; with Mitchell he was to start work on a wage basis on November 5; in neither case had he been asked for references.

On October 30 (the day of the murder) Thomas drove out to Downton and asked to be allowed to start work immediately. He was told that there was no accommodation for him before November 5. Nevertheless, he left his lodging with Mrs. Horne on November 3 and started work with Mr. Mitchell on that day. On December 21 Mitchell missed £143 from his office. He went to the local police sergeant who, very naturally, questioned Thomas, who was the most likely man to have stolen it. Thomas disclaimed all knowledge and told the sergeant that he had been employed with the Allied Transport Road Association, Bold Street, Southampton. On the following day he absconded with his wife, but on his way out of Downton he chanced to meet the police sergeant, who stopped him. He told the sergeant that they were going to do some shopping, and the sergeant let them pass. The two begged a lift on a lorry as far as Salisbury, where Thomas deposited the woman and engaged a taxi to drive him back to Downton. As the taxi drove into the village, the driver turned his head and saw that Thomas was lying on the bottom of the cab. As soon as they were clear of the village he rose and told the driver to stop and turn round. Thomas went into a field and was absent for some minutes. He returned and told the driver to take him back to Salisbury. This apparently aimless drive had been to recover the stolen money from its hiding place in the field. The couple then hired a car in Salisbury and drove to London.

A search of the rooms occupied by Thomas at Downton and the luggage they had left behind them provided a fresh clue. In a flower vase the police found a memorandum of a Manchester garage. Inquiries through the Manchester police showed that Thomas had been employed there under the name of Podmore; that he had stolen a motorcar from them and absconded on October 17—three days before he took Mrs. Horne's lodgings under the name of Thomas.

Then followed exhaustive inquiries through a dozen police forces throughout the country about this elusive person. He was traced to London, to Birmingham, and to Staffordshire. He went under the name of Podmore, no doubt with the object of asserting, in case of necessity, that he had never passed under any other name. In Birmingham he and his wife had replied to an advertisement which led to their employment at a hotel in Meriden.

The discovery of Messiter's body was published on January 10, and on that date Thomas and his wife left their employment without waiting for their wages and returned to Birmingham, where they parted company—the wife, who was known as "Golden-haired Lil," returning to her home in Staffordshire; the husband proceeding to London.

The hammer, the only weapon used in the murder, was identified by a motor mechanic named Marsh, who worked in a garage about a mile from Messiter's oil depot. Marsh said that he had bought it in France, and that a motor mechanic, whose name he did not know, had borrowed it from him. He had a watertight alibi for the day of the murder. It is right to say that, though there was no reason to doubt that Marsh was telling the truth, he failed to pick out Podmore from a line of twelve men at a subsequent stage of the inquiry as the man who had borrowed his hammer.

This case is an admirable illustration of the system of

teamwork which prevails, not only in Scotland Yard, but between the police forces all over the country. Prothero had caused a detailed description of the missing couple to be circulated to all police forces as well as to the newspapers. The police of Stoke-on-Trent at once recognized both the missing persons from their descriptions. They knew that "Golden-haired Lil" was identical with a woman named Hambleton of Sneyd Green, Hanley. All these places lie close together in the County of Staffordshire in the North Midlands. They went to find her, but were too late to catch Podmore. He had paid a flying visit to Sneyd Green, but had left almost immediately. The girl Hambleton had just arrived, having parted from Podmore only a few hours before. She stated that he had left for Southampton via London to be interviewed by the police concerning the death of Messiter. They had seen the police appeal for W. F. Thomas to come forward and had decided that he must go to Southampton to face the music. The police also got from her the address of the hotel where Podmore usually stayed; it was the Leicester Hotel in Vauxhall Bridge Road, London.

A Scotland Yard officer at once went to the Leicester Hotel and found him there. He was at the disadvantage of not knowing how much of his past history the police knew. He said, "I know what you want me for, but I can explain all my movements in Southampton." The officer told him that he must come with him to see Chief Inspector Prothero. He said, "The reason I held back was because of the Stone job." By this he meant a case in which he had been suspected of stealing jewelry at Stone in Staffordshire, but, as he knew very well, the police had exonerated him and allowed him to go.

He was taken to Southampton, where he made a statement to Chief Inspector Prothero in which he said that he had been with Messiter on the fatal morning, when Messiter was dealing with a man named "Maxton" or "Baxton." He said, "I saw money pass from Messiter to this man, and I heard the amount mentioned as two shillings and sixpence."

Later in his statement he said, "Maxton and Messiter had a book before them, and I saw Maxton make an entry." At this point he turned upon Detective-Sergeant Young and asked, "What have you got down?"

Young read over what he had said. Podmore jumped from his seat in angry excitement and paced up and down the room, saying, "I did not say that." Then he sat down and laid his head on his arms on the table, sobbing. After a moment or two he raised his head and said, "No; it was Messiter who made the entry."

The meaning of this outburst was not understood until they came to examine one of the exercise books which had been found in the car. An entry in Messiter's handwriting ran as follows:

> October 30th. 1928.
> Received from Wolf's Head Oil Co.
> Commission on order S. Gover
> 5 gals heavy at 6d,   2s6.
> H. F. GALTON.

It was, as has been said above, a perfectly innocent transaction which had really taken place at Galton's house when Messiter had delivered the oil. The outburst was due, not to this normal transaction, but to the slip which Podmore realized he had made in attributing the entry to "Maxton," as he called Galton, on whom he hoped to be able to fix the murder.

It was then found that a page had been torn out of the exercise book—the page immediately preceding that on which Galton's receipt was written. On this receipt were discovered impressions almost imperceptible to the naked eye. When the page was held at a certain angle in a strong light the impressions of the writing on the missing page could be seen and photographed. It read:

> October 8. 1928.
> Received from Wolf's Head Oil Co.
> Commission on Cromers and Bartlett
> 5 gals at 6d   2s6.
> W. F. T.

No doubt Podmore had discovered Galton's receipt with the fatal date October 30 on it when he was tearing out the missing page, and he took advantage of it in trying to throw the guilt onto Galton.

The writing on the torn receipt, which could not be deciphered, owing to the coating of grease and dirt, was treated first by Mr. Ainsworth Mitchell, the analytical chemist, and afterwards confirmed by an official chemist. They cleaned off the grease and dirt and disclosed the following words in the handwriting of Podmore:

> Possibly 36 galls. Tuesday
> 12 galls. beginning of week
> W. F. Thomas
> Call at gar—sat—10 a.m.
> or 12.30.

This explained the crumpled note found in the back room by the police:

Mr. W. F. Thomas,
I shall be at 42 Grove Street at ten, but not at noon.
VIVIAN MESSITER.

Several duplicate sheets had been torn out of an invoice book, but the two carbon sheets found at the end of the book were covered with impressions of names and addresses. On one of them it was possible to decipher the words, "Cromers and Bartlett, Bold Street, Southampton." This was the address given by "Thomas" as that of the Allied Transport Road Association, with whom, he told the Downton police sergeant, he had been working. An inquiry was made; it was found that there was no Bold Street in Southampton. All the names and addresses that were deciphered on the other carbon sheet also proved to be fictitious. These discoveries were important, for they were the first indication of a motive for the murder. "Thomas" had been giving Messiter fictitious orders for oil and had been paid commission on them. Though there was no proof (since the only person who could have proved it was dead), it was a fair deduction that Messiter had discovered the fraud and was taxing the guilty man with it on that fatal morning; that "Thomas" had a swift vision of what would happen if his employer communicated with the police—the discovery that he was the man who stole a car in Manchester—and that, having a hammer in his hand at the time, he obeyed the impulse to silence this hostile witness forever.

Few criminals are able to invent names and addresses on the spur of the moment. Well aware of this failing, the police made inquiries in the places where "Thomas" was best known, and learned that most of the fictitious names and addresses were familiar to him in the Staffordshire Potteries. Jervis was the name of a family in Stoke-on-Trent, where the Podmore family was well known. There was a firm called "Cromers and Bartlett" in Staffordshire, but they had never placed an order for oil. There were three Bold Streets in the Stoke district. "Thomas" had been arrested by a police sergeant of the uncommon name of Baskeyfield five years earlier.

The man was a strange mixture of cunning and incompetence. He had spent time in removing from the books all the pages that might incriminate him, and yet he left on the scene of the crime crumpled memoranda and the hammer with which he had committed the crime.

In England the police have no power to detain a man on suspicion for the purpose of interrogating him, but in this case fortune favoured them. They could hold their prisoner on another charge—that of stealing a motorcar in Manchester—and could continue their inquiries and put him up for identification without charging him with murder. He was sent to six months' imprisonment, and while serving his sentence he was incautious enough to tell a fellow prisoner about the money he had stolen from Mitchell in Downton—a crime in which there was no direct evidence against him. When this reached the ears of the police he was transferred from Manchester to Winchester prison to be present at the inquest on Messiter, and on completing his sentence he was arrested at the prison gate and tried for the charge of stealing money. One would have thought that he would have learned a lesson against trusting confidences to fellow prisoners; but no; during his second sentence he spoke to at least four prisoners about the "garage murder," and to two of them he made it clear that he had been the murderer. A statement was taken from each of them, and on the morning of his discharge on December 17, 1929, he left the prison gate only to find Chief Inspector Prothero waiting for him with a car, in which he was taken to Southampton to answer the charge of murder, and was committed to the Winchester Assizes.

The evidence against him was purely circumstantial, but it was a chain of circumstances from which it was difficult to escape. He was the only man with Messiter on the morning of the murder and was seeing him by appointment; he was cheating Messiter out of commission on fictitious sales. The rest of the evidence was concerned with his efforts to cover up his tracks, for when the lord chief justice was directing the jury he warned them that the evidence of the accused's fellow prisoners was of necessity tainted, and that in view of all the facts there had been no need to call them at all.

It was a curious coincidence that when the prisoner was entering the police station on his final arrest a plumber employed by the Southampton Borough Council was at the desk handing over a gold watch from which the swivel ring was missing. He had found it in the flushing tank of a public lavatory fifteen yards from the entrance to a theatre which had been attended by "Thomas" and Lil on the evening of the murder.

At the trial the defence made much of the fact that the alleged murderer should have gone no farther away than Downton immediately after the crime. The answer to that argument was that he had not sufficient money to travel far until he had robbed Mr. Mitchell. He was found guilty and sentenced to death, and in spite of an appeal to the higher court and an agitation for a reprieve the sentence was carried out in Winchester prison.

The interest in this case lies chiefly in the patience of the detectives engaged upon it. They had to sift many hundred clues; they had to check statements made by dozens of well-intentioned informants, but though days were consumed in this waste labour they never relaxed that inestimable quality in a detective—pertinacity. In point of fact, in every important case there must be waste labour if the truth is to be established.

The Podmore case is not one that can be cited as an example of quick justice in the British criminal courts. Messiter, the victim, disappeared on October 30, 1928, but was not reported missing until November 8. The execution of Podmore took place on April 22, 1929, and in the meantime he was made to serve two sentences for lesser offences than murder. Official excuses were made for this delay—excuses which did not altogether ring true; but whoever was to blame, it was not the police who were responsible.

I have been asked how long it takes to bring murderers to justice—how long from the day when the crime is first reported to the police to the day when the murderer is hanged. In an earlier part of this volume an account was given of the Voisin case, which was reported to the police on November 2, 1917. It was an intricate case because the body had been dismembered, the hands and head were missing, and there was no indication of the identity of the body, much less of the identity of the murderer, except a laundry mark on the sheet in which the trunk had been wrapped. After much patient investigation the detective police identified both the victim and the murderer, who was condemned to death and executed on March 2, 1918—four months from the discovery of the body.

In an earlier case, that of William Seaman, *alias* King, who had served twenty-eight years in prison for crimes of violence, he was caught almost in the act of murdering a Jew, aged seventy-seven, and his servant, in April 1896. In order to escape from the police he jumped from the roof onto the heads of the crowd, but this only partly broke his fall, and he was removed to hospital with a broken thighbone, which delayed his trial. But even so it was possible to execute him on the 9th of June following. This included the magisterial inquiry, the trial in the Central Criminal Court, the appeal to the Court of Criminal Appeal, and the three weeks that must intervene between sentence and execution—an interval of two months.

N O INVENTION HAS ADDED GREATER DIFFICULTIES to police work than the motorcar, first in respect of the problem of traffic in the streets of the larger cities, and secondly in the detection and pursuit of criminals.

Let us take, first, traffic control. Public carriages in London have been controlled from Scotland Yard ever since the force was established in 1829. From 1869 until 1933 the vehicles as well as the drivers and conductors were licensed by the commissioner of police. In 1933 a new public authority, the London Passenger Transport Board, was created to take over the control of all omnibuses, tramcars, trolley vehicles, and, with a few exceptions, suburban coaches in its area, which includes just under seven hundred square miles. It is the area of Greater London, which has 8,202,818 inhabitants. It is the largest city in the world, not excepting New York, which has 7,473,791, and Paris, with 4,933,855. Berlin comes fourth with 4,288,314. The salient fact about Greater London is that more than one fifth of the population of England inhabit that city and that its share of the total population of the world is about a 250th part. Imagine, then, the congestion there must be in the business quarters of the City when its breadwinners are all on wheels and the streets are no wider than they were a century ago.

It was natural that the regulation of street traffic should fall on the shoulders of the police because there was no one else to undertake it. The problem had become so pressing a few years ago that a proposal to appoint a special traffic corps of pensioned police or ex-service men was being considered; but at that moment a public benefactor came forward with the automatic traffic signals. No doubt when the police controlled traffic they did it by the prestige of their uniform. Now that mechanical signals have been installed, they are found not only cheaper but more effective. Nevertheless, for some years to come constant observation will be necessary to detect disregard of the signals. Whenever London ceases to sin against the traffic regulations the accidents to Metropolitan policemen, which have numbered about twenty-five hundred a year—over 12 per cent of the force—will be almost unknown.

The right to control traffic on special occasions was given to the police under the Metropolitan Police Act, 1839. It was perforce extended at the time of the Great Exhibition in 1851 when horse owners complained vigorously that when the police held out their arms to make signals they frightened the horses. In spite of these complaints, the police received universal praise from British and foreigners alike for their work in 1851. The early commissioners were very careful not to wound the feelings of any class. We find in 1856 an order that if a cabdriver is spoken to by a policeman he is to be called "cabdriver," and the vulgar, offensive word "cabby" is never to be used by the police.

In 1867 the Metropolitan Streets Act gave power to the commissioners of the Metropolitan City Police to make traffic regulations for the area within six miles of Charing Cross in order to remove the worst causes of congestion, such as driving cattle, leaving vehicles standing in the streets, loitering cabs, carrying advertisements, etc.; and the delivery of coal and beer in the busy thoroughfares.

Even in those remote days of the horse, excessive speed had to be checked by the police. In 1869 many summonses were taken out for furious and reckless driving, yet in the five years 1866–70 the number of people run over and killed in the London streets averaged annually 106 and the number injured about 1500. After 1900 the figures rose rapidly. In 1927 they were 1,056 killed and 48,049 injured; and in 1933, 1,441 killed and 56,912 injured.

Until 1896 a mechanically propelled vehicle on a public road had to be preceded by a man on foot with a red flag, and its speed was limited to three miles an hour. The advent of the motorcar forced new legislation on the House of Commons, and the speed limit was raised to twenty miles an hour, which, of course, no motorist would keep to. The police were forced to set traps and to prosecute people with whom they had previously had little to do. Their popularity suffered—it had always been a tradition that they did not set traps for people.

The war suspended progress in setting up a central control, and the police were kept too busy to think of speed limits, but after the war the rivalries of omnibus companies forced the pace. The Ministry of Transport was set up, and a London Traffic Act was passed to cover the area of eighteen hundred square miles that lay within twenty-five miles of Charing Cross. This Act has been of great assistance to the police in establishing roundabout systems, one-way streets, and parking places, to say nothing of clearing the streets of obstructions. In 1930 the Road Traffic Act abolished the speed limit, except for commercial vehicles, and relieved the police of the disagreeable duty of setting traps. On the other hand it created a number of new offences which Scotland Yard had to detect. Lest their activities should raise a storm of protest, Scotland Yard enforces the law in an accommodating spirit. Verbal warnings and cautionary letters are widely resorted to before prosecution takes place; in fact, out of a total exceeding 350,000 cases, 86 per cent were dealt with in this way and only 14 per cent by prosecution. The new Act entailed the maintenance of police vehicles for traffic patrols, and these patrols take cognizance of all kinds of offences, such as car-stealing or "felonious borrowing" as well as ordinary crime. The number of traffic patrols is about five hundred with 140 vehicles. They are organized in four sections corresponding with the four districts of the police area. The men selected for traffic patrol are chosen with great care. They must be competent drivers and experts in traffic law, and they must possess more than the usual tact and judgment. They are in evidence as much as possible in order that drivers may see them. Unfortunately, the accidents that the police can prevent are a very small proportion of the total. It must be remembered that the men who make regulations are not the men who have practical traffic experience. Scotland Yard has to rely upon its men in the streets; it is from them that improvements come.

The first experiment with automatic traffic signals in London was made as long ago as 1868 outside the Houses of Parliament. The apparatus consisted of a semaphore with green and red lights, and the experiment, which was widely applauded, ended in an explosion which injured the constable who worked it. After the war Scotland Yard engineers devised an apparatus for working two-way traffic in a single line past road obstructions. This made it possible for one constable to do the work of two or three. In July 1931 automatic signals were set up at all the junctions in Oxford Street. They worked far better than had been expected, for the drivers accommodated themselves readily to the lights—green, amber, and red. More than two hundred other installations have since come into use. The signals are costly to instal, but they have already saved between two hundred and three hundred police. So far police have to be employed in seeing that the lights are obeyed, and offenders are often stopped by a policeman emerging from a car to which a wireless message has been sent from the scene of their offence.

No doubt Scotland Yard will remain in the transitional stage for decades to come, since the police problems will continue to change almost month by month. In the realm of crime detection, the criminal has profited more by modern invention than the police. By stealing a car he can travel far from the district where he is known in order to break into a shop or a private house, and the Flying Squad cannot pretend to know by sight every criminal who comes from distant divisions or from provincial towns. Personal knowledge of the criminal and quiet information about his movements can never be replaced by mechanical contrivances.

As long ago as 1829 Sir Robert Peel told the House of Commons that police would be necessary to meet "the increasing mechanical ingenuity of the age." He was thinking of the railway period then in its infancy. If he had foreseen the motorcar he might have drawn a more vivid picture.

The motor vehicles of the Metropolitan Police, including all types, number about six hundred, without counting the thirty police launches and boats on the Thames. None of these is built to run at a spectacular speed. Quick acceleration, reasonable speed, and endurance are the qualities for which they are selected. The cars have hard work—policemen are not built for baby cars—nevertheless all police vehicles have to be light. In London the patrolling cars are fitted with wireless; not pocket wireless sets, because these have been found less suited to the Metropolis than to provincial towns.

For the first sixty years of the Metropolitan Police force the number of arrests for every kind of offence remained at about 80,000 a year. There was a marked increase after 1895 up to and after the South African War. In 1905 arrests amounted to 127,000, then for a few years there was a decline, but in 1913 arrests had risen to 133,000. During the war, when a large number of potential criminals were serving at the front, the number fell to half this total, and immediately after the war, when everyone expected a crime wave, the old average of 80,000 a year was resumed. Then there was a decline, until the average for the five years 1928–32 was about 54,000 as compared with the average of 126,000 a year in the five years 1910–14. The figures are not difficult to explain. They are due to the decline in drinking. In 1913 arrests for drunkenness in a public place were in proportion to population practically double what they were between 1884 and 1895. Since the war the decline in arrests has been largely due to the change in the public habit as regards drink. The cinema in its competition with the public house seems to have won the day. The arrests for drunkenness fell from 70,000 in 1913 to 13,760 in 1932. One striking result of the fall in drunkenness is that the number of police injured in making arrests is about one quarter of what it was thirty years ago.

I may be pardoned for one more excursion into figures. The criminal statistics of recent years show that about two thirds of all persons found guilty of crime in England and Wales are under thirty years of age and two fifths are under twenty-one. This fact, which has come almost as a shock to this statistical generation, has always existed. In 1785 the Solicitor-General told the House of Commons that nine out of every ten who went to the gallows were under the age of twenty. Even as late as the middle of the nineteenth century many hundreds of children under the age of sixteen were sent to prison every year, and though they were kept separate from the adult prisoners, familiarity with the interior of a prison could not fail to breed contempt. It was not until 1896 that serious steps were taken—special prisons for what were then called "Juvenile-adults" under what is now known as the "Borstal System," where education and gymnastic training combined with strict discipline was given up to a maximum of three years. The cases are followed up after discharge by Borstal associations in every part of the country. Reforms such as these can be carried out only in countries where the prisons have passed to the control of the central government, which they did in England in 1877.

The commitment to prison of children under the age of sixteen has ceased: they are now sent to reformatories. There will, however, always remain a residuum of youths, even from good homes, who seem to be proof against any reformatory treatment and who graduate into the class of incorrigible criminals.

Throughout the hundred-odd years of their existence the police have been loaded up with duties that have little relation to crime. The new factor is that they have now to do with the well-to-do classes as well as the classes that are living from hand to mouth. The motorcar has brought into existence no less than 250 new offences which are generally committed by persons of the upper classes. The acts that the police have to prosecute, whether they are acts of commission or omission, do not offend against the moral code of the good citizen; he can see no harm in them, because most of them are acts which he has himself committed, and so the policeman cannot count upon the same support that he had when he was dealing with drunkards or thieves. He is certain therefore to find himself charged with arrogance and highhandedness, although he is merely enforcing regulations, with the making of which he had nothing to do. The latest Royal Commission, 1928–29, found that there was little support for the view that the police were more arbitrary or oppressive than they were before the war. It is true that police service is rapidly becoming a profession. The policeman's new rates of pay and allowances have brought the emoluments of a constable to about £300 a year, with the prospect of promotion to a level with the earnings of what used to be called the "black-coated" professions. There is now a growing sense of *esprit de corps* and of pride in their occupation which was never shown before in their history. Probably there is little danger of their forgetting their duty towards the public or of setting themselves up as a haughty "praetorian guard"; there is certainly far less danger than there was a few years ago of their joining forces with the leaders of strike movements.

At the moment, experiment is in the air. The Royal Commission on Police Powers, of 1929, reported against any system which limited the appointment to the higher posts to those who had entered the force as constables, and it was out of this finding that the scheme for a police college grew. A constable has to serve for five years before he is qualified for the rank of sergeant; the police themselves consider that all posts, including the highest, should be filled by serving policemen who have graduated through the ranks. The police college is an attempt to effect a compromise. The college is to be filled by selected men serving in the force and young men coming direct from the universities and the secondary schools, who pass a fairly stiff examination. On passing out of the college the men will have to serve for a term as constables before passing to the rank of inspector.

Another experiment is the short-service scheme which proposes that 5,000 men—one quarter of the present force —shall be recruited on a ten years' engagement, at the end of which they will retire on a gratuity of one month's pay for every completed year of service. The object of this scheme is to rid the force of constables who are serving for twenty-five years or longer without any hope of promotion. There is much to be said both for and against this scheme; it must be left to the umpire, Time, to decide between its merits and demerits.

The Criminal Investigation Department has been little affected by these proposed experiments; nor is it likely to be, since success in the detection of crime does not come by intuition or superior education but by intelligence combined with experience and dogged hard work. Sherlock Holmes and his copyists in fiction are never likely to spring from a police college.

As has already been noted earlier in this volume, Scotland Yard took its name from a lodging of the Kings and Queens of Scotland when they visited the English Court. Adjoining "Scotland" was York Place, the London Palace of the Archbishops of York. In 1519 Cardinal Wolsey acquired from the Westminster Abbey authorities the "parcel of land formerly belonging to the King of Scotland," as the grant describes it. In 1529 Henry VIII dispossessed Wolsey of York Place and joined it to the new York Palace of Whitehall. In an Act of Parliament of 1531, defining the boundaries of the new palace, reference is made to the "Croft or piece of land commonly called 'Scotland.'" The plan of this palace, as it was in Stuart times, shows at the northern end a double court or yard named "Scotland Yard" because it included ground once known as "Scotland."

The police office set up in 1829 was at Number 4 Whitehall Place, a private house. The back of this house was converted into a police station, entered from Scotland Yard. There are official documents showing that in 1829 the new police headquarters were sometimes described as "White-hall Place" and sometimes as "Scotland Yard."

Gradually the staff overflowed into adjoining houses, and this led to the purchase in 1885 of a site on the Embankment under the shadow of Big Ben on which New Scotland Yard was built to the designs of the architect Norman Shaw. The twenty-five hundred tons of granite for the basement of the building were quarried and dressed by Dartmoor convicts. Most of the land on which it stands was reclaimed from the Thames by the construction of the Thames Embankment in 1863. It had been sold in 1874 to a Colonel Mapleson, who planned to build on it the world's finest opera house. The Duke of Edinburgh, King Edward the Seventh's brother, laid the foundation stone in 1875, but the opera house never got far beyond its foundations, which may still be seen in the basement of police headquarters. In 1890 all the police departments were transferred to New Scotland Yard and building still continued. Scotland House on the opposite side of the street was built, and still Scotland Yard is crying for more room.

CHAPTER XXVII

The Existing Organization at Scotland Yard

THE DIVISION OF POLICE ADMINISTRATION into departments began in 1842, when the detective branch was formed. In 1878 this developed into the Criminal Investigation Department, with an assistant commissioner in charge of it.

The controlling officers, consisting of the commissioner, four assistant commissioners and chief constables, continued as they were until the end of the war. It was a slender allowance of superior officers for a force of 20,000 men, and in 1933 it was decided to give to one of the assistant commissioners the title of deputy commissioner; he was to share with the commissioner the general responsibility for the control of the force. The work was redistributed among the five assistant commissioners, for an additional A.C. was appointed in 1933. There are now four departments each with its own assistant commissioner, viz.:

(A) Administration and General Duties.
(B) Traffic.
(C) Criminal Investigation.
(D) Organization.

Much of the clerical work in the Department is discharged by Metropolitan Police civil servants. They are not sworn in as police officers, but police officers are interchangeable with them. The commissioner and the assistant commissioners only are appointed by the Crown, and they are all justices of the peace.

323

THE DIVISION OF DUTIES

Assistant Commissioner A deals with all matters relating to the welfare of the force and with complaints against the police by the public. Discipline and recruiting, the mounted branch, the special constabulary, the women police, and the medical service are under him, as well as betting, gaming, and liquor licensing. Further, he has to make the promotions and the transfers from one division to another and to assemble bodies of police for special occasions. He has an experienced staff of police officers under him, formerly the executive branch, but now A2 and A3. The former controls the police personnel engaged in office work at headquarters as well as the motor drivers, wireless operators, and telegraph office. A3 prepares and issues the daily orders to be read to the men when parading for duty. The telegraph office is engaged day and night in sending messages and receiving them on the tele-printer and the telephone. By this means, together with wireless and signal lights, the men scattered over the seven hundred square miles of Greater London can be apprised immediately of the flight of criminals or of stolen motorcars.

RECRUITING

Recruiting for the Metropolitan Police is second to none in importance, for everything depends on the type of man who joins the force. In Great Britain the men are not as a rule drawn from any disciplined force; the policy has always been to get men from the agricultural counties, not only because of their superior physique, but because men who have had no previous experience of city life have always proved to be the most trustworthy policemen. Their minds are fallow without being infertile; the Londoner's mind is fertile but is usually far from being fallow. Until about 1890 the supply of rural recruits proved to be sufficient; after that date it fell off, probably because the county constabularies were authorized to pay improved scales of pensions. Moreover, the standardization of pay and service in 1919 deprived the Metropolitan Police of advantages over other forces in the matter of recruiting.

When the weekly rest day was granted, about sixteen hundred additional recruits were required, and a recruiting commission was set up in 1909 to travel through the entire country from northern Scotland to Cornwall. It was found that the best recruits came from the West Country, particularly from the Severn valley and from Devonshire, but the commission found excellent raw material in the Highlands of Scotland. Most of the local police authorities co-operated with the commission, though by some its members were regarded as poachers.

This method of recruiting ended with the war and probably will never be revived. At the Armistice, when there were several thousand vacancies in the Metropolitan force, recruiting officers were sent to France to try their luck with likely men about to be demobilized. During the next two years the force was brought up to strength, but quality had been sacrificed to quantity. The men were taken chiefly on their military records, and it was found impossible to keep many of these recruits.

The fact is that police service is not one for which it is easy to recruit men. Night duty can be performed only by men who have acquired the power to sleep in the daytime; while the duty of a uniformed constable is largely monotonous routine, at any moment he may be called upon for intelligence and discretion of a high order, and men who have these qualities do not take kindly to the other aspects of police work. Stature, muscle, and brain are not always found associated in the same individual, yet no one who has acquired an intimate knowledge of the police who were employed on the old rates of pay can deny that there were men of exceptional intelligence and ability in the force, and that when they had had training and experience they were more than equal to the best recruits found today. A system that could evolve men like the chief inspectors whose achievements in bringing to justice the criminals whose cases are described in this volume will be difficult to excel.

THE MAINTENANCE OF DISCIPLINE

The discipline code set out in the regulations of the Secretary of State for all forces specifies some fifty ways in which a policeman can offend; such as discreditable conduct, insubordination, disobedience of orders, neglect of duty, falsehood or prevarication, corrupt practices, unnecessary exercise of authority, oppressive conduct, malingering, drunkenness, untidiness, etc. These offences if proved may be dealt with by dismissal, being required to resign as an alternative to dismissal, reduction in rank, reduction in pay, a fine, or a reprimand. Any such punishment is entered on a conduct sheet and is quoted against the defaulter if he offends again, but in the lighter cases the entry may be cancelled after a prescribed term of good conduct.

The authorities empowered to deal with discipline offences are the superintendent of the division, the chief constable, and the deputy assistant commissioner of the district; a discipline board presided over by an assistant commissioner; and lastly the commissioner. In every case there is an appeal to the next higher authority. If the sentence is dismissal or compulsory resignation there is a further appeal to the Secretary of State.

Superintendents have the power of punishment by a fine not exceeding four days' pay for minor offences. District officers deal with other defaults by sergeants and constables, but the minimum penalties they can inflict are reduction in rank or a fine of a week's pay for each offence. All other offences and all cases of defaulters of the rank of section sergeants upwards are dealt with by a discipline board. The procedure before this board resembles that of a court martial. The defaulter is allowed to have the assistance of a friend and is given every facility for stating his case. If he appeals to the commissioner he can have his friend present.

No member of the force against whom a charge is pending is kept in the dark at any stage. Every adverse report that may affect his prospects must be communicated to him before going to the commissioner; and he is allowed to take copies of all reports made against him. There can be no fairer method than this.

In recent years offences against discipline have amounted to about 400 to 500 a year in the force of 20,000 men, and only one quarter of these are deemed cases that should go before a discipline board. Most of the cases relate to neglect to patrol beats or exceeding the half-hour allowed for refreshment in the middle of the eight hours' tour. If we may take the number of defaulters and the dismissals and other punishments as a criterion, the standard of conduct has improved immensely since the early days of the force. This is due, no doubt, to the care taken in weeding out unsuitable candidates and to the great decrease in drunkenness, which used to be the commonest weakness of the policeman. In the early days every pay day was followed by a string of dismissals for the "crime" of being drunk. Even fifty years ago, when the force was less than half its present number, there were as many defaulters in two or three months as there are now in twelve. In the first ten years of the force about a third were got rid of every year, and for several years afterwards the average wastage was 20 per cent; it was still as high as 10 per cent between 1870–80; at the present time it is about 5 per cent. The total number of dismissals or compulsory resignations for all offences averaged in the five years 1929–33 less than a quarter per cent of the force.

COMPLAINTS BY THE PUBLIC

It was pointed out in the report of the Royal Commission of 1908 that the maintenance of good relations between the police and the public depended upon the public being able to feel sure that their complaints will be properly inquired into and remedied as far as possible. Every complaint is investigated first by one of the district officers, and if the charge is serious the case is referred to the commissioner to decide whether it should be dealt with by a discipline board or by criminal proceedings. If the former, the complainant and his witnesses are invited to attend and are allowed the fullest opportunity to substantiate the complaint.

If the complaint amounts to a criminal charge and the evidence is conflicting, the case is generally brought before a court, where the evidence will be taken on oath. Even if there is no conflict of evidence, any serious charge against a policeman is handed over to the courts to deal with. The necessary inquiries are carried out by other members of the force, and these have always displayed impartiality in bringing guilty comrades to justice, for the force as a whole is anxious to get rid of its black sheep. In 1929, when a sergeant named Goddard was found guilty of accepting bribes from night clubs, it was the police themselves who brought the facts to light.

Assistant Commissioner B deals with all traffic questions in his five sections; these have been dealt with in previous chapters, as have also the functions of Assistant Commissioner C (Criminal Investigation). Assistant Commissioner D deals with a comparatively new set of subjects under the general heading of organization. His main functions are to initiate, examine, and develop schemes for improving or maintaining the efficiency of the force. His department is, in fact, a research department, keeping in touch with improvements in other forces in England and abroad. The D1 section deals with training, examinations, the police college, the system of promotion, and mechanical aids, such as transport and wireless. Each of the four districts has disguised "Q" cars, so named after the mystery "Q" ships of the war, to prevent or detect crime. The vans are used chiefly for conveying police and prisoners; signs are carried on police cars and vans to indicate, when necessary, what they are; some have blinds on the rear window which, when pulled down, show conspicuously the words, "Stop. Police."

The question of aliens, which loomed so largely during the war, is now far more manageable. It comes under the

sphere of Assistant Commissioner C (Criminal Investigation), but it forms a smaller element in the criminal population than it did. Between 1911 and 1931 the number of
aliens living in Greater London fell from 175,000 to 128,-
000, and they are now dispersed all over the Metropolis
instead of being congregated in special areas according to
their nationality.

The enforcement of the law in regard to licensed premises
and clubs falls on the uniformed police; most of their work
in this disagreeable and unpopular duty remains unknown
to the newspaper-reading public, unless it is a question of a
night club which seems to have a high publicity value. The
police officer on whom the duty falls is placed in an unfair
position. The law has imposed restrictions, but has not given
the police the right of entry, and to enforce the law in such
cases means that the officer has to disguise himself in dress
clothes to gain admittance. Naturally the men dislike the
duty extremely.

THE CIVIL SERVICE STAFF

Now that the pay and allowances of the police officer have
been increased to their present rate, efforts have had to be
made to relieve them as far as possible from office work, and
the civil service staff now outnumbers the police staff at
Scotland Yard by two to one.

THE POLICE IN THE DIVISIONS

The key to the success of the Metropolitan Police is to
be found in the divisional system. It would be impossible
efficiently to control 20,000 men spread over seven hundred
square miles of streets from the central office at Scotland
Yard. The huge area is split up into four districts, compris-
ing twenty-three divisions, ninety subdivisions, and 180
police stations. Each division is under a superintendent, and
the divisions are grouped in four districts, each under a
deputy assistant commissioner with a chief constable under

him. Two new ranks of inspector were created to complete the scheme of the police college. Entrants to the college take the rank of junior station inspector, and on completing their course of instruction and their practical training in a division they receive substantive appointments. The element of "educated control" which had been the aim of Sir Robert Peel had been allowed to lapse to a great extent, and the control had fallen into the hands of the superintendents promoted from the ranks. In practice the orders from headquarters went direct from Assistant Commissioner A to the superintendents, thus "short-circuiting" the chief constables, who tended to become attached to headquarters in an advisory capacity without any real control over their districts.

At present the district officers have a general oversight of the work, discipline, and welfare of the men under them, and they relieve Assistant Commissioner A of many of his duties. Every member of the force has a right of personal access to the deputy assistant commissioner or the chief constable of his district without having to disclose to any intervening superior officer his object in seeking the interview. Minor offences against discipline can still be dealt with by the superintendents; more serious cases and all complaints by the public must go before the district officers, who can if they think fit send them on to be dealt with by a discipline board at headquarters. One of the officers of the discipline board is a district officer from another district. There cannot therefore be any imputation of bias.

SUPERINTENDENTS

The superintendents are the keystone of the arch as regards discipline and the relations of the force with the public. All have entered as constables and have passed through the various ranks. They have been tried in the fire by long years of hard service. Many of them first came into notice through having been selected for employment in the divisional office, where they graduated in time to become that important functionary, the divisional clerk with the rank of clerk-sergeant who knew everything that transpired in the division. From clerk-sergeant he again passed to outdoor duty as inspector and passed through all the grades to chief inspector and later to superintendent.

As has already been related, soon after the Criminal Investigation Department was extended to every division there was some fear that it might tend to become an *imperium in imperio,* and to meet this difficulty it was arranged that the divisional detective-inspector should submit all his reports to the superintendent before they went on to Scotland Yard. Some superintendents took a keen interest in the work of the C.I.D.; others forwarded the reports mechanically; but under the present system the C.I.D. itself is broken up into districts—indeed, the reorganization has been carried a step further by the appointment, in each division, of another chief inspector—the "crime chief inspector" who is responsible for organizing and directing what is called the "anti-crime" work of the division. They are to be crime intelligence officers whose business it is to know the general state of crime in their divisions and take the necessary countermeasures. The new posts have been filled by men selected from the uniformed police as well as from the C.I.D., but as they do not undertake the investigation of particular cases it is more than possible that they may be found redundant in the future. In the meantime they may be useful in keeping the superintendent in closer touch with the crime committed in his division.

It is a fundamental principle in the British police system that when once a charge has been accepted and entered on the charge sheet the accused must be brought before a magistrate within the next twenty-four hours, but within the last few years it has become the practice to allow the station officer, on facts that have been brought to his notice, such as a mistake in identity, which would have led him to refuse the charge if he had known of it earlier, to treat the charge as having been refused unless the accused demands to go before a court.

Thus the station officer is sometimes placed in a very

awkward position. If he decides to accept a charge he has to decide whether he should keep the accused in custody or release him on bail. The hour may be too late for making inquiries. It is true that under an Act of 1925, if a person is arrested without a warrant, and the charge cannot be investigated forthwith, the station officer may release him on bail to appear at the police station at a prescribed time. But even so the station officer has to take a risk; if he refuses bail he may be detaining a man who ought at once to have been admitted to bail; on the other hand he may be setting a dangerous criminal at liberty. He may either be furnishing material for a fresh newspaper scandal about the high-handedness of the police, or he may be letting out a criminal and will have to answer for it to his superiors. It is only to this limited extent that the police have to decide between the guilt or innocence of an accused person; in all other respects the decision rests with the judicial authority.

It is perhaps worth mentioning here that the only arm carried by the Metropolitan policeman is the truncheon, secured to his wrist by a thong. He carries neither pistol nor handcuffs; these are kept in the police stations for use in emergencies.

THE CRIMINAL INVESTIGATION DEPARTMENT

Nothing is more interesting than to trace the change in public opinion regarding the detective police. During the early years of the force it was looked upon as an organization to spy upon the private lives of the citizens of London; as a disreputable body composed of "low Irishmen" who would furnish the government with information imperilling the liberty of the people. After the Good murder in 1842, and still more after the alarms of the dynamite outrages in the early eighties, the public temper changed. Detectives were regarded as necessary evils. It was not until the detective novel came into vogue and the daily press began to take an interest in the work of detectives that they came into their own. But even now, in the novels and on the stage, it is more often that the brilliant amateur steps in to show the Scotland Yard detective what a blunderer he is.

By a curious fatality, whenever Scotland Yard has been doing its best work some public scandal occurs to shake the growing public confidence in it. There was the case of Popay,[1] who attended political meetings in plain clothes as a struggling artist and was afterwards recognized in a police station; that of Titley, the chemist, to whom a policeman's wife had been sent to apply for medicine to procure abortion, which led Sir William Harcourt, the Home Secretary, to declare that the police must not "set traps for people." "This," he said, "is not consonant with the temper of the English people, even though they know that they have to pay the price in the defectiveness of their detective system." In 1874, when the C.I.D. had proved their usefulness, came the Benson frauds and the scandal of three detectives being in his pay, and straightway the public adopted the absurd view that the detective force was in league with criminals. Happily all this prejudice has been lived down, and the public seems now to be satisfied that it has the best detective force that it is humanly possible to organize.

The opponents of Sir Robert Peel's scheme, it will be remembered, foretold that Irishmen would flock to the New Police. Apparently they did not know that the first commissioners, Colonel Rowan and Sir Richard Mayne, were both Irishmen. One of their most gifted successors, Sir Edward Henry, who introduced fingerprint identification, was also Irish, and a few years ago all the best men in the Special Branch were Irish, as were their predecessors in the days of the dynamite outrages. The fact is that Irishmen have a special bent for police work, especially work of a confidential nature like that of the Special Branch. In the first place Irishmen are unsurpassed in being able to keep secrets, and they are always loyal to their salt. The only case of leakage in recent years was traced to two officers, of whom one

[1]See Chapter X.

was a Londoner and the other a Dutchman. The Dublin Metropolitan Police in the most troublous times was staffed by Irishmen exclusively; their work, dangerous as it was, seemed to attract men who were as fearless as they were honest, loyal, and incorruptible.

Sir William Harcourt's dictum that the police must not "set traps for people," in the sense of obtaining evidence against people who commit unlawful acts behind closed doors, has not stood the test of time. The police do not set traps, nor do they incite people to break the law, but when they know that the law is being persistently broken and no prosecution is possible without evidence, they cannot fold their hands and do nothing merely because the law is being broken behind closed doors and the legislature has not given the police the right of entry. In such cases the police have to dress in the same garb as the lawbreakers, even if it be in dress clothes.

The C.I.D. has more than justified its creation by the official figures. The number of arrests by detectives in the Metropolitan area rose from 13,128 in 1879 to 15,472 in 1880 and to 17,522 in 1883.

The Irish dynamite scare in 1869 had been largely responsible for the enlargement of the C.I.D., and when it died down in 1885 its place was taken by the anarchists of the type of Polti and Farnara, who were tracked to their "arsenal" and cleverly arrested. The year of Queen Victoria's first jubilee in 1887 was full of anxiety for the Special Branch, who never knew how many among the myriad foreigners who crowded into London for the ceremonies might be anarchists armed with bombs. Happily the Italian anarchists had acquired a prudent respect for the British police, and the celebrations passed off without a hitch.

In 1888 the crimes of "Jack the Ripper"—so named from a bogus letter signed by that name which reached the police among hundreds of others—filled London with horror and apprehension. Most of the murders were committed in the poor district of Whitechapel, and the women victims were of the "unfortunate" class. There was a strong feeling against the C.I.D. for its failure to arrest the murderer; it was not realized that an isolated maniac with a blood lust makes no confidants, and therefore the starting point for investigation—the police informant—was lacking. The only clue was the fact that the man who ripped women up with what must have been a surgical knife had probably been at some time a medical student. In the belief of the police he was a man who committed suicide in the Thames at the end of 1888. Though there was one other murder of the same kind in the beginning of 1889, it was considered that this was one of the imitative crimes so often committed after a series of crimes has deeply impressed the public mind.

After 1890 the C.I.D. settled down to a quieter period and built up a world-wide reputation for efficiency. During this period the old prejudice against the detective disappeared, though there is still in some quarters a strong feeling that the employment of police in plain clothes should be restricted as much as possible.

The starting of all detective work is "information received," in other words information received from a member of the underworld who has abandoned his criminal career in favour of honest employment, but is still on friendly terms with his old associates.

In Paris and in a number of American cities, to cite no other instances, the police have scientific laboratories which are an attraction to visitors, even if they serve no useful purpose, but Scotland Yard has a good reason for not incurring this expense. No trained laboratory chemist is capable of covering all the branches of science on which an expert opinion may occassionally be indispensable if a conviction is to be obtained, and British juries are always apt to discount the evidence of officials as compared with that of independent scientific authorities. One failure to obtain a conviction through the alleged mistake of an official expert would throw doubt upon his evidence for years to come. The Yard has a list of experts in every branch of science, who receive a fee for each case when they are called in.

Only in the matter of fingerprints is the expert an official, but he brings with him photographic enlargements of the prints concerned, with the points of resemblance, and these are handed to the judge and jury, who are able to make the comparison for themselves.[1]

Only once in the history of the C.I.D. was the experiment tried of appointing to the department men of superior education without previous police experience. They were not a success. The detective drawn from the most intelligent of the uniformed force has had the advantage of meeting criminals in their own haunts, of studying their habits and associates, and of being able to keep in touch with informants. Experience has shown that the policeman-detective can deal successfully with the complicated accounts of City swindlers like the Mandevilles and Horatio Bottomley as well as any university man could do—in fact that he can rise to any emergency, but the root of success lies in his personal knowledge of criminals. The juniors have learned the more complicated aspects of their work by serving under seniors who are carrying on the traditions of the men who went before them.

Contrary to what one would expect, it is not the outlying suburbs that suffer most from the housebreaker, but the inner suburbs, which are closely built over. Most of the crime which goes undetected, however, is petty crime, in which the property stolen is worth less than £5.

The Lee Commission of 1929 went so far as to deprecate the practice of arresting a man on a minor charge while inquiries into a major charge are proceeding. This, it was said, "contains elements of subterfuge"!

If the legislature had given the findings of the commission the force of law, Smith, the murderer of the "Brides in the Bath," Podmore in the Messiter Murder, and Browne and Kennedy in the more recent murder of the constable Gutteridge might never have been brought to justice. The sense

---

[1]The authorities are now considering the question of setting up a police research laboratory instead of using the government chemist and the Home Office pathologists and analysts. For the reasons given above it seems doubtful whether the expense would be justified.

of fair play for the criminal blinds some excellent people to the injury they may be doing to the community by meddling in matters they do not understand. What difference can it make to a guilty person whether he is arrested a week earlier on another charge if eventually he is to be arrested on the major crime? For the good folk on the commission do not go so far as to advocate that the man guilty of a major crime should go scot free, though that would often be the logical consequence. The motive of these well-meaning people appears to be to strew the path of the detective with difficulties, forgetting that he is a public servant discharging a difficult and often dangerous duty in the interest of the public. It is an aspect of the British character which caused a wit to observe that in England the people of sound common sense have to spend the greater part of their lives in undoing the harm wrought by people of good intentions.

THE END

WORKS CONSULTED

The Bow Street Runners, Gilbert Armitage.

The Chronicles of Bow Street, Percy Fitzgerald.

Treatise on the Police of the Metropolis, Dr. Patrick Colquhoun (1796).

The Annual Register.

A History of Police in England, Captain W. L. Melville Lee, M.A.

A Police Encyclopaedia, H. L. Adam.

How Criminals Are Made and Prevented, Canon J. W. Horsley.

Reminiscences of Ex-Chief Inspector Littlechild.

Scotland Yard, Past and Present, Ex-Chief Inspector Cavanagh.

At Scotland Yard, John Sweeney, Ex-Detective Inspector, C.I.D.

Dictionary of National Biography.

The Lighter Side of My Official Life, Sir Robert Anderson.

The Trial of George Joseph Smith, Eric R. Watson, LL.D.

For the Defence: The Life of Sir Edward Marshall Hall, K.C., Edward Marjoribanks.

Forty Years of Scotland Yard, Frederick Porter Wensley, O.B.E.

Scotland Yard, Sir John Moylan, C.B., C.B.E.

The History of the C.I.D., Margaret Prothero.

Scotland Yard, George Dilnot.

The Real Detective, George Dilnot.

British Encyclopaedia.

State Papers.

Fifty Years Ago, Walter Besant.

Bygone Punishments, Robert Andrews.

She Stands Accused, Victor McClure.

Mysteries of Police and Crime, Arthur Griffiths.

Last Studies in Criminology, H. B. Irving.

Sidelights on Criminal Matters.

INDEX

INDEX

Abbott, Lord Chief Justice, presides at the trial of the Cato Street conspirators, 49.
Abolition of: stocks, 94; hanging in chains, 94; public flogging, 96; transportation, 158; capital punishment for housebreaking, 90.
Acton highway robbery, 144.
"Aeronauts" at the Great Exhibition, 144.
Alexandra, Princess, casualties at wedding of, 158.
Aliens Department: improved after Sidney Street Siege, 196; now under Assistant Commissioner C, 329.
Arcos Ltd., Russian trading delegation premises, raid on, 298.
Arrests, decline in, 318.
Assistant Commissioner, statutory authority over department, duties of, 324, 328.

Bankes, Isabella, poisoned, 155.
Barrett, Michael, Fenian: blows up Clerkenwell prison, 169; last criminal hung in public, 171.
Barrow, Eliza, murdered, 202.
Beck, Adolf, 211.
Benson, Harry, forger, 174.
Bentham, Jeremy, on the need of police, 15.
Bertillon system of body measurements, 211, 216.
Birnie, Sir Richard, deals with rioters at Bow Street, 86.

Bishop, Bow Street runner, apprehends Thistlewood, 48.
Blackstone's *Commentaries* quoted: on need of police, 15; on inconsistencies of criminal code, 94.
"Blood money," payment of, to informers, 46.
Borstal system, 319.
Bottomley, Horatio, 276.
"Bound over," term explained, 275 footnote.
Bow Street: runners, 34; premier police court, 95.
Bradbury, Sir John, "forges" notes, 240.
Bradford, Sir Edward: made Commissioner, 191; retired, 192.
Brereton, Colonel: tries to pacify Bristol rioters, 101; court-martial and suicide after Bristol riots, 103.
Brett, Sergeant, shot dead, 167.
Brides in the Bath Case, the, 248.
Bright, P. C., murdered, 130.
Bristol riots, 101.
Bucknill, Mr. Justice, in Seddons case, 205.
Burking horses, 124.
Bullock-baiting, 40.
Byng of Vimy, Lord, 257.
Bywaters, Freddie, 284.

Cambridge, Duke of, in favour of amalgamating Metropolitan and City Police, 158.
Capital punishment for house-

CPSIA information can be obtained at www.ICGtesting.com
Printed in the USA
BVOW07s1129061213

338377BV00012B/397/P

9 781162 789200